It Happened to Me

Series Editor: Arlene Hirschfelder

Books in the It Happened to Me series are designed for inquisitive teens digging for answers about certain illnesses, social issues, or lifestyle interests. Whether you are deep into your teen years or just entering them, these books are gold mines of up-to-date information, riveting teen views, and great visuals to help you figure out stuff. Besides special boxes highlighting singular facts, each book is enhanced with the latest reading lists, websites, and an index. Perfect for browsing, these books contain loads of expert information by acclaimed writers to help parents, guardians, and librarians understand teen illness, tough situations, and lifestyle choices.

1. *Epilepsy: The Ultimate Teen Guide*, by Kathlyn Gay and Sean McGarrahan, 2002.
2. *Stress Relief: The Ultimate Teen Guide*, by Mark Powell, 2002.
3. *Learning Disabilities: The Ultimate Teen Guide*, by Penny Hutchins Paquette and Cheryl Gerson Tuttle, 2003.
4. *Making Sexual Decisions: The Ultimate Teen Guide*, by L. Kris Gowen, 2003.
5. *Asthma: The Ultimate Teen Guide*, by Penny Hutchins Paquette, 2003.
6. *Cultural Diversity—Conflicts and Challenges: The Ultimate Teen Guide*, by Kathlyn Gay, 2003.
7. *Diabetes: The Ultimate Teen Guide*, by Katherine J. Moran, 2004.
8. *When Will I Stop Hurting? Teens, Loss, and Grief: The Ultimate Teen Guide to Dealing with Grief*, by Ed Myers, 2004.
9. *Volunteering: The Ultimate Teen Guide*, by Kathlyn Gay, 2004.
10. *Organ Transplants—A Survival Guide for the Entire Family: The Ultimate Teen Guide*, by Tina P. Schwartz, 2005.
11. *Medications: The Ultimate Teen Guide*, by Cheryl Gerson Tuttle, 2005.

12. *Image and Identity—Becoming the Person You Are: The Ultimate Teen Guide*, by L. Kris Gowen and Molly C. McKenna, 2005.
13. *Apprenticeship: The Ultimate Teen Guide*, by Penny Hutchins Paquette, 2005.
14. *Cystic Fibrosis: The Ultimate Teen Guide*, by Melanie Ann Apel, 2006.
15. *Religion and Spirituality in America: The Ultimate Teen Guide*, by Kathlyn Gay, 2006.
16. *Gender Identity: The Ultimate Teen Guide*, by Cynthia L. Winfield, 2007.
17. *Physical Disabilities: The Ultimate Teen Guide*, by Denise Thornton, 2007.
18. *Money—Getting It, Using It, and Avoiding the Traps: The Ultimate Teen Guide*, by Robin F. Brancato, 2007.
19. *Self-Advocacy: The Ultimate Teen Guide*, by Cheryl Gerson Tuttle and JoAnn Augeri Silva, 2007.
20. *Adopted: The Ultimate Teen Guide*, by Suzanne Buckingham Slade, 2007.
21. *The Military and Teens: The Ultimate Teen Guide*, by Kathlyn Gay, 2008.
22. *Animals and Teens: The Ultimate Teen Guide*, by Gail Green, 2009.
23. *Reaching Your Goals: The Ultimate Teen Guide*, by Anne Courtright, 2009.
24. *Juvenile Arthritis: The Ultimate Teen Guide*, by Kelly Rouba, 2009.

Reaching Your Goals

The Ultimate Teen Guide

Anne Courtright

Illustrations by Peg Raasch

It Happened to Me, No. 23

The Scarecrow Press, Inc.
Lanham, Maryland • Toronto • Plymouth, UK
2009

SCARECROW PRESS, INC.

Published in the United States of America
by Scarecrow Press, Inc.
A wholly owned subsidiary of
The Rowman & Littlefield Publishing Group, Inc.
4501 Forbes Boulevard, Suite 200, Lanham, Maryland 20706
www.scarecrowpress.com

Estover Road
Plymouth PL6 7PY
United Kingdom

All illustrations on chapter opening pages are by Peg Raasch.

British Library Cataloguing in Publication Information Available

Library of Congress Cataloging-in-Publication Data

Courtright, Anne, 1941–
Reaching your goals : the ultimate teen guide / Anne Courtright ; illustrations by Peg Raasch.
p. cm. — (It happened to me ; no. 23)
Includes bibliographical references and index.
ISBN-13: 978-0-8108-5572-4 (cloth : alk. paper)
ISBN-10: 0-8108-5572-0 (cloth : alk. paper)
1. Success—Psychological aspects. 2. Imagery (Psychology) 3. Visualization.
I. Raasch, Peg. II. Title.
BF724.3.S9C68 2009
155.5'138—dc22 2008042229

™ The paper used in this publication meets the minimum requirements of American National Standard for Information Sciences—Permanence of Paper for Printed Library Materials, ANSI/NISO Z39.48-1992.
Manufactured in the United States of America.

For Maa,
and for my husband, Robert,
and my kids, Tony, Annie, Mark, Lizzy, and Chrissy
with great love.

Contents

Acknowledgments

Along my journey in writing *Goals*, I have had the privilege of walking with many significant friends, all who have helped me in their own unique way.

First I want to thank the dearest of friends and illustrator for this book, Peg Raasch (who never gave up hope this book would be finished some day). I must thank Tina Schwartz for introducing me to Scarecrow. Who can forget that cold winter's day in New York when you introduced me to Arlene, my future editor? (You also shared so many of my high and low moments, always with a cheerful smile.) I would also like to thank all of my other SCBWI (Society of Children's Book Writers and Illustrators) buddies, including the following: Esther, one of my first mentors, you've always so gracious to me (Thanks!); Heidi, celestial!; Lorijo, who spent many hours editing my edits (even up to the end you have been there for me); Denise, always encouraging even though you knew how much work was involved; Suzanne, thanks for your personal insights and examples of how you handled similar problems; Hal, my inspiration on how to be inspired; Mary Beth (your enduring spirit touches me); Ilyse, Dawn, Whimsey, Jeff, Shawn, Chris, Pam, and the other mad-ones from Ready Writers (my hat is off to you ruthless writers!); Mary, one of the first guides who believed in me, and your ever-faithful writer's group including, Laurel, Susan, and some of my other above mentioned pals (you were all my first editors who helped me to reach higher); and Laurie Korte (who gave me the lovely opportunity to share my art with her students); Deepti, who I am indebted to because you did an amazing job on the graphics; and Natalia B. (you are so talented!).

I also want to thank Frank and Shirley, two of my oldest friends, and a very special person, Marlene who shared her pals, including Trish, MaryAnn, Mini, Francine, Nina, Joan, and Linda (sisters in spirit who bring me so much joy!) and the unselfish reader, Libby, Janice and Mary among others in my critique groups. You guys are so cool!

I also would like to thank all of the young adults who have come from far away points such as India (thanks, Sukruthi), Japan (thanks, Himi!), and Paris (thanks, Aurelie!). Thanks to you, one and all, including: Kalpita Ainapure, Cheryl Barnes, Olga Berger, Natalia Bulsza, Becca Courtright, Joachim Courtright, Pearl Courtright-Shucow, Erin Courtright, Victor Courtight, Ellie Crouch, Preeti Deshpande, Annie Dolbeau, Martin Eagan, Aurelie Epie, Evon Ford, Ivy Ford, Tyler Freeman, Alex Goodman, Whitney Freeman, Rahul Gorawara, Sunjay Gorowara, Samuel Gray, Della Hansmann, Keela J. Hansmann, Sukruthi Jois, Kate Leaver, Neha Manchade, Georgia Metz, Josh Metz, Jay Miller, Stepen Naidu, Chrissy Nottoli, Mark Nottoli, Lorenzo Nottoli, Nicholas Nottoli, Victor Pacini, Amy Palace, Gina Polozzi, Aurora Roeker, Max Schewitz, Kayla Schultz, Tina Schwartz, Shelby Shrake, Chuck Skinnman, William Starsiac, Panjri Shukla, Himika Tanaka, and Carreen Toland.

A second special thanks to those who were brave enough to appear on the book's covers. They are (front cover, from left to right) Max Schewitz, Joachim Courtright, Sam Gray, Shelby Shrake, Kayla Schultz (also on the back cover).

My hat is off to all of you for your great unselfish effort and your fun-loving spirit!

I would like to give my heartfelt thanks to the professionals who helped me. First and foremost to Arlene, who did seven complete edits on my book and never got mad at me for my many mistakes (thank you, Arlene)! Kim Tabor, Corinne Burton, Stephen Ryan, and Jayme Bartles—a thanks for your professionalism and patience (even though I was always late with my edit returns). And a huge hug to one of the most influential people in my writing career, Dee Konrad, my professor at Barat (who knew I would get published someday.)

I would also like to thank those amazing people called my family members, including Cay, my inspiration; JR (my childhood best friend); Tony, Annie, Mark, Lizzy, and Chrissy (and their significant others); and Christophe, Bella, Oliv, Sophie, Nick, Mason, Margot, Vincent, Gio, Enzo, Terry, and Bill; and my sweet and very patient husband, Robert.

And I would like to acknowledge my Maa (who inspires me daily) and my source, my ever-beloved, Baba.

To each and everyone, I humbly acknowledge your part in making this book possible.

Part 1: GET READY

Life is meant to be happy—even your life. Maybe that's a hard thing for you to believe, but could there be some truth in it? Are you happy in your daydreams? Do any of them appear over and over again? Daydreams are unspoken wishes—tiny glimpses of something you long to do someday. Do you have a hidden life goal that is calling you?

Have you ever found yourself in your car, stopped at a traffic light, thinking about nothing in particular? You glance at a Navy billboard where an F-16 is blasting off an aircraft carrier, and just for an instant, you think, "It would be so cool to join the Navy." Or maybe you saw a TV commercial for Sea World where whales and dolphins were flying, not swimming, followed by the word "Believe," and for an instant you thought, "Hey, I'd love to work with them!" Those might be daydreams, but they might also hold a seed for a real goal!

In section 1, "Get Ready," you'll learn many things about goals. This will include what goals are and the five steps to reach them, how to find your path in life, how to stay on course to meet your goals, how to turn failure into success, and how to embrace change.

Tucked away in the pages of this book, you'll find self-help exercises. Some are nicknamed No Sweat Exercise so you won't stress over them. Others are designed to lead you through journaling, doodling, or drawing. They're all designed to help you uncover your goals, to discover your dreams, and to give you new ways to make them come true.

Are you dreaming of a happy, successful life? Then the answer is simple—let's GOAL!

1 What Are Goals?

Goals are dreams that come true. They are both the journey and the magical end. Along the way something about you changes as your goals define you. When you reach your destination, you are ready to accept it. You have longed for it so much that you become it.

In this story about goals, *you* are the main character, and you get what you really want in life. It becomes reality. Sound impossible? It's not. In this chapter, you'll learn tools to help you realize your dreams—everything from examining what a goal is, to using a Goals Notebook, to writing lists, to discovering the difference between crazy things you might want to do someday and envisioning lofty goals. You'll even play with the idea of your own success to experience how great it feels.

ARE GOALS DREAMS THAT COME TRUE?

You might wonder, "Are goals really dreams that can come true?" The amazing answer is, yes! Once you've learned how to make

"Goals are dreams we convert to plans and take action to fulfill."—Zig Ziglar, motivational speaker

your dreams and goals become real, you can do it over and over again your whole life.

We're not hoping that by some miracle millions of dollar bills will fall out of the sky. We're talking about reality—about a simple formula anyone can learn that can make things happen in a tangible way. Are you interested? If so, get ready.

Creating goals is fun and easy. It's like having a secret—one you think about all the time—one you'll want to share with a special person in your life at the perfect moment. Maybe the goal you accomplish will be a surprise for your best friend or your parent, or maybe it's something you've always wanted to do for yourself.

Perhaps you're at a low point in your life right now or you've had a string of bad luck. Here's the first idea to learn in the journey of success: you actually create your own good luck.

Azriela Jaffe believes that, too, and wrote a book about it entitled *Create Your Own Luck: 8 Principles of Attracting Good Fortune in Life, Love, and Work.*[1] She suggests you open your mind and actually expect good luck. Laurie Beth Jones makes the same suggestion in her book, *The Path: Creating Your Mission Statement for Work and for Life.*[2] She explains that when you expect good things in life, your emotions seem to carve a path for the universe to come right to your door. In other words, your belief becomes a prophecy that helps to create your future.

Maybe you're discouraged right now or even thinking, "My life is so messed up, why should I even try?"

When you were a toddler just learning to walk and you fell down, you didn't think, "Okay, that does it. I'm never walking again." No, you picked yourself up and tried again until you mastered that one particular step that was giving you trouble.

"When life throws sudden changes at you, don't let it intimidate you. It happens to everybody. We all experience hard knocks, things that deplete you of your spirit, drain your energy, and sap your courage. You have to dig deep into yourself at those times."
—Les Brown, author[3]

Your goal was to get around faster by walking—you fell, you tried again, and you did it. You have been setting goals all your life. Now it's time to learn to plan your goals as a young adult.

Maybe someone, like your coach or counselor or parent, says to you, "What you need is a goal. Sit down right now, and in the next half hour, write one out."

You look around the room and think, "Okay, what's my goal?" Obvious answer: "To get out of here asap." But you can't. You've got twenty-five more minutes to kill, and if you can't come up with something, maybe you'll have another thirty minutes to stare at the blank page after that. Or, in your heart maybe you know that it's time to do something constructive with your life. The problem is, you don't know where to begin or how to create a goal.

Let's begin with the basics to create a goal. What exactly is a goal? A goal can be a lofty idea or something simple that makes common sense. What is goal worthy? Almost anything you desire can become a goal—whether it's earning a million dollars before the age of thirty or losing five pounds by the start of summer vacation.

Write your goals.
Illustration by Peg Raasch.

"I'm taking driver's ed right now, which is really easy. It was the first goal I set for myself when I got back from a nine-month rehab. I'm having fun in the class, except for when we have to watch the films on gory accidents. If they're supposed to scare you into driving carefully, they really work.

"The other part is I've got a driving permit, which is cool with me. But when I drive with my mom she freaks out if I don't turn a certain way, when I already have the situation under control. So her freaking out causes me to freak out, too. But, little by little I'm getting the hang of it."—Alex, 16 years old

THE GOALS NOTEBOOK

For you to get the most out of this book you'll need a Goals Notebook—from a spiral notebook to a cloth hardcover book, any kind of notebook will do. When prompted in each chapter, you'll open it and copy the format described in the text for the No Sweat Exercises. Keep the notebook with you in your backpack to jot down notes and read over your goals.

Right now, take out your Goals Notebook and on a clean piece of paper write, "Today is the first day of the rest of my life." It may sound cliché, but do it.

Underneath that write, "Today I will begin to reach my goals." Then, write today's date and sign it. This is all you will put on the first page.

Next, take a breath, settle yourself in your chair, turn over the page, and begin again—only this time you should feel more in charge because learning to set and achieve goals isn't about the people who seem to control your life at this moment; it's about you. Now, relax, open your mind, and be yourself. Then we'll get started with lists.

LISTS, LISTS, LISTS

It's trendy to get into lists. Why? Here are some reasons:

- **Writing lists is a form of brainstorming.**
- **Brainstorming helps reveal your inner thoughts and goals.**
- **Daily lists help you focus on your daily schedule.**
- **Weekly and monthly lists place your goals into action steps.**
- **Writing yearly lists brings deep thoughts to your planning.**
- **Life lists are the ultimate life-goal revelation.**

Crazy Things I Want to Do Someday

Let's look at goals as life lists. For fun, take three minutes and scribble out a short list of eight things you want to do "someday." Why eight? There's a kids' card game that's been around forever called Crazy Eights, and I thought it would make goal setting

EXAMPLE: NO SWEAT EXERCISE 1—CRAZY THINGS I WANT TO DO SOMEDAY

1. Visit Nepal and watch the sunrise from Mount Everest.
2. Go to culinary school and graduate as a dessert chef.
3. Move to Zimbabwe in Africa and help kids with AIDS.
4. Swim under a waterfall in the rain forest.
5. Learn fly-fishing—then go to Alaska and fish with my dad.
6. Go camping with my friends in the Rockies for a week.
7. Create some new gismo and become a millionaire.
8. Ride the waves for an entire day in Hawaii.

Here is an amazing way to empower yourself—write a life list. Look at Stephanie La Grossa, who is a "survivor" in every sense of the word. Not only did she outlast every member of her team on the reality TV show *Survivor: Palau*, but also she was voted first runner-up in December 2005 on *Survivor: Guatemala*.[4]

Bill Ervolino, a journalist for the *Sunday Record*, a New Jersey newspaper, wrote about Stephanie in an article on January 1, 2006. Stephanie told Ervolino that while at Palau, she asked herself, "Where had I been? What had I done? So, one day I went off by myself and wrote a list of all the things I wanted to do when I got home, and all the things I wanted to do with the rest of my life."

In the same article, Ervolino says,

> **Life-lists have been called wild, crazy, affirming, and the new "must- haves."**
>
> **. . . They "are serious compilations of the things you want to do, see and experience in your lifetime."**
>
> **The items on your list could be as adventurous as flailing around at the end of a bungee cord in New Zealand or zipping off to Norway to see the aurora borealis. . . . Go back to school. Complete an unusual collection. It's your list. You're the only one who can write it, and the only one who can bring the items on your list to fruition.**
>
> **It isn't a Life-list until you've written it down. Having it on paper serves as a focus and a constant reminder. It makes it real, and it makes it more likely that you will realize the items on your list.[5]**

more fun to think of these exercises as a game. Also, eight is two less than ten, which makes things easier. Remember, this is a "No Sweat" Exercise, so relax as you get a little wild with your ideas. On the previous page is an example of the first No Sweat list to help you to think about yours.

Maybe you're not a person who likes to do quizzes, lists, or exercises. This book is meant to shatter your old ideas, to help change your mind, forget that you're mad, sad, indifferent, bored, scared, furious, exhausted, or whatever! You can write eight more words that describe how you feel at this very instant. Go ahead. No one will even notice.

Feel a little better? Good. Now crumple up the second list, and toss it in the trash. That was a just-for-fun exercise to get you in the mood to write. Now for a real laugh, try and write out your crazy goals. There's only one rule: you have to do it quickly—

One rainy afternoon in 1939, an inspired fifteen-year-old boy named John Goddard sat down at his kitchen table in Los Angeles and wrote three words at the top of a yellow pad: "My Life List." Under that heading he wrote 127 goals and since then he has completed 108 of them. These were not simple or easy goals; they included climbing the world's major mountains, exploring the longest rivers of the world from source to mouth, piloting the world's fastest aircraft, running a mile in five minutes, and reading the entire *Encyclopedia Britannica*.

Today he is known as the World's Greatest Goal Achiever. [6]

three minutes max! That way you can't overanalyze your own thoughts. Plus, remember it's a game that's supposed to be fun and yes, just a little "crazy."

To review, for each No Sweat Exercise you'll copy the format found in the text into your Goals Notebook. Be sure and number every exercise so you can go back and reread your answers because one idea for a goal will often lead to another.

Now you begin to see why setting goals can be fun. But setting goals has a serious side as well. You are, after all, pursuing something that could be a life-long dream.

FOUR REAL IDEAS FOR A GOAL

Your next mission is to figure out which of your dreams can be converted into a goal versus those which are simply lofty concepts.

What exactly does *lofty* mean? According to the dictionary, lofty means something that is "sublime" or "elevated" or eloquent," such as lofty principles or lofty discourse.[7] We all have

NO SWEAT EXERCISE 1—CRAZY THINGS I WANT TO DO SOMEDAY

Directions: To start, write the exercise title at the top of the next blank page. Then number lines from one to eight and begin to write whatever comes into your head.

1. ______
2. ______
3. ______
4. ______
5. ______
6. ______
7. ______
8. ______

lofty ideas. However, to turn a goal into reality, it can't be something lofty you want to do someday. It needs to be tied to a time and a place in your life—something you can begin to work toward immediately.

From time to time you'll flip from something that is crazy, like the previous No Sweat Exercise, to a more serious subject where

"We can't all get the lead in the school play, be class president, be the star on the basketball team, or be in the national Honor Society. But we all have the ability to lead dynamic lives by pursuing our own unique goals and dreams. . . . We must believe that it is possible to achieve our dreams and then commit to achieving those dreams. Without that belief, every dream will turn to dust."—Stedman Graham, author[8]

"In my first year of college, I wasn't sure what my special interest would be or what I should major in. Although I loved English, I lost sight of my goal to become a teacher as I felt there must be something better for me. I kept looking until I took a class in General Psychology, which I loved. It was so much fun, I just couldn't get enough developmental psychology; it was great! As I thought about it with the help from an advisor, I thought I might become some kind of Early Childhood Family Counselor.

"After much research, I stumbled across a college in my state that specializes in different medical fields including therapy. I fell in love with it, but I wasn't about to choose yet another goal only to lose interest a week later as my heart took over my head. It turns out that it is affordable, so I'm filling out my application and sending it in.

"If all goes well, I will be moving to a tiny studio apartment sometime this summer to get ready for the fall semester. Until then, it's going to be me and whatever jobs I can find, to get enough to cover my costs by the fall!"—Lynda, age 18

you can turn inward to see what is really important to you. Take a few minutes right now and do just that. Brainstorm to jot down some of your dreams; try to examine what might be a lofty idea floating around in your head versus a real potential goal you can begin to work on immediately. Although it's important to think about your dreams and goals, it's more important to begin the

Some people just know when their destiny is to become an entertainer. Avril Lavigne remembers, "I always knew this [singer/song writer thing] was what I had to do. I remember when I was really young, standing on my bed like it was a stage, singing at the top of my lungs and visualizing thousands of people surrounding me."[9]

NO SWEAT EXERCISE 2—FOUR REAL IDEAS FOR A GOAL

Directions: To begin, write the title on the top line. Then number the next four lines for the remainder of the exercise. That's what is called the format. Now jump in and write.

____

1. ______________________________
2. ______________________________
3. ______________________________
4. ______________________________

process. How? Start to put something down on paper—even if you just stare at your notes. That's the first step toward making your goals a reality.

Whether your goal is to set a record for the most hoops in one game, be the best batter on your softball team, or find a new best friend—in your mind's eye put yourself there.

Best friends, Georgia and Himika.

GIRLS WHO MET THEIR GOALS TO BECOME SUCCESSFUL ENTERTAINERS IN THEIR TEENS

- **Alicia Keys, at seventeen, signed her first recording deal with Arista Records, and she wrote, produced, and recorded her own albums singing R & B and soul.[10]**
- **Charlotte Church appeared on *The Oprah Winfrey Show* at age thirteen and debuted her first U.S. album, *Voice of an Angel*, which went double platinum in six weeks in the United Kingdom.[11]**
- **Beyoncé Knowles, the lead singer in Destiny's Child at age sixteen, won nine Grammy Awards—six for her solo work and three as a member of Destiny's Child.[12]**
- **Raven-Symoné cut her teeth on *The Bill Cosby Show*, then became the main star on the TV show *That's So Raven*. At thirteen, she was the youngest person ever to sign with MCA Records.[13]**
- **Hilary Duff starred on the Disney TV sitcom *Lizzie McGuire* at age thirteen and made *The Lizzie McGuire Movie* by the age of sixteen. Her first album, *Metamorphosis*, became number one on Billboard and sold over 2 million copies.[14]**
- **Avril Lavigne went on her own to become a recording star at sixteen and was a worldwide featured entertainer at the closing of the Winter Olympics in February of 2006.[15]**

If you think this is bunk, look at kids your age who made it into the spotlight. Hollywood boasts of many entertainers who followed their dreams and became famous during their teens.

Exactly how did they do it? What was the magical formula that helped them to reach their goal? The main word is

D-E-T-E-R-M-I-N-A-T-I-O-N

plus they all set out with a plan on how they would reach their goal to become an entertainer.

If you long for success, you must first learn the fundamental steps to create your goal:

Five Steps to Create a Goal

1. **Desire the end result—you've got to really, really want it.**
2. **Write out action steps and a time they will be completed.**
3. **See the goal completed—every day act as if it's already happened.**

4. **Feel the excitement—how will you feel when you meet your goal?**
5. **Track your progress—grade yourself on how well you completed each step.**

MY FIRST GOAL

You'll need to speed things up because you've been taking baby steps to get to this point. Ready? Now it's showtime.

Congratulations—you are on your way to achieving your goals. Now that you have written out your first goal, you'll need to do some more digging to find other hidden wishes. Why? Wishing is the fuel you'll need to reach your goal. There's power in a heart-felt wish because it gives you the drive to try one more time when you feel defeated.

A wish is different from a daydream—it's more emotional. When you listen to your inner voice and clarify your wish, you find it's a powerful magnet. Your goal is your destination; your wish is the fuel that pushes you toward it.

You'll discover ideas you long to experience that may be hidden. That is the real purpose of these exercises—to help you see and listen to your heart's desires. Allow yourself to feel what's

NO SWEAT EXERCISE 3—FIVE STEPS TO CREATE A GOAL

Directions: First write the title, then number lines from one to five. Then take three minutes and copy Five Steps to Create a Goal from the text into your notebook. Place this simple formula on index cards and scatter them where you can read the steps day and night.

____

1. ______________________________________
2. ______________________________________
3. ______________________________________
4. ______________________________________
5. ______________________________________

pulling at your heart—that is the first clue to find out what you really want.

Remember step 1 to create your goals—you must desire the end result. You've got to be passionate about it. Since most of us fear the disappointment of failure, we're afraid to take the first baby steps—we're even scared to listen to our inner voice. Sometimes when we try too hard, nothing comes to us but a bunch of mumble-jumble ideas that have nothing to do with our heart's desire.

Life is so simple when you allow things to come to you—ideas, events, even people. When you tune into this amazing force, anything can happen. That's because when you begin to set your goal, you become a magnet for positive things to come into your world. Open your mind—look at what is waiting for you to "see."

Since you are reading about how to set goals, you might not have a lot of experience in the real world—you know, that foreign place existing outside your inner circle of friends and daily environment. That's why learning to set goals exactly where you are at this moment is the key to success. That's how you get ahead of the pack.

Check out the illustrations in this book. Can you see yourself in the pictures, meeting your goals? Whether you envision yourself graduating from college, purchasing your first car, or even delivering an acceptance speech for an award, put yourself in the picture.[16]

Play with the idea of your own success. Try to film yourself using your digital camera, webcam, or phone. Turn yourself into a big video production, staging "lights, camera, action!" and then put your video on MySpace or YouTube. You've got to try this

"You have to ask yourself, 'Who am I creating this goal for and why am I really doing it?' To please your parents so you can get a new car? To win over your teacher so you'll get a better grade? No! You are creating this goal for yourself and don't ever lose sight of that. Forget impressing others—impress yourself and meet your goals."—Anne Courtright

NO SWEAT EXERCISE 4—MY FIRST GOAL

Directions: You are now ready to write out your first goal using the five steps from No Sweat Exercise 3. Pay attention to steps 2 and 5 where you'll track your daily progress. To be in sync for this first experiment, take a typical goal that every teen wants to achieve—to get his or her driver's license. If you already have your license, substitute another goal such as the college of your dreams.

On the first line write the title. Next, number five lines for your goal. Create your own tracking system by using a check mark, or paste stickers in the boxes to monitor the steps of your goal. Pay special attention to steps 2 and 5. Make a corresponding mark on your calendar to remind yourself to check your progress daily. Give yourself five minutes to complete this exercise.

Still hesitating? Here are the basics of the five steps to get you started. Now you just need to fill in the blanks.

____

1. I really want . . . [to get my driver's license]

   ____________________________________ ☐

2. To achieve it I will do the following each week: [get my permit, go to driver's ed class, etc.]

   ____________________________________ ☐

3. How I see myself when I achieve my goal: [how I look driving my car]

   ____________________________________ ☐

4. How I feel when I've reached my goal: [how I feel behind the wheel]

   ____________________________________ ☐

5. I track how well I completed the above steps: [Before I go to bed I check off my progress.]

   ____________________________________ ☐

idea out to see how great it feels to put yourself in a crazy scene of the future. By trying new experiments like this, you'll see what you enjoy and reveal hidden goals as you try to discover your true path in life.

Hold on tight—the journey's just beginning, and your path is beckoning you!

NOTES

1. Azriela Jaffe, *Create Your Own Luck: 8 Principles of Attracting Good Fortune in Life, Love and Work* (Holbrook, MA: Adams Media Corporation, 2000).

2. Laurie Beth Jones, *The Path: Creating Your Mission Statement for Work and for Life* (New York: Hyperion, 1996).

3. Les Brown, *Live Your Dreams* (New York: William Morrow, 1992), 211.

4. Stephanie La Grossa competed on the *Survivor: Palau* reality TV show (May 2005.) She was voted first runner-up in *Survivor: Guatemala* (December 2005), http://en.wikipedia.org/wiki/Stephanie_LaGrossa(accessed September 2, 2006).

5. Bill Ervolino, "Six Steps to Writing a To-Do List of a Lifetime," *Sunday Record*, January 1, 2006, 4.

6. John Goddard, "The World's Greatest Goal Achiever," www.johngoddard.info/life_list.htm (accessed January 8, 2007); Michael Kaplan, "99 Things to Do before You Die: How to Make Your Own Life-List—and Start Achieving Your Goals," *Mens' Journal*, June 2005, 82–90.

7. *The New Lexicon Webster's Dictionary of the English Language* (New York: Lexicon Publications, 1988), 582.

8. Stedman Graham, *Nine Steps to Success: Teens Can Make It Happen* (New York: Simon & Schuster, 2000), 13–14.

9. "Avril Lavigne biography," BiggestStars.com, www.biggeststars.com/a/avril-lavigne-biography.html (accessed June 22, 2006).

10. "Biography for Alicia Keys," The Internet Movie Database, www.imdb.com/name/nm1006024/bio (accessed October 29, 2006).

11. "12-Year-Old Inductees: Charlotte Church," The Kids Hall of Fame, thekidshalloffame.com/CustomPage6.html (accessed October 29, 2006).

12. "Beyonce," AskMen.com, www.askmen.com/women/singer_150/197c_beyonce.html (accessed October 15, 2007).

13. "Biography for Raven-Symoné," The Internet Movie Database, www.imdb.com/name/nm0712368/bio (accessed October 29, 2006).

14. "Bio," Hilary Duff, www.hilaryduff.com/ (accessed October 29, 2006).

15. Corey Moss, "Avril Lavigne: Usher, Hilary Duff, SpongeBob Take Home Orange Blimps From Kids' Choice Awards," VH1, April 4, 2005, www.vh1.com/artists/news/1499525/0 042005/lavigne_avril.jhtml (accessed October 3, 2006).

16. You'll learn how to place yourself in any picture in chapter 7, "Create Goals by Visualizing a Picture Map."

2 Find Your Path in Life

Shelby on Dreamer.

Whether you were born to sing, like Kelly Clarkson;[1] speak out for the world's refugees, like Angelina Jolie;[2] or simply follow your heart—your path awaits you. It leads the way to your true calling—to your life's goal. So, what will you need to do to get there?

As you understand more about goals, you will see the need to dig deeper to make them meaningful. Therefore, we will examine more in-depth reasons why you need goals, what is meant by the *big picture*, how to take advantage of goals that are part of your school curriculum, and how friends can support you to meet your goals.

WHY DO YOU NEED GOALS?

It sounds simple, yet it can be complicated. If you're a horseman, there are a lot of steps to master to become an accomplished rider. Whether it is learning to tack and brush your mount, jump a triple hedge, or trot in front of hundreds of people, every step is comprised of smaller steps. When you put them all together, you function as an expert equestrian. That is why you need goals. Goals are like steps—they will help you see your way clearly through all of the decisions you'll have to make along the way.

"The bottom line of why you need to set your goals is to find your path in life—to figure out what you really want to do and who you want to become."—Anne Courtright

THE "BIG PICTURE"

Maybe you were pushed into meeting goals that somebody else set for you so you could see the big picture for your life. This could come from your parents, who want you to get straight As, or your coach, who drives you during team practice so you can win an athletic scholarship. It makes you think, "What's the fuss about the big picture?"

The *big picture* is a term used to describe the realm of possibilities of a subject when all the smaller pieces fit together. It's what the adults in your life feel you should focus on for your future—areas that they think are important that you haven't thought about. They might be things outside of your everyday

"After I finished high school I worked at my dad's restaurant, but it didn't seem right, or what my heart was calling to me to do. So I applied to nursing school.

"Now I have finished three semesters of school. Although it is very difficult, I still like it a lot. My schedule is a bit crazy though, because I take classes at school for six weeks and then I work at the hospital for four weeks. I like to work in all the different floors of the hospital. Last week I worked with patients who had heart murmurs—it was sad but challenging.

"After this semester, I'll start my second year and I still have time to decide what I want to specialize in. I think I want to work with sick children. They seem to need me the most." —Aurelie, age 19

world. Eventually these goals will help you to live on your own and enjoy success. More than likely you will merge your own goals with their hopes for you. However, realize that your goals might never merge with what adults have in mind for you, and that's okay, too.

"Why do adults always talk about the 'big picture' and push you into things you already want to do? When they cram it down your throat who wants to do it then?"—Becca, age 16

A great example of this scenario comes to mind in the 2004 Hilary Duff movie *A Cinderella Story*.[3] A moment of truth comes for the star athlete, Austin Ames (played by Chad Michael Murray), during the homecoming football game. His dad is on the field with him and keeps reminding him, "This is the big one—stay focused. Everyone is counting on you." (Austin's dad dreams of his son going to college at the University of Southern California even though Austin dreams of going to Princeton.) Finally, Austin splits during the final huddle to find Sam (played by Hilary). His dad yells, "Where are you going? . . . You're throwing away your dream." Austin yells back, "No, Dad, I'm throwing away yours." He runs into the stands and kisses Sam in front of the entire crowd while a teammate scores the final touchdown. At the end of the movie, Sam and Austin both reach their goal of going to Princeton.

It's time for a reality check here—the big picture usually boils down to you becoming independent and being happy. Well, great news . . . that's exactly what you want, too. So, rather than fight this point of view, which can be a very big source of family conflict, why not try a different approach? Laugh at the whole idea. Using your sense of humor, slightly distort the next eight examples to fit your family's issues. Then, write a second list for yourself and see if there is any point where the two lists might merge.

Looking at the big picture, which is simply another term for your future, boils down to the way you "see" certain things versus

EXAMPLE: NO SWEAT EXERCISE 5—THE BIG PICTURE

Here are eight pieces of the big picture some adults might want for you:

1. Get a job.
2. Buy your own car.
3. Pay for your own car insurance.
4. Get better grades in school.
5. Go to college.
6. Join a religious youth group.
7. Train to become a professional athlete.
8. Enlist in the military.

NO SWEAT EXERCISE 5—THE BIG PICTURE

Directions: Are you game to tackle this big issue? If so, grab your Goals Notebook and prepare your page for this two-part exercise. You will have two separate titles: Exercise 5A—Their Big Picture and Exercise 5B—My Big Picture. Next, number one set of eight lines under each title. Now enjoy the adventure of creating the two lists and remember to laugh at the entire scenario.

Exercise 5A—Their Big Picture

1. ____________________
2. ____________________
3. ____________________
4. ____________________
5. ____________________
6. ____________________
7. ____________________
8. ____________________

For you to see your own big picture, you have to make goal setting a priority. This is why your goals need to be your heart's calling, not someone else's. It is important to never stop striving to be the real you. Since you are sincere about your goals, you can use the check boxes to mark your progress

Exercise 5B—My Big Picture

1. ____________________ ☐
2. ____________________ ☐
3. ____________________ ☐
4. ____________________ ☐
5. ____________________ ☐
6. ____________________ ☐
7. ____________________ ☐
8. ____________________ ☐

the way your parents "envision" them unfolding for you. If you're feeling more empowered, tell your parents about this exercise and ask them to write down eight things they hope will become part of your big picture. Compare their answers with the fictitious list you wrote for them in No Sweat Exercise 5A. Then compare it to your real list in 5B, and see where you have similar ideas. If there's a difference maybe the gap is due to terms and language used, not the core ideas.

One young man wrote a book on the big picture. In doing so he didn't discover how to succeed, but the reasons to succeed. In his book, *The Big Picture: Getting Perspective on What's Really Important in Life*, Ben Carson came to realize that his big picture was about broadening his perspectives. He describes how "finding a vision for your own life can reframe your priorities, energize your efforts, and inspire you to change the world around you."[4]

HOW I SEE MY FUTURE

Because you do not have a lot of experience in life, it's difficult to see how your plans might unfold. That is why you might turn to your parents or guardian for guidance, even though their advice might be painful to hear. Believing they know what is best for you, your parents might limit your choices. They might put subtle pressure on you to pursue a certain profession or maintain a strict academic or moral code.

An example of this can be found in the heart-wrenching movie *The Notebook*.[5] The story unfolds through the memoirs of Noah, played by Ryan Gosling, as he remembers the summer he and Allie, played by Rachel McAdams, fell madly in love. Because Noah is from a lower social class, Allie's parents disapprove of the

"Dare to do this simple thing: Make a list of what you really want—not what somebody else thinks you should have. As you make your list, dare to please only yourself, remembering that 'the highest is the nearest.' Then keep your list private, a secret between you and your own (higher) self."—Catherine Ponder, author[6]

NO SWEAT EXERCISE 6—HOW I SEE MY FUTURE

Directions: Try to imagine what you will be doing ten years from now. Write the title on the first line and number one to eight on the next eight lines. Next write down eight possibilities to this intriguing question.

____

1. ____
2. ____
3. ____
4. ____
5. ____
6. ____
7. ____
8. ____

relationship and decide to end their summer vacation early, resulting in the couple's traumatic break-up.

Seven years later, Allie reunites with Noah, but she is engaged to marry another man. Allie is in turmoil over what to do, so Noah challenges her: "Stop thinking about what everyone wants—what your parents want, what he wants, what I want. What do you want?" That seems to be the crucial question. Whether it's signing up for a military career or marching for social justice, it's hard to see what decisions will lead you to your ultimate goal.

To convince yourself and your parents that you can begin to envision your own big picture, why not develop habits that show you are responsible and start working toward achieving them? Here are eight possible ways to do this:

1. **Get a part-time job.**
2. **Don't blow off work for social events.**

3. **Come home from a party at the time you agreed upon.**
4. **Create a budget and be accountable to yourself for the way you spend money.**
5. **Set up a repayment plan if you owe your parents money, and stick to it.**
6. **Save for the deposit on your next car.**
7. **Put additional money aside for car insurance.**
8. **Watch your spending sprees on clothes, iPods, and other impulsive "must-haves" (especially resist those flashy ads on the Internet that target teens).**

Why not take the first step and open a bank account (if you haven't already done so). You can open a savings account at any age. In most states, you must be eighteen to open a checking account. You will need a driver's license and a social security card for ID. Most banks issue ATM debit cards with your checking account within two weeks from your opening date. The amount you can debit (or withdraw) is tied to the balance in your checking account. Record every debit into your check register and treat it like a check or a withdrawal. (Later you can move to online banking but start with a good paper trail to keep track of your records.) Have your paycheck deposited automatically into your bank account by filling out the necessary paperwork. Your savings account can be connected to your checking account so you can save a given amount from every paycheck.

If you already have a bank account, make it a habit to save at least 10 percent of your weekly earnings. Simple things like that make you feel successful, especially when you see how quickly your balance can grow. Little by little you'll see your big picture start to come to life whether at home, with friends, or in school.

SETTING GOALS IN SCHOOL

Setting goals in school is so overdone that it can make your skin crawl. You might think that only nerds go for goals in school and that turning over a new leaf will cause other kids to tease you. But getting serious about your own success can win new respect from others.

In *The 7 Habits of Highly Successful Teens*, Sean Covey (son of the famous business guru Stephen Covey) applauds his younger brother, David, who was determined to become a successful athlete.[7]

Even though David was scrawny in his freshman year, he was strong-willed and he wrote down some goals he wanted to achieve during high school. First he worked on getting proper nutrition and rest so he would grow bigger and stronger. In football, David set a goal to be the starting wide receiver on the varsity team, and in track to be an all-state sprinter. He envisioned himself as the captain of both the football team and the track team.

Although David went through many trials and tribulations, he reached most of his goals with only a few minor setbacks. It took time and determination, but by his senior year David was six feet tall, weighed 180 pounds, and was able to bench press 250 pounds. He learned firsthand that the seven principles (or "habits" defined by his father) really work.

Having goals imposed on you in school is hard to take because they are not your idea in the first place. Consequently, you start turning yourself off on the first day of school. But what if one of the goals mentioned in class was actually one of your dream goals?

In your first period, you probably have a 95 percent chance of hearing a teacher say, "This year, our goals as a class are . . . blah, blah, blah." You go into the zone, turn up the volume of your favorite tune in your head, and probably even tap out the beat. You're in a groove, and there's no room there for your teacher.

***The 7 Habits of Highly Successful Teens*, written by Sean Covey, adapts the principles created by Stephen Covey in his best seller *The Seven Habits of Highly Successful People*.[8] Stephen's book reveals the main concepts of the Franklin Covey system. These include habits such as being proactive in daily life and using day planners, as well as other ideas expanded through leadership-centered workshops. Sean adjusts these winning principles, or habits, to reflect the attitudes and problems that face teens.**

If you wonder how this could benefit you, think of it as your first glimpse into the corporate world that awaits you in the near future. If you're curious how Sean's dad, Stephen Covey, is regarded in the business world, consider this: Stephen R. Covey is chairman of the Covey Leadership Center and the nonprofit Institute for Principle-Centered Leadership. "The firm holds leadership and training and development seminars worldwide. It has over 100 of the Fortune 500 companies as its clients and thousands of midsize and small companies, educational institutions, and all levels of government."[9]

What if this semester you become open-minded? When you hear the goals-for-this-year talk, what if you turn down the volume in your head and listen to your teacher instead? What if one of the goals mentioned is one of your daydreams, one you've been afraid to try on your own. What if, at that exact moment, you make it your own goal?

Try this scenario: What if you are sitting at your desk on the first day of English class and Mrs. Matthews, the teacher, starts rattling off all of the work for the semester from a syllabus she is passing out. She might have a list including when assignments will be due from your text, how often you can expect an exercise, when term papers should be started, and how important it is to do well in English if you want to get a high score on your SATs. She might wrap up her spiel with a list of workshops and a writing contest to be held in your region during the semester.

Fortunately for you, your ears pop just in time to hear her describe a regional short-story contest where the first place winner will be awarded a free trip to New York to meet an editor and art director. Just as you sit up and pay attention, she staples the notice to the bulletin board in the back of the room, saying, "If anyone's interested, let me know so you can earn extra credit for this."

Whoa! Did you really hear that right? You look up to see if anyone notices that your ears are tingling, because one of your deepest desires is to go to New York where you could meet an editor and be discovered like Christopher Paolini, who wrote *Eragon* when he was fifteen.

If you can accept the idea of setting goals in school as a possibility, you could take a kernel of your dream, look at it from every angle, remold it to fit into your school agenda, and give it your own spin. The advantage is that you would have all the support and the tools to do this in class. All it would take is self-motivation and the courage to go for it. If you would just make the simple decision to do this for yourself, dramatic changes would happen in your life.

You might say to yourself, "My goal this year is to raise my grades by a whole point," or "My goal is to be an exchange student," or "My goal is to get accepted into my first choice of colleges." The possibilities are endless. What if you decided it was an excellent idea to succeed and stupid to fail? The next time you hear the word *goal* in school, pay attention. Listen to see if you

One of the most amazing teen authors who has met early success is Christopher Paolini, who began writing his fantasy novel, *Eragon*, at the age of fifteen. First published independently in 2002, *Eragon* was republished by Knopf, a large New York publishing house, in August 2003 and went on to become a *New York Times* best seller.

***Eldest*, the second book of the Inheritance trilogy and also set in the mystical land of Alagaesia, was released in August of 2007.**

***Eragon*, the movie, was released in December 2006 along with all the hype that goes with today's movies including websites, games, clothes, and fan clubs.[10]**

***Brisingr*, the final book of the Inheritance series, was released in September 2008.**

Although you might admire Christopher Paolini as he continues to write his fantasy novels and enjoys the journey of being a young adult success, ask yourself if you would have the courage to visit 135 schools dressed in a medieval costume to promote your book as he did!

can adapt the goal and create five steps to achieve it. Then try to change your habits, putting them into doable action steps that will give you more time to study and succeed. Maybe you can make your goal to study abroad like one teen did.

Wake up and pay attention to your everyday habits. It's time to think about your life at school from a different angle. Why not make it more successful by pretending it's another goal-setting project? To start, jot down some ideas on your different subjects. Then move into one specific area where you could shine, if you gave yourself an edge. How do you begin such a huge

"If you want better grades, then you have to work on 'time management.' Set goals to give yourself one extra hour a day for study."—Jay McGraw, author[11]

"Last summer I had a chance to go to Japan as an exchange student, which was really exciting. I stayed with a family on one of the smaller Japanese islands and attended a private school. I made a lot of new friends and if I ever get the chance to study abroad again, I would do it in a heartbeat, because it helped me develop my self-confidence.

"Traveling across the world was a whole new experience for me and when I arrived I couldn't speak the language. It was hilarious because I had to learn to bridge the communications gap. I would carry around a notebook with me and draw out what I was trying to say, or I would act it out, like charades.

"When I got home I had fun telling my friends about my experience in Japan."—Pita, age 17

Pita visiting Japanese students.

NO SWEAT EXERCISE 7—SETTING GOALS IN SCHOOL

Directions: Flip back to review No Sweat Exercise 4—My First Goal and use it as your guideline. After you write the title of this exercise on the top line, pick one specific subject where you could make four small changes to help you to understand it better, such as turn your homework in on time or pay attention in class. Put that subject on the line below the title to focus on it. Then, number the next four lines and write possible changes you could make. Give yourself three minutes to complete this exercise.

____

____

1. ______________________________
2. ______________________________
3. ______________________________
4. ______________________________

undertaking? Simple! Grab that Goals Notebook and brainstorm to shed some light into the murky parts of your brain.

It's important to let your family and friends know you are serious about improving your life. Maybe you'll need to be more selfish about your time and stay after school to work in the library to get your homework done. That could change your duties at home, so somebody else would have to walk the dog or feed the

"I like the extra-curricular activities at my school, because they're a lot of fun. I'm a member of Future Business Leaders of America (FBLA). We do a lot of different things there and two weeks ago I won first place in Parliamentary Procedure.

"We learn a lot of other things about how to be a leader and about business in general. This has helped me become very focused on meeting my goals in school."—Jay, age 17

Here are some positive ideas to share with the adults in your life. Use them to discuss how the adults can help you meet your goals.

- **"The best way to help your teen succeed in school is to help him see the role difficult subjects and situations play in reaching personal goals. . . .**
- **"A student who approaches school with a sense of purpose will usually succeed.**
- **"Your job is to help your teen clarify her goals, help her make new connections with old subjects, and encourage her to do her best."[12]**

"Last year I didn't think I'd have a chance to go away to college. It seemed out of reach in every way and I just couldn't see how I could swing it financially. My mom's a single parent and well, there's not a chance in the world I could ask my dad or his family for help.

"My school counselor told me she thought I could do it and I should make it my goal. I didn't know what I was doing, but I followed her advice. I wrote the name of the college on 3" × 5" cards with notes to myself on how to get there. I stuck them everywhere—on my bathroom mirror, in my school notebooks—even on my alarm clock. I looked at them day and night.

"I wrote a biography on myself for the application that my English teacher corrected for me, which helped a lot. A couple of other teachers wrote letters for me, saying what kinds of grades I got, and that I was good in track and other stuff. Then my mom's secretary helped me with the actual scholarship application. In the end, I got a partial scholarship as well as a state grant and together the two were enough to convince my mom I could handle the living-away-from-home college scene.

"Now I've got my eye on the dean's list (which will help me get next year's scholarship) and I'm learning more about this goal thing because I can see that it really works."—Erin, age 18 cat when you can't be counted on to do those chores. You'll be amazed how people will help you in little ways when they see you are trying to do more for yourself to achieve your goals.

So, don't be afraid to announce your plans for success. This creates a way for events to happen that will support you in reaching your goals.

As you mentally prepare yourself to reach your goals this year, maybe you'll need more supportive friends to get there. Sometimes you may not feel you're really acting like yourself but doing things to impress others kids. That can make you feel miserable. It's hard to break away from old friends and be true to yourself.

FRIENDS THAT SUPPORT MY GOALS

There are times when a friend means everything to you, especially when you are going through tough times. Sometimes you'll find

"SWEEP ACROSS THE SKY"

by Elizabeth, age 17

**I alone lay on my thin, white beach,
Staring up at my deep, dark sky.
It's here I find my quiet side,
As I gaze into sparkling eyes.
These billion eyes dive into mine,
And take me far away.
When I get there the sky is mixed,
The colors are blue and gray.
Another dreamer then comes nigh,
We smile, then dance, then fly.
We sweep across the sky by night,
My new-found friend and I.**

Here is a timeless magazine quiz that could be a definite eye-opener.[13]

"Is It Time to Break Up with a Bud?"

	Yes	No
If you're hanging with a group of girls and the chatting turns catty, your bud usually joins in on the trash talk.	☐	☐
Your family isn't a huge fan of her. You avoid telling them when you're meeting up with her.	☐	☐
She's really hurt your feeling when she's spilled a secret with your crush.	☐	☐
You're psyched about a new interest like yoga. She tells you to sign up for dance instead because that's her new thing.	☐	☐
Hanging with your pal has gotten you into trouble—like when she cooked up a not-so-smart scheme and convinced you to join her.	☐	☐
When it comes to tricky territory like dating older guys and smoking, you think maybe your bud's heading in the wrong direction.	☐	☐
When you're having a heart-to-heart, she seems to talk about herself a lot more than she listens to your problems.	☐	☐
Last year, you and your bud were digging the same tunes, friends, and styles. This year, you can't believe you used to be so similar.	☐	☐

you need to reach out and make new friends. This can be a scary thing, but it also can have amazing results.

You have to wonder, "Will my old friend be there for me if I change while I meet my goals?" Maybe you've had a best friend for several years and you feel you are drifting apart. If you dread hanging out, maybe you need to make your break-up official.

Guys, you also need to be honest about what it takes to meet your goals. What could help the most is to find a supportive friend who could share your ideas, hopes, and dreams. Together you could help each other grow in ways you could not dream of by yourself.

DARE TO DREAM

A great example of guys helping each other reach their goals can be found in the hilarious 2005 movie *Napoleon Dynamite*. Its popularity came from the simple humor found in its nerd-hero, Napoleon (played by Jon Heder), and his best friend, Pedro (played by Efren Ramirez). They were treated as high school outcasts until they forged a common goal of Pedro running for class president. Magically, this proved to be the key that brought each one success.

To test out this concept of bonding with a friend for support, here are some practical steps. Find a friend you can trust. Together write down a common goal. Create simple steps you can both do on a weekly basis. Write down a checklist and e-mail it to each other twice a week.

Dare to be like Napoleon Dynamite, who grew from a wimp to a hip-hop star to win his goal, and have the courage to believe that "your wildest dreams will come true!"[14] Forget impressing others—impress yourself and meet your goals.

"MY DREAMS"

by Victor, age 20

I want to take you on a journey.
It all starts inside of you.
Close your eyes and visualize
All the things you can do.
Like the lion in the jungle,
Or the eagle in the sky,
Your possibilities are endless.
You're free to roam and try.
I believe in myself.
There's nothing I can't do.
I'll follow my dreams,
I'll make them come true.
No matter what people want me to be,
My dreams are my dreams,
And no one can take them from me.

Victor singing at a high school visit.

When Victor Pacini was asked to entertain kids in summer camp, he dreamed that someday his real job would be writing and singing for kids. Now he is booked professionally through Parent Teacher Organizations and other school groups where he brings kids his message of hope. Victor's enthusiasm gets kids to sing his songs, follow their dreams, and never give up despite any obstacles they may confront.[15]

Allow yourself to dream—to become all you can be—and you will achieve your goals.

NOTES

1. Kelly Clarkson was winner of the 2002 season of the TV program *American Idol.*

2. Angelina Jolie took on a radically different role as a goodwill ambassador for the United Nations High Commissioner for Refugees in 2003. Her memoirs of activities in this role can be found in her book *Notes from My Travels: Visits with Refugees in Africa, Cambodia, Pakistan and Ecuador* (New York: Simon & Schuster, 2003).

3. *A Cinderella Story*, Warner Brothers, www2.warnerbros.com/acinderellastory/index.html (accessed May 12, 2007).

4. Ben Carson, *The Big Picture: Getting Perspective on What's Really Important in Life* (Grand Rapids, MI: Zondervan, 1999), back cover, www.amazon.com/gp/reader/031023834X/ref=sib_dp_pt/103-0849810-1015842#reader-link (accessed March 5, 2008).

5. "*The Notebook*: Synopsis," New Line Cinema, www.thenotebookmovie.com (accessed February 22, 2007).

6. Catherine Ponder, *Open Your Mind to Prosperity* (Marina Del Rey, CA: De Vorss & Company, 1984), 53.

7. Sean Covey, *The 7 Habits of Highly Effective Teens* (New York: Simon & Schuster, 1998), 99–101.

8. Stephen Covey, *The Seven Habits of Highly Effective People: Restoring the Character Ethic* (New York: Simon & Schuster, 1989).

9. "Stephen Covery," Jeri Charles Associates, www.lecturenow.com/People/StephenCovey.htm (accessed November 19, 2003). To learn more on Stephen Covey's Institute for Principle-Centered Leadership and find Franklin Covey products, go to www.stephencovey.com/about/about.php (accessed February 22, 2007).

10. "Christopher Paolini," Wikipedia, en.wikipedia.org/wiki/Christopher_Paolini (accessed December 12, 2006); for the Inheritance trilogy, go to Alagaesia, www.alagaesia.com/christopherpaolini.htm (accessed December 11, 2008); for *Eragon* (the movie), go to Eragon, www.eragonsite.com/ (accessed December 20, 2007).

11. Jay McGraw, *Life Strategies for Teens* (New York: Fireside, 2000), 171.

12. Biff Barnes, "Talk about Goals, Not Grades," *Parenting Today Magazine*, September 2003, 13.

13. "Is It Time to Break Up with a Bud?" *QuizFest*, November/December 2005, 30.

14. *Napoleon Dynamite*, www.foxsearchlight.com/napoleondynamite/ (accessed November 28, 2008).

15. To learn more about Victor Pacini's school visits where students share their goals and dreams, go to www.victorpacini.com (accessed May 24, 2007).

3 Staying on Course

To meet a new goal always involves some kind of change in your life. Once you embrace this, you'll begin to see endless possibilities for your future. You'll see that anything is possible and setting a goal is the "ticket" to creating a new life.

In this chapter you'll examine various ways to stay on course. You'll look at how to improve your life in small ways through creating realistic steps, how to meet and defeat major causes of stress, how to cope with peer pressure using your intuition, and how to use new tools such as planning, determination, and practice.

The goal you choose to focus on should be significant but not on so high a level that you'll never be able to reach it. The new task is to take a specific goal and define it through a process of action steps. So, if you select a goal to do something practical, such as keep your room tidy, and put up a small chart to check off every time you put your dirty clothes in the laundry hamper, then your goal will become real. Then one small step can lead to a larger step and soon you will be leaping into success!

STRIVING TO ACHIEVE GOALS

Don't underestimate the importance of your daily routine. When you strive to achieve your goals, staying on track with the small day-to-day activities allows you to focus on what's important and moves you forward. These could be simple events like waking up on time, getting showered and dressed for the day, eating a healthy breakfast, and leaving for school or work early. Your routine can make your day run smoothly, or it can give you something to focus on if you are dealing with major life changes. Small steps

"After high school a lot of different things happened I didn't plan on. First of all, at the last minute, I just didn't feel ready to live on my own. So I decided to stay at home and enroll in our local junior college.

"I'm in my third semester now and I've found that I really like the science classes. I felt I wanted to go into health care, perhaps nursing, so I'm taking both biology and chemistry as well as a couple of other classes. I also have a part-time job one day a week, so I have a busy schedule.

"I'm reaching small goals and figuring things out as I go, and that feels right for now."
—Gina, age 19

done with a purpose add up to big steps, which lead to one thing—reaching your dream.

Planning everyday events helps you feel empowered. It's great if you make lists. This way, instead of letting little things pile up to become as big as mountains, you keep your "to do" stack the size of a mole hill.

Consider little things as an important part of your objective. This way they become small steps to help you reach your goal. If your goal is to get a raise at work and you are continually late because you had to stop on the way to work to put gas in your car, you are not really planning for success.

To overcome this kind of setback, play a game with yourself. Set your alarm clock ahead five minutes so you'll be on time for work, stop for gas on the way home the night before, and then reward yourself for being proactive. Buy a new pair of flip-flops

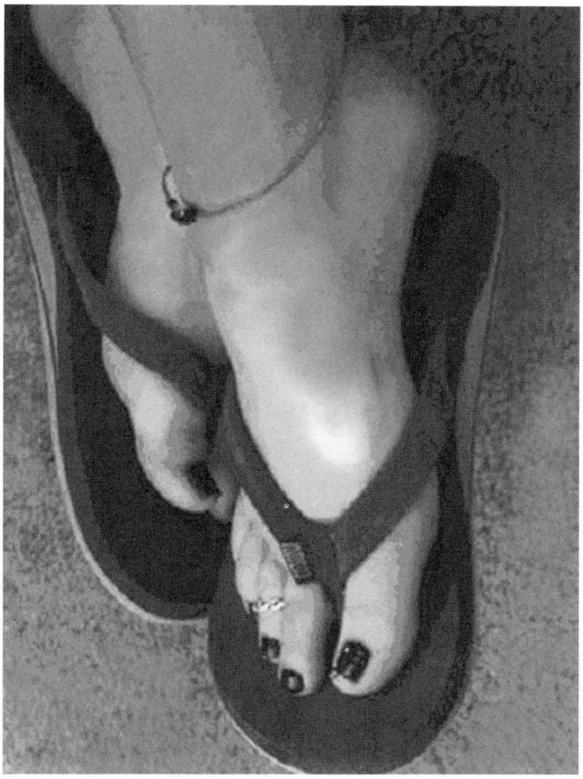

Kay's fun reward—new flip-flops!

or a fun knickknack for your car. Try and find a reward buddy (like a workout buddy) who'll help you celebrate in little ways and won't sabotage your goals. Remember, life is meant to be happy so find ways to make yourself smile!

"Most of us tend to be more motivated toward success when we have both internal and external reward systems. The internal reward is the feeling of success; the external reward is something outside of ourselves, e.g., crossing off the objective on the check list, a (good) grade on a paper, recognition from a group of friends, dinner at a special place, a new outfit."—Dr. Diane Sukiennik, Dr. Bill Bendant, and Lisa Raufman, authors[1]

FOUR STEPS TOWARD A REALISTIC GOAL

You can find quirky games to play and ways reward yourself, but you will never reach your goal if it is not realistic to achieve. How can you determine this aspect of goal setting in advance? Simple. Learn to put steps in place that will help you.

Because shorter goals can have long-term results, you would continue to break down your goal into other action steps until your book is completed.

Now it's your turn. Make your points simple steps that will move your one idea into focus as a realistic, achievable goal; be sure to check off your daily progress.

Action steps are a simple way to put you in control and reduce stress. If you eliminate excessive routines, you'll reduce some of the stress in your life, too.

HOW TO DEFEAT MAJOR CAUSES OF STRESS

Life's pressures can overwhelm you and create a lot of daily stress. Stress makes you anxious and takes your attention away from meeting your goals. Ask yourself, "Is it really worth it?"

EXAMPLE: NO SWEAT EXERCISE 8— FOUR STEPS TOWARD A REALISTIC GOAL

Your next task has two steps. First you will identify a goal that you feel you can reach easily. Sound simple? Great news, it is! Next, you'll find four ways to work this idea into your everyday life.

Let's review an example of this. Just for a minute, pretend you are fifteen-year-old Christopher Paolini and your realistic idea is to write a novel for teens based on a character who lives in a fantasy world and discovers he has magical powers. If you put yourself into this scenario, here are some action steps you can use to move your idea into reality:

1. I write three pages in my journal every day to clarify my ideas.
2. I listen to teen TV shows and read teen comics weekly.
3. I talk to other kids to get their opinions on controversial subjects.
4. I organize and rewrite what I've learned to fit into my manuscript.

NO SWEAT EXERCISE 8—FOUR STEPS TOWARD A REALISTIC GOAL

Directions: As a starter, write the title on the top line. Next, flip back in your Goals Notebook and select one idea from No Sweat Exercise 2—Four Real Ideas for a Goal. Copy it on the second, or focus, line of the exercise. Finally, number the next four lines and write down four ways to work this idea into your everyday life. This exercise should be fast, so limit your time to five minutes, max.

____

____

1. ______________________________
2. ______________________________
3. ______________________________
4. ______________________________

Do you find there are times when you are ready to blow a fuse? Perhaps this happens after school, when you are at work and you are asked to stay late because a coworker has an emergency. Maybe you blow up at a customer or grumble in an unprofessional way. Blowing up is immature and not acceptable in the working world. You need to find new ways to cope with your stress.

Try and think of a thirty-second plan to de-stress when negative things pop up. It could be simple, like hum a tune, or go to the restroom and splash cold water on your face and count to ten, or any other trick that will calm you down.

The secret is don't overdo your commitments—create down time when you can relax. If a glitch pops up, you won't get stressed if you leave spaces in your day to help you get back in control. Then one important activity (such as work) does not spill over into another, and you are not caught in an impossible situation—you can stay on track to meet your goals.

If the stress you face is ongoing, maybe it's time to take action and change your situation. Your school counselor can help you form a plan to do something positive and adjust your schedule. Why? Meeting your goals always involves change. See this as a turning point to grow and meet new goals in your life.

"When I found out I was going to be a dad at seventeen, it was a huge shock. My goals went completely out the window and I dropped out of school.

"I found myself working all the time to support my family delivering pizza and working other jobs that didn't pay very well. But I did whatever I could for us. I won't deny that it was a struggle and we moved around a lot.

"Right now, things seem to be getting back on track. I've taken time out to get my GED and complete a course in loan processing so I can get a license to work in that area. That feels good because I've always had a goal to learn about finances. I feel I've a knack for it.

"Now I see things differently. I realize winning takes courage. I've stood up for my family and feel like I did the right thing. My friends still like the party life, but for me, it has lost its appeal. I'd rather spend time with my daughter while she's little. Maybe someday I'll go back and get more out of school, but for now, I'm doing okay and feeling positive about what choices I have made."
—Chuck, age 19

PEER PRESSURE CAN SABOTAGE YOUR GOALS

You hear a lot about the term *peer pressure*. Is this one of those parental control topics that's a huge turn-off for you? You have to develop a plan in advance even if you feel you can follow your intuition and avoid those sticky situations.

Peer pressure is sneaky. It comes in all sorts of disguises, such as teasing, manipulative control moves, gushy attention, and a host of other weird actions from the kids around you.

Sometimes you need to act on your intuition. If you get an eerie feeling that it's time to slip away from the crowd, pay attention to your inner voice. When you stay on target and work your plan to reach your goal, you rise above an undertow of negativity that can come about when peers try and pick your goals apart.

MAJOR CAUSES OF STRESS

- **"Big change. The death of a loved one. Moving. A new job. Earth destroyed by moody aliens in flying saucers. All that sort of thing. El Majoro stresso.**
- **Gnarly, unsupportive, dysfunctional people. Toxic people. Mean people. Subtly mean people. Not subtly mean people. People who don't wish the very best for us. People who think we need to change or improve ourselves. Negative people. Abusive people. People who make us feel crazy, yucky, inadequate, or like we need a bath. Or like they need a bath.**
- **Life pressures and obligations. From school, from coaches, from jobs, from teams we're on, from theater casts we're part of, from parents and their not always wise expectations."[2]**

There's one more important fact to learn about peer pressure. It doesn't stop when you leave your teens. Throughout life, people are bombarded with pressure from others to give up their principles. Even your parents deal with pressure from family members, adult friends, and their coworkers. It can literally lead you to a life of misery and undermine every single goal and decision you make.

When you understand how peer pressure can ruin your goals and keep you from becoming the person you dream of being, you will never be defeated.

ASK YOURSELF, "IS THIS TRUE FOR ME?"

"Kids say peer pressure makes them feel they're being pulled in two directions. They may not want to do what they're feeling pressured to do, but they're also afraid of losing their friends if they say no. Kids worry about being on people's bad sides and really want to avoid feeling like outsiders."[3]

"A couple of years ago I spent a fantastic three months in the Pacific Northwest. It was to help me gain outdoor survival and leadership skills but truthfully, my parents felt I needed something to change my view on life and find some new friends.

"Several things I'll never forget, like spending a month sailing in a 36' sailboat with the entire group of twenty kids and instructors. We explored the Straights of Oregon and lived on a deserted island for two weeks. We also went kayaking along the outer coast of Vancouver Island. Then we backpacked and climbed in the Northern Cascade Mountains. This made me really appreciate how beautiful the earth is.

"The whole experience was so invigorating. Now I feel I can accomplish anything."
—Jay, age 17

Jay McGraw thought the subject of peer pressure was so important it became part of the conclusion in his book *Life Strategies for Teens*.

He cautions you to think for yourself. Don't be drawn into a stupid reason to try something just because everybody you know is doing it. This kind of reasoning is the way peer pressure starts, and most of the time the stories aren't true.

He concludes, "If we are caving into peer pressure to do drugs, have premarital sex, blow off school, defy our parents, or just generally be pissed off because 'everybody is doing it,' we have stopped thinking. My opinion is that if you are going to be independent, if you are going to be your own person, then do that."[4]

According to the *Book of Lists for Teens*, a "study was conducted by the Horatio Alger Association of Distinguished Americans to celebrate the lives of Americans who have overcome adversity. This organization publishes *The State of Our Nation's Youth* report, which collects the results of surveys to show more sensitivity to the concerns of young people. The 2003 survey was conducted by phone and included 1,014 students aged fourteen through eighteen across the country."[5]

The State of Our Nation's Youth Report

	Problem	Not a Problem
Pressure to get good grades	62%	38%
Pressure to look a certain way	46%	53%
Family pressures	46%	54%
Financial pressures	42%	57%
Pressure to do drugs or drink	36%	64%
Loneliness or feeling left out	33%	67%
Pressure to have sex	30%	69%

All students did not respond to all questions.

PLANNING, DETERMINATION, AND PRACTICE

So far you've looked at what goals are and why you set them. Now the challenge is to incorporate those two aspects into making your goals become a reality. You can accomplish that by learning the finer points of planning, determination, and practice.

By now you might be saying under your breath, "Planning? I'd die before I'd drag around a planner. And leave my PDA out of this—that's for my social life only!" It's hard to be different, but kids who carry around agendas or constantly use their PDAs for planning (because they've hooked into an organizer PC program) are sometimes labeled as nerds. They keep checking their schedule because they don't want to forget anything.

But, hold on a minute—you're already using a planner, but maybe you call it by a different name, such as a school agenda, a school handbook, or a Day Runner. The ins and outs of using a planner are such a huge part of goal setting that it cannot be ignored. Take a look at how the idea helps you in goal setting.[6]

"From the moment people found out that I was a vegetarian, I was mocked and taunted. Many people called me gay and stupid, and for a time, I could not go out with my friends without being made fun of. One time in particular comes to mind.

"I was at lunch when one of my friends who knew I was a vegetarian started telling everyone about it and they all laughed and made fun of me.

"The way I handled this situation, along with many others, was just as bad as the people laughing at me. When someone confronted me, I either denied it or I said that my parents forced me to. This was terrible because I let something that I believed in get to me and I did not hold fast to my beliefs.

"I have learned from this that I should not be worried about what other people think about something so stupid as what I eat. I should hold fast to a belief that I feel strongly about, and that it is better to admit something from the start then to try and change it later, just like lying."—Josh, age 16

Planning is just plain smart. Most high school kids use the school's agenda pages to keep track of when certain assignments have to be handed in. If your school offers a school management software program such as Power School,[7] get to know the program because it will be a huge time-saver and can be hooked up to your handheld for extra convenience. Your calendar can be linked to the school's main schedule and to your teacher's monthly agenda to access activities, assignments, and other important information. There's an access for parents as well.

In *The Sure Thing*, one of John Cusack's early films,[8] Daphne Zuniga's character, Allison, and John's character, Gib, meet in a college English class. Being total opposites in personality, they dislike each other immediately. When they both respond to a ride-share notice posted on the bulletin board, Gib and Allison find themselves stuck as they drive out with another couple to spend Christmas break in California. Gib has a blind date waiting that's supposed to be a "sure thing," while Allison is set on visiting her boyfriend.

When one disaster happens after another, the couple find themselves stranded, broke, and exhausted. Although Allison carries a planner that contains every important detail of her life (and where she stashes her cash), she loses it. Gib yells, "How could you lose your schedule book? That's the most important thing in your life. That stupid little thing . . . you wouldn't even know your name without it."

The point of the story is that there's an over-the-top dependency on a planner versus a sensible use of one. If you're like Allison, you might worry that you'll fall apart without some written reminder. However, if used sensibly, your planner is another tool to keep you on task to meet your goals—something that makes your life more fun as things happen just the way you "planned."

When you're patient, you allow your dreams to surface. You might wonder how this can happen. Easy. Just listen to your voice within when you're daydreaming or doing something that is routine. That's the time to pay attention and find a time and place for your goals to become more concrete. Then through the step-by-step method of planning, you can watch your dreams materialize.

How can your day planner help you? The Premier *discoveragenda* suggests, "It can help you do better in school and be a better person in life. Of course you might be able to get through the school year without it, but why wouldn't you want a hand in making your life easier? This agenda doesn't hold you down; it frees you up to do what you want to do. Think about it. Then decide."[9]

If you didn't finish your Four Steps toward a Realistic Goal in No Sweat Exercise 8, open your Goals Notebook and give yourself a few minutes to complete it now because you will build on that next.

Create an Action Plan

It's important to understand why you are becoming more focused on your goal and how this point of concentration brings

EXAMPLE: NO SWEAT EXERCISE 9—CREATE AN ACTION PLAN

To create an action plan, you will need to have your school agenda or day planner with you. First you will flip back in your Goals Notebook and select an action step from No Sweat Exercise 8—Four Steps toward a Realistic Goal. Next you will write eight steps for your action plan in your Goals Notebook. Finally, you will take a stab at micromanaging your time. How? No sweat! Simply transfer your ideas into your planner.

To illustrate, we will use the No Sweat Exercise 8 example involving Christopher Paolini. Under his goal "to write a novel for teens based on a character who lives in a fantasy world and discovers he has magical powers," step 2 was "I listen to teen TV shows and read weekly teen comics." Following is a list of eight steps Christopher might have created as part of his action plan to accomplish step 2:

1. Block off Thursdays from 6 to 7 pm to watch the TV program *Smallville*.
2. Take notes for episode name, main characters, activities, and plot.
3. Buy latest issue of *Smallville Magazine* for new info on Tom Welling (Clark Kent), Kristin Kreuk (Lana Lang), and other main characters.
4. Write one paragraph about the death of Jonathan Kent, Clark's dad (from the one hundredth episode) on the night he won the election to the Kansas state senate.
5. Get teens' views on certain episodes and compare them to letters posted in the magazine.
6. Research different episodes for good and bad aspects of the character, Lex Luthor.
7. Read similar teen magazines, such as *Heroes* or *Supernatural* for plot comparisons.
8. Talk to other teens about their favorite comic or TV characters.

your goal from a fuzzy idea into something real in your everyday life. Understand that writing out detailed steps serves an important purpose—skipping over them will make it more difficult to reach your goal.

NO SWEAT EXERCISE 8—CREATE AN ACTION PLAN

Directions: To begin, mark off ten lines, then write the title on the top line. Next, turn back in your Goals Notebook to No Sweat Exercise 8; choose one of your small steps and write it on the second, or focus, line.

You will use the next eight lines to break down your chosen step into activities that you copy into your agenda. Because this is practice for using your day planner, limit your planning time, so you won't dread it in the future.[10] Give yourself five minutes, max.

____

____

1. ______________________________
2. ______________________________
3. ______________________________
4. ______________________________
5. ______________________________
6. ______________________________
7. ______________________________
8. ______________________________

It can be frustrating to learn a new skill, such as breaking down a goal into action steps and putting them into your agenda. When you keep it up every day, you can make it a habit—then it becomes easy. The most important part of an action step is the obvious—do it at the time and place when you told yourself you would.

There's nothing like determination to help you reach your goal. It helps to get physical, too. When Preeti drew a picture of her friend, Katrina, playing softball, she captured that look of determination.

Katrina playing softball.
Art by Preetit Deshpande.

Maybe you can decide to do twenty sit-ups every morning or run an extra mile every day. This challenges you to gain the discipline you will need to mentally meet your goals as well.

A great example of discipline was demonstrated on the TV show *The Biggest Loser* in the spring season of 2006, when the Senti family was pitted against the Sapienzas to see who could lose the most weight as a team. Although all members of both teams lost significant weight, two of the greatest winners were the teen daughters, Emily Senti and Alexa Sapienza. But the biggest change came to Emily, sixteen, who lost sixty-four pounds, reversing the onset of juvenile diabetes.[11]

To find other examples of teens that turned their failures into success, read various biographies of athletes.

Although Michael Jordan was a kid who experienced a lot of failure, we never remember anything but his tremendous success as a basketball player. He led the Chicago Bulls to six NBA titles between the years 1990–1998. But back in his sophomore year in

Skateboard kid.
Art by Anne Courtright.

high school, Michael didn't even make the basketball team. Today's teens still consider Michael to be one of the most successful NBA stars. Maybe you would like to have his motto as a plaque on your computer desk to motivate you to reach your goals. Then you could remind yourself each day, "Don't be afraid to fail. Be afraid not to try."[12]

If you love a sport, such as skateboarding or basketball, you practice and practice for hours because you enjoy playing and having fun. You are doing what you love to do, and desire is the first step in achieving a goal.

MICHELLE WIE

Do you love the sport of golf? Michelle Wie does. As a young teen, she got a lot of attention not just for her height, which had reached six feet one inch, but for the length she was able to drive the ball and the form of her golf swing. As for Wie's potential impact on the sport, Arnold Palmer stated in 2003 that "she's probably going to influence the golfing scene as much as Tiger [Woods], or more. She's going to attract people that even Tiger didn't attract, young people, both boys and girls, and families."[14]

LANCE ARMSTRONG

Lance Armstrong has always thought like a winner. He used a planner by the time he was in the eighth grade. He always recorded his workouts and the things he planned to do for the next day faithfully in his planner pages.

In high school he won the national sprint-course triathlon championship twice. By the time Lance was eighteen, he was living on his own. He worked out and traveled with the U.S. amateur cycling team. Lance turned pro after the 1992 Olympics, where he finished fourteenth in the road race.

In 1996, at the age of twenty-five, Lance was stricken with testicular cancer. The disease had advanced into his lungs and brain. He wrote a book with Sally Jenkins about his experience: *It's Not about the Bike: My Journey Back to Life*. He wanted the public to know that going through his illness was not a pretty picture, and his story was not about heroes and miracles, but hard work and "blind luck."

Did you know that there was a period after Lance beat cancer when he felt defeated? In 1998, when he had pulled out of the Paris-Nice race after riding only two stages, he went into a slump. But his former coach, Chris Carmichael, convinced him to go on a weeklong training in North Carolina (where he had scored a smaller victory in the 1995 Tour Du Pont) to turn things around in his head, and it worked.

"The ascent (up the mountains) triggered something in me. As I rode upward, I reflected on my life, back to all points, my childhood, my early races, my illness, and how it changed me. 'Move,' I told myself. 'If you can still move you aren't sick.'"[15]

"As long as we live, the future will come. Be it good or bad. We will always have yesterday to think about. But the quality of our journeys will ultimately be determined by how we travel today. . . . So, a long time ago, whenever I found myself living in yesterday or tomorrow, I started calling myself back to today. I called out to myself, '. . . Come back. Come back, GregAlan.' Saying this to myself reminded me that I needed to pay attention to that day's journey. We need to stay mostly in today because that's the day we're journeying in."—GregAlan Williams, author[16]

Another amazing athlete, Lance Armstrong, held the title of Tour de France champion for seven years. When he specialized in the triathlon in high school, Lance decided he wanted to be a cyclist. When that became his goal in life, he trained 342 days out of the year to meet it.[13]

Another success story is Michelle Wie, the sixteen-year-old golfer who turned pro. If you want to be like Michelle and other winning athletes, you'll need to set a time each day to practice going through the five steps of creating your goals as you practice your sport.

Whatever goal you want to achieve, remember to include your objectives in your day-to-day planner activities and you'll soon find out that you can move your goal from lofty to real.

NOTES

1. Diane Sukiennik, Bill Bendant, and Lisa Raufman, *The Career Fitness Program: Exercising Your Options* (Scottsdale, AZ: Gorsuch Scarisbrick, 1986), 95.
2. Mark Powell, *Stress Relief: The Ultimate Teen Guide* (Lanham, MD: Scarecrow Press, 2002), 3–4.
3. Philip Morris USA, *Peer Pressure & Smoking* 2, no. 2, www.philipmorris usa.com/en/prc/activities/downloadresources.asp (accessed January 6, 2007).
4. Jay McGraw, *Life Strategies for Teens* (New York: Fireside, 2000), 235.
5. Sandra Choron and Harry Choron, *The Book of Lists for Teens* (New York: Houghton Mifflin, 2002), 285–86. To learn more about *The State of Our Nation's Youth* report, visit the Horatio Alger Association, www.horatioalger .com/pdfs/state03.pdf (accessed July 16, 2007); for the 2005–2006 reports, visit www.horatioalger.com/pdfs/state05.pdf (accessed November 25, 2008).
6. To learn about different planners, go to the following sites:

    a. *My Calendars and iCal*, PowerSchool, www.kingsford.org/ powerschool/my_calendar_ical.pdf (accessed November 7, 2006).
    b. Premier Agendas, www.premieragendas.com/ (accessed November 7, 2006); http://premier.us/movies/ontrac.Theme (accessed January 24, 2009).
    c. E Campus.com, www.ecampus.com/newbk_searchresult.asp? qsearch=planner&qtype=combo (accessed November 21, 2008).
    d. Day Runner, www.dayrunner.com/webapp/wcs/stores/servlet/ category3_10053_10004_50702_-1_Y_50701_10053_Y (accessed December 1, 2008).
    e. Jennifer Johnson, "Palmtops/PDAs Blog," About.com: Palmtops/PDAs,palmtops.about.com/cs/pdafacts/a/Palm_Pocket_PC.ht m (accessed December 19, 2007).

7. Power School, www.powerschool.com/ (accessed October 23, 2007).

8. *The Sure Thing* was rereleased in August 2003 as part of MGM's 12-DVD Best of the Eighties set: "*The Sure Thing*: Special Edition," DVD Journal, www.dvdjournal.com/reviews/s/surething.shtml (accessed November 3, 2006).

9. Premier high school ***discoveragenda***, 2002/03 edition (Bellingham, WA: Premier Agendas), 2; Premier Agendas, www.premieragendas.com/ (accessed November 7, 2006).

10. To be successful it is recommended that you plan you activities for your next day before you go to bed at night. Discover Zone, discoverzone.com/my/time/weekly.html (accessed November 7, 2006).

11. *The Biggest Loser* reality TV show in January 2006 featured two obese families, the Sentis and the Sapienzas, who both owned restaurants and had teenaged daughters. At the age of fourteen, Alexa Sapienza's start weight was 191 pounds. After six months she had a total weight loss of twenty-five pounds. Her family was beaten by the Senti family whose teen daughter, Emily, lost a total of sixty-four pounds. NBC.com, www.nbc.com/The Biggest_Loser/ (accessed May 3, 2006).

12. Michael Jordan quote taken from Tadpole Crossing, www.tadpolecrossing.com/vilmain_don_t_be_afraid_paperweight_dbapw_c406_p28371.htm (accessed November 5, 2008).

13. "Lance Armstrong," Wikipedia, en.wikipedia.org/wiki/Lance_Armstrong#Early_career (accessed November 2, 2006).

14. "Michelle Wie," Wikipedia, en.wikipedia.org/wiki/Michelle_Wie#2005:_Turning_pro (accessed November 7, 2006).

15. Lance Armstrong, with Sally Jenkins, *It's Not about the Bike: My Journey Back to Life* (New York: Penguin Group, 2000), 202.

16. GregAlan Williams, *Boys to Men: Maps for the Journey* (New York: Main Street Books, 1997), 127–28.

4 Turn Failure into Success

We often fail in the area where we are destined to have our greatest success. Success doesn't come overnight—it usually arrives after years of hard work and sometimes with a little luck.

Here are examples of people who became successful after overcoming failure:

1. **The famous Wright brothers, Orville and Wilbur, experienced four years of failure before they flew the first airplane successfully at Kitty Hawk in 1905.[1]**
2. **Michael Jordan, who didn't make the basketball team in his sophomore year of high school, went on to lead his team to a state championship in his senior year.[2]**
3. **Alexander Fleming, a British scientist, created penicillin by accident when he left an unwashed culture plate in his lab while he went on a two-week vacation.[3]**
4. **Ruth Wakefield created the famous chocolate-chip cookie when she added chips that didn't melt because she had no cocoa for her chocolate cookie recipe.[4]**

"If success were easily won, the prize would not be so precious."—Anne Courtright

5. **J. K. Rowling was rejected twelve times by editors before her first manuscript of *Harry Potter and the Sorcerer's Stone* was finally accepted.[5]**

MY MAP—REVIEWING MY FAILURES

Look at some things you have done where you were disappointed with the results. It could be the time you went blank in the opening performance of a school play, or you fell doing an amazing gymnastic routine, or you choked at the home plate. When you take responsibility for your mistakes, you gain the respect of your peers, which motivates you to try harder.

"Remember . . . failures can work for us if we listen to the lesson that they can teach us. Failure will always be a very real part of our lives. Past failures are part of our map as future ones will be part of our destiny. . . . Sometimes the experiences that lie behind us, the mistakes that we've made, appear too ugly to look at. They bring back a lot of anger and shame and stuff we'd rather not spend time looking on. But what's real for me is this: If I don't look at my maps, I mean hold it in my hand and look closely at it, then much of what I've experienced in my life has simply gone to waste. Even if I've taken some wrong turns and built some bad obstacles, my earlier journey can be of great help to guide me on my journey today. Even the fatal mistakes of others can be of great value if I look at those mistakes closely."—GregAlan Williams, author[6]

In his book, *Making Peace with Your Past: The Six Essential Steps to Enjoying a Great Future*, Dr. Harold Bloomfield discusses the topic of shame. He calls it a cancer of the spirit wherein past emotional traumas, undigested feelings, and repressed memories reappear when left unexamined. He feels we tend to recreate failures we have not worked through. They pop up as glitches when you try to move forward and create a new goal.

Dr. Bloomfield feels it is important to distinguish between guilt and shame. Whereas guilt is "the remorseful awareness of having done something wrong, . . . shame is a sense that something is inherently wrong with us, that we are basically flawed, that we are a sham."

He explains further "that remorse is a healthy emotion that enables us to feel and express genuine sorrow when we do something wrong [and] . . . it helps us to develop a strong sense of conscience and produces strength of character."[7]

It's time to look at some of the things you've done where you were disappointed with the results. If you think of these events as the failures in your life, shine some light on them now. When you decide to carve out some goals for yourself, it's important not to get caught up in your past because it causes you to feel a sense of guilt or shame. These negative emotions can keep you from meeting your goals.

Learning from your failures can help you turn a new page in your life and give you a positive way to change your past. You know the old expression about what to do when you fall off a horse—you get right back into the saddle. So, if you think you

"I'm in a program right now because I've had a few problems. And what drives me crazy is that everyone keeps pushing me to set a goal.

"So, I decided—my goal for right now is to stay in this program and take it one day at a time. I figure if I can do that, I'm okay."—Alex, age 16

EXAMPLE: NO SWEAT EXERCISE 10—MY MAP: REVIEWING MY FAILURES

Don't let failure sit in your mind as a memory, but take a positive step to change the impact of each event. It takes courage to take an honest look at your past mistakes. Put yourself in the picture and see if any of these embarrassing situations ring true:

- I sent an article to our school paper where I ranted about new prom rules, and it was rejected.
- I insulted a friend by mistake in front of a group of friends, and she ripped into me.
- I snubbed my brother when I had tickets for a basketball game because he forgot my birthday.
- I quit the gym after training for two years and now I'm out of shape.

NO SWEAT EXERCISE 10—MY MAP: REVIEWING MY FAILURES

Directions: Turn to a new page in your Goals Notebook. Write the title on the top line then number four more lines. Don't get in a stew over your past mistakes, but take a few minutes and allow your failures to surface without judging yourself. Then write down four events that wander across your mind.

____

1. ______________________________________
2. ______________________________________
3. ______________________________________
4. ______________________________________

"Last fall I traveled all over the country to visit universities. I spent long hours writing and revising admission essays, hunting down teachers for recommendation letters, and scouring the Internet for scholarships.

"To my disappointment, I was rejected from my top two college choices, Duke and Northwestern. Plus I was put on a 'wait list' for my next two choices even though I was in the top two percent of my class with many extracurricular activities. I finally got accepted at the University of Iowa, which I had dubbed my last-minute 'safety-school,' because it had the easiest application with no essays or recommendations needed. It's funny that this was the one school I hadn't bothered to visit.

"What's ironic is that I'm enrolled there for the fall and I am incredibly excited to begin college. I now have the chance to go to college with one of my best friends and I have a guarantee of at least $6,000 a year in scholarships. What I consider my greatest victory is that I will be in residency in an exclusive writer's community and my goal is to be an English major."—Amy, age 18

failed before, now is the time to take steps that will put you on a new path that points you in the right direction.

Your failures and victories can be great or small. They can be anything from failing your driver's ed written exam and passing the road test, or gaining fifteen pounds and deciding to lose ten in time for prom. The point is you cannot change and reach new goals unless you are first willing to see where you have gone off course in the past.

PLANNING SUCCESS

The next step is to build on your success. In No Sweat Exercise 11—Planning Success, you'll put your so-called failure on the left side of the page and turn it into success by adding an action step. Once you have listed something you remembered as an old failure,

EXAMPLE: NO SWEAT EXERCISE 11—PLANNING SUCCESS

- If you spouted off on new school policy—write a comic twist and send it to your school paper.
- If you insulted a friend in front of a group of other kids—e-mail him or her an apology.
- If you snubbed your brother because he forgot your birthday—break the ice with a gag gift.
- If you quit the gym after training for two years—go back and start to use the track and pool.

be creative with the solution that will make you feel better as you rectify the situation. Remember, you don't have to be like Jason Lee from the TV sitcom *My Name Is Earl* and make amends to all the people on your "bad karma" list.[8] No, the person you are forgiving in this project is yourself. For an example, put yourself in this picture and stretch your mind with these solutions.

To embrace this new positive mind-set, relax and be honest with yourself. This will help clear out the cobwebs from your past.

NO SWEAT EXERCISE 11—PLANNING SUCCESS

Directions: To begin, write the title of the exercise on the top line. Next, number four lines and copy your answers from the previous exercise, your so-called mistakes, on the left side of each line and turn them into success by adding an action step.

____

1. ______________________________
2. ______________________________
3. ______________________________
4. ______________________________

Don't be surprised if you feel a huge weight is lifted and you experience a new sense of freedom. That's how to make room so you can plan for success.

If you let this exercise get you pumped up, you'll get on a "victory roll." Then challenges that used to paralyze you will seem to dry up and blow away.

It is important to review this statement: we often fail in the area where we are destined to have our greatest success. Why? Because when you create new goals to mend a past mistake your victory means so much more to you. Bingo! You've reached the first step to achieve your goal: you have to really want it.

EXPAND ONE VICTORY INTO FOUR TEMPORARY GOALS

To implement this idea, you will select one success from No Sweat Exercise 11 and turn it into four temporary goals. Why temporary?

EXAMPLE: NO SWEAT EXERCISE 12—EXPAND ONE VICTORY INTO FOUR TEMPORARY GOALS

To illustrate this idea, we will expand on the following failure/success: "If you quit the gym after training for two years—go back and start to use the track and pool." Here are the objectives (or short-term goals) you can focus on.

1. Find a buddy who will run two miles on the track with you two days a week.
2. Show up by yourself two extra days and do laps in the pool; work up to fifteen.
3. In your planner, check off days of training at gym, both by yourself and with your buddy.
4. Keep your gym bag stocked with your favorite vitamin water and workout clothes.

From the above steps, you can see this is not that hard to do. How will you feel when you've reached four short-term goals? Fabulous!

"I've been trying as hard as I can to earn some money. My goal is to move out and get my own apartment. I work two jobs every day—they're both in cleaning. It's a challenge to keep on top of my two shifts because I only have a short break in between them and I have to change into my uniform for the second job. But I like the second job a lot because I clean the offices of executives and they joke around with me.

"Last week when I went to the bank, I jumped for joy and thanked God right in the lobby because I had never had such a large balance in my bank account before. I must admit I'm really proud of myself for working so hard and turning my life around."—Cheryl, age 19

"One of the most sublime moments that anyone can experience is to live through a storm."—Maximiliano's blog, Veracruz, Mexico[9]

NO SWEAT EXERCISE 12—EXPAND ONE VICTORY INTO FOUR TEMPORARY GOALS

Directions: Write the title on the top line. On the next line, write out the success you chose from the previous exercise, and then number four additional lines to complete the exercise. Allow three minutes max.

____

____

1. ______________________________________
2. ______________________________________
3. ______________________________________
4. ______________________________________

Something that is temporary is short-lived and easy to accomplish. You will find that short-term goals are activities that can be quickly attained. We will examine them further in chapter 11, "The Long and Short of Goals."

It's one thing to write an exercise out on paper; it's another to make a commitment to do it. To make your idea concrete, grab your Goals Notebook.

When you realize that your new goals were once failures, you'll be free from the disappointment you felt in the past and you'll feel empowered to try new challenges.

"I started to play sports through our local park district. I like basketball. I was a pretty good player, but I didn't make the varsity team at school.

"So, when an opening came up in the park district to be a referee, I jumped on it. It's really fun and I get paid pretty well. The only bad part is when the parents yell at me because they don't like my calls. But the kids don't seem to mind. Plus, I'm still involved in the game. For now, until I can try out again for the school team, this suits me fine."—Sunjay, age 16

You might think that failing is the most embarrassing thing that could happen when you are trying to reach your goal. It depends on how you look at it that counts. Everyone faces some kind of setback during his or her life, especially the most successful people. Setbacks can motivate you and make you try harder—if you learn from them.

A good example of an embarrassing failure happened during the 2002 Winter Olympic Games held in Salt Lake City, Utah. Apolo Anton Ohno, a nineteen-year-old member of the men's U.S. speed skating team fell in the 1,000 meters short-track event. He was skating in his first event and was one turn away from winning a gold medal when he found himself flat on the ice, sliding head over heels into the sideboards, bleeding. Apolo crawled on his hands and knees on the ice the last few yards to finally swing his injured leg over the finish line. Did he fail? Absolutely not!

Apolo showed his winning attitude when, during his crisis, he made the decision to cross the finish line. He said it was one of the best efforts of his life! He didn't win a gold medal in that race, but he did win silver. Apolo overcame his failure with a turn-around action. He showed the spirit of a real champion by coming back to win gold in the 1,500 meters. He also won the hearts of many young Americans.

"I struggled and faced every challenge to get to the Olympics because I believe it is all part of my journey. Some people work toward getting rich, others want to be stronger, faster, smarter, better looking. If I have just one goal, then when I reach it my life will be over. My journey is always about getting to a place, then passing and surpassing it. . . . There's no ultimate destination—It's the journey that I love."[10]

"I always tell young people: Do not ever give up on your dreams. Do not ever let other people tell you what you can or can't achieve. You can achieve whatever you want to. You are the only one who sets the limits."[11]—Carl Lewis, U.S. Olympian.[11]

We all fail at something in life. The difference between winners and losers is that winners, like Apolo, pick themselves up and try again. We are human, not machines; we have human emotions and feelings. The wonderful thing you learn when you goof up is that life goes on. Your real friends still like you, and failing gives you a reason to try harder the next time.

If you're worried about failure as you set your goals, avoid the following pitfalls. Failure can come from self-sabotage, hanging with dead-beat friends, fear of success, and destructive habits.

SELF-SABOTAGE

Self-sabotage is a hard thing to spot. It happens when we're feeling negative and we trip ourselves up. It's infuriating because we don't do it on purpose. In her book *Negaholics: How to Overcome Your Addiction to Negativity and Turn Your Life Around*, Cherie Carter-Scott describes how to identify the problem of being negative.[12] She feels it can be either conscious or unconscious thoughts or actions that can create a glitch so you don't reach your goal and get what you want. She suggests you try and listen to your words and catch yourself if you say negative things like the following: "I can't." "It never works for me." "Why try?" "Who cares?" "I'm not smart enough." To overcome these negative thoughts, you can visualize a more positive scenario.

You might wonder how to overcome your negative habits and trick your subconscious mind into accepting your goal as real. When you practice the five steps to create a goal (chapter 1), pay attention to step 4. When you feel the excitement as you are nearing your goal, you'll convince yourself to accept your goal as real.

"Visualization is seeing with the mind's eye what you want to become a reality. . . . You close your eyes and fantasize the ideal situation which you desire, in order to regroove the brain, see the image, feel the feelings, and hear the words associated with it."—Cherie Carter-Scott, author[13]

In her book *The Artist's Way: A Spiritual Path to Higher Creativity*, Julia Cameron brings positive solutions to help us overcome our acts of self-sabotage: "We may tune into the voice of the creator within, hear a message and then discount it as crazy or impossible. Instead we draw very limited amounts of the power available to us. . . . More often, what we are talking about seems to be a conscious partnership in which we work along slowly and gradually . . . clearing away the wreckage of our negative partnering, clarifying the vision of what we want, learning to accept small pieces of that vision from whatever source."[14]

If you start out having a bad day because of some little thing—like your favorite jeans are dirty and that makes you mad—you'll just get angrier as the day goes on. You don't have to give in to negativity. You can become positive and turn things around. You're in charge of your own attitude.

How can you change the situation? Simple! Take a time-out and mentally review the action steps you need to meet a specific goal, such as throwing a fifty-yard touchdown pass. Imagine yourself actually throwing the ball over and over until you can visualize yourself fulfilling your goal, and see how your mood changes. As you stick to your plan, you build a new internal belief system that accepts your goals as real. If that doesn't work, laugh at your life. Humor is a "cure all" for negativity.

HANGING WITH OLD FRIENDS

Can your old friends be your true friends? Maybe you've been through a lot together, which can be comforting. But some friends don't want you to change for selfish reasons.

The movie *Good Will Hunting* examines what true friendship means. Released in 1999 with an "R" rating, it was the first script written by Matt Damon and Ben Affleck. Together they won an Oscar for the Best Original Screenplay in 2000.[15]

The story revolves around Will Hunting (Matt's character), who was beaten by his dad as a kid. After he ran away, Will moved from one foster home to another, which made him hate any change. The only things in his life he could count on were his three childhood buddies, Chucky, Morgan, and Bill. With a job as

"I was hanging around with some old friends and I did some stuff that landed me in a lot of trouble—things I wouldn't do on my own, just to impress them. I took the rap for it and got sent away for nine months, while they stayed home.

"I didn't like the new kids where I was sent, but I did pretty good in school there. I earned a lot of credit hours. Now my goals are live at home with my mom and go back to school because I only have a few more credit hours left and I'm finished with high school.

"Before all of this trouble began, I had a job in pet grooming. I liked working with the animals but it was a family-run business, and I mean family! It was too personal and I felt like an outsider. So now I would like to work for a pet store, or even a grocery store. It doesn't matter, just any place where I can get into a routine.

"Once I have my diploma I can do anything, and I'll have a clean slate. I think I'd like to move to South America and live in the rain forest. That's my real goal."—Marty, age 17.

a janitor, Will mopped the floors of the famous university, Massachusetts Institute of Technology in Cambridge, Massachusetts. His mathematical genius flourished there as he solved complex problems left on a hall chalkboard for the students to solve. When the math professor saw Will at the chalkboard, he called to him, but Will ran away.

After a run-in with a south-side gang, Will wound up in court. There he was given a choice to study math with the professor and go through counseling, or serve time in jail. Will chose math and counseling.

Together with Sean McGuire (the psychiatrist played by Robin Williams), Will sorted through the problems of his love life, his work, and his friends. When Will's girlfriend, Skylar (played by Minnie Driver), decided to move to California after graduating from Harvard, Will was afraid to leave his neighborhood and his best friend, Chucky (played by Ben Affleck). He was torn between following his dream of becoming a mathematician and living with Skylar or hanging with his old friends.

Chucky was an unselfish and true friend. He told Will, "You're better than this. If you're still here doing construction for the next twenty years, I'll . . . kill you 'cause you've got something none of us have. Hanging around here is a waste of your time. . . . You're sitting on a lottery ticket and you're too much of a #@&* [chicken] to cash it in." He told Will how to leave, saying, "The best part of my day is when, for ten seconds I knock on your door and pray you won't be there. No goodbye. No see you later. You've just left."[16]

When Will couldn't figure out what to do, Chucky helped him to see his true path—to go after Skylar and become a mathematician in California.

Unfortunately, not everyone has true friends like Chucky. If you wonder why your friends don't want you to change, maybe they fear you will move on someday without them. Only you can tell who is a true friend and who isn't. That is why you have to believe in yourself and find positive things to focus on. As you go forward in your life and find new interests, new friends will be there for you—people who will want you to be the real you.

DESTRUCTIVE HABITS

Your bad and destructive habits can feel like an old friend, too. But they can betray your new plans and goals before you realized you have goofed up.

Jay McGraw warns, "If you want to get rid of some destructive habits—smoking, weekend drinking, casual sex, whatever—then you've got to manage your way out of them. . . . You need to have a very specific goals about how to keep yourself out of situations where the peer pressure is going to be intense."[17]

HOW CAN YOU BUILD GOOD HABITS?

"Don't count on your friends or teachers to remind you of assignments.
Look for inner motivation and discipline to meet deadlines.
Take the blame for your actions and hold yourself accountable.
Keep your commitments.
Replace your bad habits with good ones.
Repeat new habits until they become part of your routine."—Anne Courtright

In her book ***Stop the Pain, I Want to Get Off! Meditations for Teens***, Dale Carlson explores various ways to deal with your problems. She suggests when you're going crazy because you want something or someone too much, it's time to examine the rest of your life and find a way to live it better. Dale offers the following meditation exercise as a way to find relief.

> SALUTE TO THE SUN
>
> Place a lighted candle three feet in front of you. Sit in your meditation posture. Gaze at the flame for two minutes. Close your eyes and press your palms gently against your closed lids. You will see the image of the flame. Concentrate; don't wander from the image for a minute or so. Rest in your meditation posture quietly and follow your thoughts for five minutes, dropping the words desire and longing into your silence.

She suggests that during the meditation you try and discover your desires and try and work through them rather than just longing for what you want. She also reminds the meditator to not just settle for one desire, but to think big and enjoy the spectacular show one can "see" or experience during their meditation.[18]

Olga in meditation.

A bad habit that brings havoc in your life can be simply wanting too much or the wrong thing or the wrong person. Desire in itself is not wrong; it's actually healthy and is a strong motivator in pushing us toward our goals. It's when desire gets out of hand that we come face-to-face with misery.

FEAR OF SUCCESS

Do you have a fear of success? A few people actually do. It's normal to be concerned about how your life will change once you have met your goal. When you visualize your goals, you'll need to train your mind to accept how you will feel when you have attained it.

Maybe you have dreamed so long about meeting your goal you can't imagine how success will feel. Self-awareness and joy come with success! It's hard to measure self-confidence; it's something you feel inside when you feel right about yourself.

Flip back to the beginning of this chapter to review the No Sweat Exercises where you turned failure into success and created crazy action steps. Pull out your school agenda (or go to your PDA calendar) to mark a time and date to fit these activities into your daily schedule. Give a daily check, or sticker, to mark how consistently you are working on your new action steps.

You can also use mental imagery or incorporate a spiritual overtone to your goals. It is important to make time for this more personal aspect of your goal setting. This will help you examine what good came out of your failures. As you weed out disappointment, you'll respect the new person you are becoming.

To begin this process, go to a quiet place—perhaps a playing field—and lie down in the grass. Close your eyes, empty your

Les Brown gives a very real example of the problem of fear of success in his book *Live your Dreams*. "When you become fearful of success you may become your own worst enemy. Mike Tyson is a prime example, of course. . . . He won the title [of world champion boxer], but never became a true champion.

"Tyson was equipped to become successful but in the end, his career was destroyed by his fear of success. He sabotaged it himself."[19]

Are you prepared to meet all of the fame that success can bring? When you live your life recklessly without changing your self-destructing habits, it can be embarrassing. Here are a few individuals whose destructive habits impacted their lives, causing them a lot of pain.

- **Richard Hatch from the first season of *Survivor* went to jail because he failed to pay income tax or prize money.[20]**
- **Macauley Culkin got married at seventeen and divorced at twenty.[21]**
- **Robert Downey Jr. served three jail terms due to drug addiction.[22]**
- **Wynona Ryder was caught stealing from a department store on a security camera.[23]**

mind, and relax. If you train in a sport such as track and field (or whatever your passion might be), see yourself doing it now. In your mind, practice reaching your goal.

We'll use tennis as our model for this mental exercise. Imagine you're seventeen-year-old Maria Sharapova at Wimbledon 2004.[24] Feel the tension she must have felt as you face off to meet Serena Williams in the final match. Take each step as though you were freezing each frame of action, like in a film you've seen before. Watch yourself prepare to ace a serve. Say the number of each step you visualize—1-2-3-4. See yourself moving in perfect balance and rhythm. Don't choke or miss a step. Over and over again, see the movement of your body as you breathe; feel the rhythm in your step; know the power in your arms as you flip the ball above your head; feel the pinch of your fingers as you grip the handle of your racket. Hear the whiz of the ball as it cuts through the air with a new force the instant it smashes against your racket strings. See your body twist in the release of the serve. Hear the crowd roar. Feel the joy as you watch yourself jump up, then kneel with your arms raised. You know you've aced the serve and won the tournament.

You are the champion! You are winning at the game of life and meeting your goals.

NOTES

1. "The Wright Story," Wright Brothers Aeroplane Company, www.first-to-fly.com/History/Wright%20Story/wright%20story.htm (accessed May 27, 2007).

2. "Michael Jordan's Biography," 23Jordan, www.23jordan.com/bio1.htm (accessed November 4, 2006).

3. "Alexander Fleming," Wikipedia, en.wikipedia.org/wiki/Alexander_Fleming#Accidental_discovery: (accessed November 4, 2006).

4. Mary Bellis, "The History of Chocolate Chip Cookies—Ruth Wakefield," About.com: Inventors, inventors.about.com/library/inventors/blchocolatechipcookies.htm (accessed November 2006).

5. "Career Reminders from Harry Potter Author J. K. Rowling," Scribd, www.scribd.com/doc/201425/5-Career-Reminders-From-JK-Rowling?from_email_04_friend_send=1 (accessed November 28, 2008).

6. GregAlan Williams, *Boys to Men: Maps for the Journey* (New York: Main Street Books, 1997), 125–126.

7. Dr. Harold Bloomfield, *Making Peace with Your Past: The Six Essential Steps to Enjoying a Great Future* (New York: HarperCollins, 2000), 65–66.

8. In the popular TV sitcom *My Name Is Earl*, Earl has to redeem his karma. Go to www.nbc.com/My_Name_Is_Earl to find amusing ways to redeem your "bad karma," take the karma exercise, send "Earl" e-cards, or try your hand at various karma games, exercises, and other "stuff." *My Name is Earl*, NBC.com, www.nbcuniversalstore.com/?v=nbc_my-name-is-earl&SESSID=c94ec7cd2f6c6e86164d3bdfafc41d95 (accessed November 4, 2006).

9. Maximiliano's blog (Veracruz, Mexico), "The Reader Has the Floor," *Warrior of the Light Online*, no. 135, www.warriorofthelight.com/engl/index.html (accessed December 15, 2006).

10. Apolo Anton Ohno and Nancy Ann Richardson, *A Journey: The Autobiography of Apolo Anton Ohno* (New York: Simon & Schuster Books for Young Readers, 2002), 130.

11. Dave Anderson, *The Story of the Olympics* (New York: HarperCollins, 1996), 4.

12. Cherie Carter-Scott, *Negaholics: How to Overcome Negativity and Turn Your Life Around* (New York: Ballantine, 1990), 124.

13. Cherie Carter-Scott, *Negaholics: How to Overcome Negativity and Turn Your Life Around* (New York: Ballantine, 1990), 124.

14. Julia Cameron, *The Artist's Way: A Spiritual Path to Higher Creativity* (New York: Putnam, 1992), 92.

15. "Academy Award for Writing Original Screenplay," Wikipedia, en.wikipedia.org/wiki/Academy_Award_for_Writing_Original_Screenplay (accessed November 6, 2006).

16. "*Good Will Hunting* Summary," Starpulse.com, www.starpulse.com/Movies/Good_Will_Hunting/Summary/ (accessed May 29, 2007).

17. Jay McGraw, *Life Strategies for Teens* (New York: Fireside, 2000), 171.

18. Dale Carlson, *Stop the Pain, I Want to Get Off! Meditations for Teens* (Madison, CT: Bick Publishing House, 1999), 101–102.

19. Les Brown, *Live Your Dreams* (New York: William Morrow, 1992), 61.

20. The Associated Press, "'Survivor' Winner Richard Hatch is a Loser with Supreme Court," www.nydailynews.com/gossip/2008/10/15/2008-10-15_survivor_winner_richard_hatch_is_a_loser.html (accessed January 20, 2008).

21. "Macaulay Culkin," Wikipedia, en.wikipedia.org/wiki/Macaulay_Culkin (accessed November 7, 2006).

22. "Robert Downey, Jr.," Wikipedia, en.wikipedia.org/wiki/Robert_Downey_Jr (accessed November 4, 2006).

23. "Winona Ryder," Wikipedia, en.wikipedia.org/wiki/Winona_Ryder (accessed November 4, 2006).

24. "Maria Sharapova," Wikipedia, en.wikipedia.org/wiki/Maria_Sharapova (accessed November 4, 2006).

5 Embrace Change to Meet Your Goals

Since you are reading a book on how to achieve your goals, chances are you might be in the midst of change, too. Change is the one constant thing you can plan on happening in life. When you look at nature and see how one season moves into another, you realize that's just the way life is.

In this chapter, we will look at various aspects of change and how they affect you; for example, why change helps you to meet your goals, how a crisis is a turning point in change, why it is important to consider the deep questions of life, and how to recognize and prepare for the seasons of change. Finally we will go through some exercises where you can vent about things you wish you could change in your life.

CHANGE HELPS YOU TO MEET YOUR GOALS

You might wonder, "What does any of this have to do with reaching my goals?" It is only through creating something new that you can meet your goals. Adjusting to that change is the core idea, because you grow and become different than you were before. If you didn't meet a goal you set in the past, perhaps you didn't change enough to become successful.

We can still learn from ancient and modern philosophers, as many of the deep questions of life they pondered still haunt us today.

ACCEPT CRISIS AS A TURNING POINT

When change comes, don't resist it. Don't moan and groan about it. Instead, accept it. Know it is for your best and that you are creating your future by the way you embrace the present moment.

Almost three millennia ago, Greek civilization ruled supreme. What propelled its success? The Greeks were deep thinkers. One thing they realized is that life constantly changes.

Today, our modern philosophers still question the meaning of life: "The divine plan often brings changes. There is nothing new about this idea. Plato knew there was a divine plan for man's life. He called it the 'divine design' and said: 'Everything changes according to a divine design. We live in transition.'"—Catherine Ponder, author[1]

Let's take a huge leap into the subject of reaching your goals in life. I think anyone who is facing death would admit in the end that he or she wanted to lead a good life. So, that must be one of life's goal—to lead a good life. Ask yourself, "What is my ultimate life goal? Is it to lead a good life? Is it to be all that I can become?"

When you encounter drastic change in the form of the death or serious injury of someone close to you, the important thing to

"What feels like a crisis is, in truth, a turning point, a moment of judgment, of decisiveness, of transformation, when we have an opportunity to separate from an old reality and chart a new course."—Barbara De Angelis, author[2]

remember is that this makes you reflect on your own life. If you ever get a chance to be present with your friends or family in their last days, do it! It will open your eyes to the real meaning of your life. Take that time to look within and see what changes you can make so you can lead a better life, too.

During the time of significant loss, you may be sad or depressed or even angry, and the experience might lead to a crisis in your life. Sometimes the best thing to do is simply not freak out, and let your family know how you feel. It is important to support each other, because crisis is nothing more than a turning point.

When I was at a turning point in my life, I found I was at a dead end and felt helpless. I had already learned about positive imaging and affirmations and what benefits we can reap from using them to change the conditions that are making us miserable.

"When my grandfather was sick, and I knew he was close to death, I would visit him a lot in the hospital. Sometimes I would skip school to do it, but I figured he was more important. I went there because I knew from all the family stories I heard he had led a hard life. Instinctively I knew he needed prayers.

"Most of the time we were by ourselves in his room and I tried to talk to him about God and forgiveness. I was hoping he would pray with me. He did a little, but he was hard headed and stubborn, so I think he prayed in his own way.

"After he died, I made up the poster boards for the memorial service. I found a special picture of both of my grandparents and placed hearts on each side of them. My grandma's read, 'love,' and my grandpa's read, 'hope.' When the funeral was over, I got out all of the pain I felt by journaling."—Kay, age 16

So, I affirmed my situation would change and my life would get better. Over and over I prayed for change.

When change came, I had to hold on tight. In just one day, we lost our house to a fire that gutted everything. We had no clothes, no food, no furniture, nothing! But my family and I survived without a scratch. So, at least we had something—our lives. That's how many families must have felt during the Gulf Coast hurricanes in 2005.

Now I realize that the moment I lost everything was the beginning of my new life. Today, I am grateful for the drastic change that occurred. My kids thank me, too, because we moved

RELIGIOUS FIGURES WHO ACHIEVED LIFE-CHANGING GOALS

1. **When Moses saw the burning bush on Mt. Sinai, he wrote the Ten Commandments that he heard from God and left his life as a shepherd to lead the Israelites from Egypt into the Promised Land. The Ten Commandments remain the basic tenets of Judaism.[3]**
2. **When Jesus left his home to wander through Jerusalem and preach the words he heard from his father, he was considered a rebel and a heretic. His teachings are found in the gospels of the New Testament and remain today as the basic tenants of Christianity.[4]**
3. **Mohammed, a trading merchant from Mecca, saw Archangel Gabriel around 610 AD and wrote the words of Allah, creating the Koran. By accepting his divine mission, the prophet taught others a new way of life and thus founded the religion of Islam.[5]**
4. **Around 500 BC, Prince Siddhartha Guatama gave up his kingdom in Tibet to reach his goal of meditating until he became enlightened. He changed his way of life and his teachings are practiced today as Buddhism.[6]**
5. **Chief Handsome Lake became a religious leader of the Iroquois people after receiving three visions in 1799. His teachings, a blend of Christian dogma and Native American traditions, are still followed today as the Longhouse religion.[7]**
6. **Joseph Smith wrote the first *Book of Mormon* when he was eighteen, which he claimed was dictated to him by an angel in a dream; then he left home to follow the teachings. This book became the foundation of the Church of Jesus Christ Latter-day Saints.[8]**

to California and had an amazing adventure that shaped our lives into a beautiful experience. We learned to make Treasure Maps, visualize, and say affirmations together. Ever since then we have been showered with abundance and blessings beyond our wildest expectations.

DEEP QUESTIONS OF LIFE

When huge events happen in your life, you can be miserable adjusting to the new changes, or you can accept them and move

"I was raised as an atheist from a young age. Atheism was my dogma. I was convinced there couldn't be a god because I couldn't see him, and after all it just wasn't logical that there would be some divine presence floating in the universe somewhere, . . . and I considered all organized religions to be based on blind faith and fear. Nevertheless, I was always yearning for something more fulfilling. There was an aching in my heart—one that I never understood how to heal.

"Last summer my mom sent me on a two-day retreat to an ashram [a secluded building, often the residence of a guru or teacher, used for a religious retreat] in the mountains of southern Colorado. Upon my arrival, I felt really out of place and disconnected. People were chanting, and meditating. This was a foreign world to me, and I didn't know what to do, or how to fit in. I resented my mom for sending me and I resented the ashram and its inhabitants.

"Eventually, we were taken to meet the guru of the ashram. She sat down and started to talk to each of the youth one by one. When it was my turn to speak, I told her that I was amazed at how much love I felt in the room. 'This love you are feeling,' she said, 'is your own love.' I was so moved that I spent the entire day with her.

"I wondered, is this what I've been yearning for all my life? I had closed myself off to anything beyond my worldly comprehensions. I realized how heavily my own beliefs were rooted in fear—fear of not knowing, of not being right—fear of losing the control I had over my own world.

"For me, life requires a certain degree of skepticism, but also a large amount of trust. Now . . . I am free to experience the divinity of myself, the divinity of my fellow human beings, and the beauty of the world. To me, this is god."—Alex, age 16

on. The choice is yours. To find your life goals, why not take time to ponder some deep questions about life. This will help you think about who you are, where your life is headed, and what you really want out of life.

A wise eastern philosopher, Sai Maa, posed these questions to young adults.[9] Ask yourself the following:

> **Who am I?**
>
> **What am I and what am I not?**
>
> **What is my purpose on this planet?**
>
> **What are the qualities that I am really?**
>
> **Where do I go from here?"**

If these deep questions haunt you, grab your Goals Notebook for this powerful exercise.

"Who am I? If I had already resolved this question I would be enlightened. So I intend to share with you the flow of thought that this question produces in me.

"In my essence I am indescribable, just as all the greats saints say. That which I am does not differ from that which you are. We have the same essence. The silent witness, pure consciousness dwells within all. . . .

"Because right now in my experience I am aware of a consciousness witnessing the world, my mind deduces that 'I AM.' I am aware.

"The mind is that which creates my world. I am not the mind. The energy of pure consciousness fuels the mind. Without the self the mind could not be. The mind, out of longing for the self and out of a habit of trying to make everything an object of knowledge, creates a false self, a false identity, based upon worldly experiences (memories, emotions, patterns, wounds, and imprints, etc.). That is what I am not.

"I am not the mind-made self. I am not William who was born on February 27 in 1986, NO! I AM pure consciousness. That is my face before birth.

"What other purpose can I have other than to Love? Anything else is just not satisfying. From here I work to stay in the remembrance of Love."—William, age 20

NO SWEAT EXERCISE 13—DEEP QUESTIONS OF LIFE

Directions: Put the title of the No Sweat Exercise on the top line, then pick one deep question from the previous list and copy it on the second line. Give yourself ample time to freewrite on the next four lines to more clearly define the hidden yearnings in your heart. Write more, if you wish.

It is normal to wonder what is happening to you as you change and grow into adulthood. When you begin to know yourself, you will be unmoved when change occurs. You will realize it is simply a part of life that happens to everyone.

If you don't think that major changes will come into your world sometime, that you won't see the domino effect (how one change causes several stable parts of your life to topple)—think again. When you have already planned a few goals in your life, you have something to hold on to in the whirlwind of change. In spite of change, you will have your eye set on your goal and you will meet it.

"KNOW THYSELF: Every schoolboy today knows about the sun, the moon, the stars, about the outermost regions of space; but, not even the most encyclopedic scholar knows the answer to the very elementary query, 'Who am I?' *I* is the most frequently used word; it recurs many times every second in conversation. I said, I saw, I went, I heard, I have this, I am King, I am peasant, I am a child, I am a scholar, I am tall, I am lean, but who is this 'I' that has these attributes and possessions?"—Sathya Sai Baba, Indian guru[10]

The first step to understanding change is to see what is happening. When you are in a field and you are looking for the path to take you back to your home, you don't spin wildly around, hoping some familiar thing will catch your eye. Of course not—you turn slowly, looking at what is in front of you, making mental points of reference. You do the same with life's changes. Look around and take comfort in the changes in nature—the snow is melting, flowers are beginning to bud, and grass is coming out of its dormant brown stage. You may think things are at a crisis, but it is not the end of the world for you. Life is still going on all around you.

"Why are we here? If you haven't asked yourself this question yet, guaranteed you will soon enough. As humans, with a brain, heart and soul, we simply need to know why we do what we do everyday. Why not step back and think about what you want in life? Do you have a vision for your life? Do you know where you're going?"—Premier high school *discoveragenda*[11]

Could you be like the historical figures that changed their path in life to pursue a goal that impacts society? Identify what motivates you, and you will find your passion and see your vision.

THE SEASONS OF CHANGE

Today families can lose their savings because of tough economic times, or become homesless due to a hurricane. Maybe you have lost a loved one through a senseless act of war. How can you come to grips and accept these changes?

"We must be the change we wish to see."
—Mohandas Gandhi

One of the best descriptions that deals with the subject of change for teens comes through the writing of Stedman Graham in his book *Nine Steps to Success: Teens Can Make it Happen.*

In chapter 7, "Pilot the Seasons of Change," Stedman explains that the best way to deal with change is to take action yourself and help create it. His analysis of the four distinct aspects of change is as follows:

- **"Understand the natural process of change.**
- **Navigate the seasons.**
- **Seek change, rather than just letting it happen. . . .**
- **Manage change, including controlling your anger, developing patience and handling crisis."[12]**

Mr. Graham continues, "Sometimes people react to change in their lives as though it is a rare and shocking experience. But our entire lives are a cycle of constant change."[13] He then expands this concept through quoting a familiar passage on the seasons of change, as reflected in the Book of Ecclesiastes taken from the Judeo/Christian Bible:

> **To every thing there is a season, and a time to every purpose under the heaven: A time to be born, and a time to die; a time to plant, and a time to pluck up that which is planted; A time to kill, and a time to heal; a time to break down, and a time to build up; A time to weep, and a time to laugh; a time to mourn, and a time to dance; A time to cast away stones, and a time to gather stones together; a time to embrace, and a time to refrain from embracing; A time to get, and a time to lose; a time to keep, and a time to cast away; A time to rend, and a time to sew; a time to keep silence, and a time to speak; A time to love, and a time to hate; a time of war, and a time of peace.[14]**

Since you have been learning about achieving your goals and turning your dreams into reality, maybe it's time to compare your skills to other teens who are dream seekers like yourself. In the book *The Road to Teen Vision: How to Find Your Passion and Realize Your Dreams*, authors Kristi Stoll and Gidget Clayton share their discoveries. They took a road trip throughout the United States to meet more than a dozen youths who have turned their ideas into reality, either by starting small businesses or by motivating others.[15]

Another remarkable teen was Max Schewitz. Although he died at the age of twenty from a little-known illness called sudden

Would you change your life to express your opinions? Do you have strong feelings about war? About peace? Could you make your cause become your goal?

Several historical figures changed their path in life to pursue a nobler goal. Mohandas Gandhi, known as Mahatma or "great soul," used his legal training to help India become independent through passive resistance. As an example to his countrymen of nonviolence, he fasted until rioting ended among the Indian Hindus, Muslims, and Sikhs.[16]

Dr. Martin Luther King Jr. became the leader of the nonviolent movement for racial equality during the 1960s in the United States. This activism brought about changes through the Civil Rights Act of 1964 and the Voting Rights Act of 1965 and won him the Nobel Peace Prize in 1964.[17]

Rosa Parks, considered the "mother of the civil rights movement," is remembered for refusing to give up her seat on a bus to a white patron in Montgomery, Alabama, which led to the Montgomery bus boycott. In 1999, Rosa was awarded the Congressional Gold Medal for her courage.[18]

cardiac arrhythmia, Max left a legacy of caring for reptiles and endangered species through the company he founded, Max and the Wild Things. As a passionate member of the Wildlife Discovery Center (WDC) in Lake Forest, Illinois, he spent much of his free time at the center caring for reptiles and bringing them to local schools for other kids to admire. Max's website states, "He loved teaching children about animals and conservation; he accumulated hours for his venomous animal license; he traveled extensively; and he went skydiving." The website concludes, "He would be very proud that his work was carried on after his death."[19]

The Max Schewitz Foundation has been established for a twofold purpose: to continue to fulfill Max's goal of wildlife conservation and to bring awareness to the community of the sudden cardiac arrest deaths in youth. Plans are being laid to establish a biological research station in Max's name at WDC. The foundation also works with the Midwest Heart Foundation to bring confidential EKG screening (an EKG, or electrocardiogram, is a test that records the electrical activity of the heart) and automated external defibrillator machines (that shock a failing heart back into normal rhythm) to local schools.

"Right now I work part time at a health food store while I take classes in environmental science at our local community college. My goal is to transfer to a college next fall where I can learn more about permaculture and nurturing the soil.

"This has become my passion since last year when I volunteered for three months in Hawaii to learn organic farming. That's when my buddy and I worked making topsoil for a citrus farm for the first month. Then the next two months we spent grafting trees on a small two-acre farm. That was cool because it was part of an ashram, so we learned about chanting and eating organic foods there, too.

"My dad found the information online and I'm really glad my parents were supportive of me finding my own path because up until then I had no idea what I wanted out of life."—Jay, age 19

How do you feel about leaving a legacy that would carry on your hopes and dreams? Are you passionate enough to change your life to reach your goals? How do you meet change in your everyday life? Do you resist it? Empower yourself today to face change and embrace it.

"When I left for college last fall, I was very upset. I had to leave my boyfriend behind. But as fate would have it, I ended up with a great roommate who had exactly the same problem. I told her, 'We can get through this together.' You know what? We have." —Sally, age 18

Max living his dream.

One teen describes how she turned to a friend for support during a major change that happened in her life.

LESSONS FOUND IN *WHO MOVED MY CHEESE?*

Life is easier to accept with laughter, and Spencer Johnson, the author of *Who Moved My Cheese? for Teens*, lets us look at the changes in our life with a smile.[20] Adapted from the original best-selling book, *Who Moved My Cheese?* which sold over 5 million copies, the teen story begins in an all too familiar scene—the high school cafeteria.

There, a teen named Chris tells six of his friends how two mice, Sniff and Scurry, and two Littlepeople, Hem and Haw, try to find their way in the maze (of life) and find their cheese. Since the cheese is simply a metaphor for what the teens want to have in their lives, the book opens the door to discussing change and other challenging teen subjects.

Some of these topics include the following:

What does the cheese mean to you, or what makes you happy in life?

Why should you change to adapt to a new situation?

What is your usual reaction to change?

What would you do if you weren't afraid to change?

What can you learn by paying attention to small changes in your life?

How can your past experiences help you to deal with change?

How do you feel when you move in a new direction in your life?

Ridiculous Things to Change in My Life

Since *Who Moved my Cheese?* shows "a-mazing" ways to reach your "cheese" and win your goals, realize that the point of the story is to accept change. To allow change to become a reality, you will use the next two No Sweat Exercises in this book to learn

EXAMPLE: NO SWEAT EXERCISE 14—RIDICULOUS THINGS TO CHANGE IN MY LIFE

1. My hair: I wish it were red and straight.
2. My size: I'm 5'7" but I want to be a 5'9" buff vegetarian.
3. My room: I dream of living in the attic using cubbyholes for closets.
4. My car: Give me the keys to that red Porsche. Farewell to my boring Chevy.
5. My siblings: Can I trade in my whiny little sister for a fun older brother?
6. My dad: Will he ever dump his polyester zigzag shirts?
7. My cat: Can she just give me some space?
8. My best friend: Will she ever get the nerve to stop people-pleasing?

what has been keeping you from success in the past and how to react more positively to change in the future.

Can you put yourself in this scenario to see some ridiculous ideas you might wish to change in your life? Consider the following possibilities.

Maybe these examples don't seem that ridiculous, but ask yourself, "Wouldn't my life would be infinitely better if I changed one third of the things that drive me nuts? How can I make that happen?" Put yourself in the picture and see how to handle that problem.

Let's take the second item from the previous list—my size—and analyze it.

Since many teens might want to eat healthier, let's find ways to tackle this issue. Whereas you can't make yourself grow taller or shorter, you definitely can work on your diet and physical form. To start this process, consider four small changes that can make a big difference.

If you pick this last activity as one of your changes, realize you don't need a lot of money to join a health club because most schools today have a workout area in the gym. Talk to your physical education teacher or coach and find out when the school equipment is available. A good time might be after team practices. Why not grab your gym bag, vitamin water, and just show up?

No Sweat Exercises 14 and 15 work together. First you ridicule and make fun of yourself in exercise 14, and then in exercise 15 you come up with small changes you can make.

EXAMPLE: NO SWEAT EXERCISE 15—SMALL CHANGES CAN MAKE A BIG DIFFERENCE

1. Rent the Robert Spurlock movie *Super Size Me*.[21] (If that doesn't inspire you, nothing can!)
2. Check out your diet and write down everything you eat for one week.
3. Get books on the Mediterranean diet and vegetarian cooking from the library.[22]
4. Go to the gym and work out three times per week.

NO SWEAT EXERCISE 14—RIDICULOUS THINGS TO CHANGE IN MY LIFE

Directions: To start, pull out your Goals Notebook. Write the title on the top line of the next blank page, then number eight lines. Make a list of eight outrageous scenarios; take some person, thing, or condition in your life that you don't like and exaggerate it. Time yourself for five minutes. Are you game to take this ridiculous exercise and let the real you out? Be extreme and let your imagination run wild.

____

1. ______________________________
2. ______________________________
3. ______________________________
4. ______________________________
5. ______________________________
6. ______________________________
7. ______________________________
8. ______________________________

It's always an emotional release to allow yourself to vent a little at the conditions in your life that seem ridiculous and are driving you nuts. Did you realize that small changes can bring enormous results? Some of the greatest failures in history became triumphant due to small changes.

HOW DO YOU RATE?

Because you see the importance of embracing change to reach your goal, try to rate yourself. This is not an exercise but a way to mentally check how you're doing. See which column you fall into. Are you mostly 2s? Then based on your results, reward yourself. Maybe its time to put a new Bobble Head on your dashboard.[23]

NO SWEAT EXERCISE 15—SMALL CHANGES CAN MAKE A BIG DIFFERENCE

Directions: Turn to your Goals Notebook for No Sweat Exercise 15—Small Changes Can Make a Big Difference. In this exercise you will pick one of the ridiculous things from exercise 14, and write down four ways you can make the changes happen.

To begin, write the title of the exercise on the top line. Next copy your ridiculous thing on the second line, and number four additional lines for ways you could work this into your daily routine. Since you are becoming an expert in goal setting, mark these small changes in your daily agenda, and remember to check off the action steps when they are completed.

____

____

1. ______________________________________
2. ______________________________________
3. ______________________________________
4. ______________________________________

How did you do with this target practice? Is your score laughable? Is it pathetic? Are you ready to get serious and hit the target as you aim for your goal?

Now that you've taken a brief look at your progress, you can see where you are falling short. This is powerful stuff—powerful enough to change your life.

"We live in a world that is constantly keeping score. . . . Just like the scorekeeper at your high school basketball games, the world doesn't care if you meant to do something. The world only cares about what you have actually done. So start keeping score for yourself. . . . Take action to improve your life and get the things you want. Nobody will do it for you. You have to do it, and you have to start now."—Jay McGraw, author[24]

HOW DO YOU RATE IN HITTING YOUR TARGET?

Directions: **Using a scale of 1 to 5 (1 being the least, 5 being the highest), rate yourself in two categories.**

A. How well do I understand the concepts of creating my goal?

1. I can say the five steps needed to create a goal.

1 2 3 4 5

2. I relate the most to step 1—I really want my goal.

1 2 3 4 5

3. I relate the most to step 2—I write out action steps.

1 2 3 4 5

4. I relate the most to step 3—I see my goal completed.

1 2 3 4 5

5. I relate the most to step 4—I feel the excitement.

1 2 3 4 5

6. I relate the most to step 5—I track my progress.

1 2 3 4 5

My total ____________

B. Why do I want my goal?

1. I want it to impress my parents or authority figure.

1 2 3 4 5

2. I want it to impress my girlfriend or boyfriend.

1 2 3 4 5

3. I want it because my life is a wreck.

1 2 3 4 5

4. I want it because I feel it is my calling.

1 2 3 4 5

5. I want it because it is the best thing to do.

1 2 3 4 5

6. I want it because I am serious about my life.

1 2 3 4 5

My total _______________

Since this is your life, you can decide to change it. How can you tackle such a grand idea? Take a moment to reflect on the changes discussed in this chapter—then quietly make a pact with yourself to integrate one small thing you have identified. If learning the many aspects of goal setting seems too serious for you, consider this final step: smile and the whole world smiles back, especially when you reach your goal.

NOTES

1. Catherine Ponder, *Open Your Mind to Prosperity* (Marina Del Rey, CA: DeVorss & Company, 1983), 121.

2. Barbara De Angelis, *How Did I Get Here? Finding Your Way to Renewed Hope and Happiness When Life and Love Take Unexpected Turns* (New York: St. Martin's Press, 2006), 53.

3. "Ten Commandments," Wikipedia, en.wikipedia.org/wiki/Ten_Commandments (accessed November 7, 2006).

4. "New Testament View on Jesus' Life," Wikipedia, en.wikipedia.org/wiki/New_Testament_view_on_Jesus%27_life (accessed November 7, 2006).

5. "Qur'an," Wikipedia, en.wikipedia.org/wiki/Qur'an (accessed November 7, 2006).

6. "Gautama Buddha," Wikipedia, en.wikipedia.org/wiki/Gautama_Buddha (accessed November 7, 2006).

7. "Handsome Lake," Wikipedia, en.wikipedia.org/wiki/Handsome_Lake (accessed November 3, 2007).

8. Wesley P. Walters, "New Light on Joseph Smith's First Vision," Institute for Religious Research, www.irr.org/mit/first-vision/fvision.html (accessed November 7, 2006).

9. Sai Maa, lecture at the Ebenezer Baptist Church, Indianapolis, Indiana, July 17, 2005.

10. McMartin, Grace J., ed., *A Recapitulation of Baba's Teachings: As Selected by Grace J. McMartin* (Hyderabad, India: Avon Printing Works, 1982), 97.

11. Premier high school ***discover**agenda*, 2002/03 edition (Bellingham, WA: Premier Agendas Inc.), 41.

12. Stedman Graham, *Nine Steps to Success: Teens Can Make It Happen* (New York: Simon & Schuster, 2006), 145.

13. Graham, *Nine Steps*, 145.

14. Ecclesiastes 3:1–8, www.bibleexplained.com/poetry/eccle/ec03.html (accessed June 18, 2007).

15. Kristi Stoll and Gidget Clayton, *Teen Vision: How to Find Your Passion and Realize Your Dreams* (Hillsboro, OR: Beyond Words, 2005).

16. Gandhi's own words taken from the biography of Mahatma Gandhi. The movie highlights the significant events of the lawyer who led the civil revolts through his philosophy of nonviolent protest, as India reached independence

from British rule. "*Gandhi*," The Internet Movie Database, www.imdb.com/title/tt0083987/ (accessed November 5, 2006).

17. "Martin Luther King, Jr.: Civil-Rights Leader, 1929–1968," Lucidcafé, www.lucidcafe.com/library/96jan/king.html (accessed November 5, 2006).

18. To learn more about Rosa Parks, go to "Rosa Louise Parks Biography," Rosa and Raymond Parks Institute for Self Development, www.rosaparks.org/bio.html (accessed November 28, 2008).

19. To learn about Max Schewitz's mission, go to www.maxandthewildthings.com/ (accessed February 27, 2007).

20. Spencer Johnson, MD, first wrote *Who Moved My Cheese? An Amazing Way to Deal with Change in Your Work and in Your Life* (New York: Penguin Group, 1998). He followed this with three other books on change:

a. Spencer Johnson, *Who Moved My Cheese? for Teens* (New York: Penguin Group, 2002).
b. Spencer Johnson, *Who Moved My Cheese? Little Nibbles of Cheese* (Kansas City, MO: Stark Books, 2001).
c. Spencer Johnson, *Who Moved My Cheese? for Kids: An A-Mazing Way to Change and Win* (New York: Penguin Group, 2003).

21. *Super Size Me* is a documentary film in which the director, Robert Spurlock, exposes the dangers of eating at fast food restaurants and the resulting obesity epidemic in America, particularly with today's youth. Spurlock won the Director's Award for documentary at the 2004 Sundance Film Festival. You can find out more about the movie at the following website: *Super Size Me*, The Internet Movie Database, www.imdb.com/title/tt0390521/ (accessed November 22, 2008). There is also a website with fast food facts from the movie: "Fast Food Facts from the *Super Size Me* Website," www.vivavegie.org/101book/text/nolink/social/supersizeme.htm (accessed November 22, 2008).

22. Here is selection of good cookbooks to use for a healthy diet:

a. Dede Heal, *The Starving Students' Vegetarian Cookbook* (New York: Warner Books, 2001).
b. Moosewood Collective, *Moosewood Restaurants Cook at Home: Fast and Easy Recipes for Any Day* (New York: Simon & Schuster/Fireside, 1994).
c. Carol Ann Rensley, *Nutrition for Dummies* (Hoboken, NJ: Wiley, 2005).
d. Suzanne Havala, *Vegetarian Cooking for Dummies* (Hoboken, NJ: Wiley, 2001).
e. Rachael Ray, *365: No Repeats—A Year of Deliciously Different Dinners (A 30-Minute Meal Cookbook)* (New York: Crown, 2005).
f. Nancy Harmon Jenkins, *Mediterranean Diet Cookbook: A Delicious Alternative for Lifelong Health* (New York: Bantam Books, 1994).

23. Bobble Head World, www.bobbleheadworld.com/ (accessed July 2, 2007).

24. Jay McGraw, *Life Strategies for Teens* (New York: Fireside, 2000), 129.

Part 2: GET SET

In part 1, "Get Ready," you explored goals—what they are and how you need a plan to reach your destination. You learned that the secret to reaching your goals lies in your ability to change.

Now, in part 2, "Get Set," you'll find creative ways to achieve your goals. These will include analyzing creative imagery, visualizing goals through constructing a picture map, examining more tools for self-discovery, and speaking goals with affirmations.

Developing these faculties will help you reach your goal and become the person you long to be.

Before we dig into this new concept, let's review the basics of every goal.

Remember the five steps to create a goal?

1. **Desire the end result—you've got to really, really want it.**
2. **Write out action steps and a time when they will be completed.**
3. **See the goal completed—every day act as if it's already happened.**
4. **Feel the excitement—how will you feel when you meet your goal?**
5. **Track your progress—grade yourself on completing each step.**

Do you want your goal enough to change? Are you ready to leave an average life and unravel your hidden dreams? If your answer is yes, move on to part 2, "Get Set," where you'll attain your goal through visualizing your victory.

6 Achieve Your Goals with Creative Imagery

There are many ways to have fun while reaching your goals, and they are as different as your creative spirit can imagine. One of the first steps is called creative imagination or creative imagery. What an amazing concept this is!

CREATIVE IMAGERY IS A VISUAL THOUGHT

Creative imagery isn't difficult to understand once you look at the words and let your mind digest them. It's simply a visual thought.

To understand creative imagery, you'll look at both elements—being creative in the way you express yourself and examining imagery, where you can expand your imagination. Later, you'll blend both ideas together.

YOUR SIXTH SENSE—CREATIVE IMAGINATION

"The reality of a sixth sense has been fairly well established. This sixth sense is creative imagination. . . . Those who use this faculty voluntarily, and with understanding of its functions, are geniuses.

"The faculty of creative imagination is the direct link between the finite mind of man and Infinite Intelligence. All so-called revelations referred to in the realm of religion, and all discoveries of basic or new principles in the field of invention take place through the faculty of creative imagination."

—Napoleon Hill, author[1]

FINDING YOUR CREATIVE SIDE

Most kids get hung up on this word *creative*, but there's no need to work into a frothing panic over it. In fact, creativity is such a big subject you can find books written for teens just like you.[2]

You are being creative all the time but don't realize it. Maybe you express yourself through your clothes, matching stripes with layers of clashing colors, mixing today's trends with vintage, or going berserk with earrings or nose rings.

Do you like to create new video games or mechanical toys?[3] How about your bedroom? Do you have a stack of throw pillows to plop on the floor when your friends stop by, or have you made orange crates into stacking tables or bookcases? Your bedroom will always give a hint about how creative you are.

Your music is also an extension of your sense of creativity. Are you a virtual reggae,[4] or can you mix up other sounds, such as R & B, with your favorite tunes? Do you program in specific ring

"My room is not very big. My parents never come in and said I can decorate it anyway I want.

"Two walls are full of photos of friends and family and people that I care about. Another is my writing wall. I've used magic marker to write the things that people have said to me that lift me up when I am down—and other things I want to always remember. The fourth is my memorial wall to special people. I've taped dried roses here and there, next to a picture of a family member or friend I love who has passed on. It reminds me of what we shared.

"Then there's my Prayer Door. I started it one day by just writing, "Dear Lord," and then I began my prayer. Now I add to it anytime, especially after my friends come over and read it and ask me to place them onto it, too.

"The rest of my room is a mess most of the time, but it's me."—Kayla, age 17

Conductor kid.
Illustration by Peg Raasch.

tones on your cell phone for each friend or family member? Of course, if you play an instrument or sing, that's huge because you are showing your creativity in an auditory way. Maybe your goal is to be a conductor and lead a symphony. Was that on your crazy list of things to do "someday"?

In screening the seven learning styles and various ways of showing creativity, we should mention that certain teens might have challenges that could frustrate their efforts in reaching goals. It's important to see them in a positive light.

As a teen, you've probably heard the terms *ADD* and *ADHD*, which stand for attention deficit disorder and attention deficit hyperactivity disorder. If you think you might fall into one of these categories, take heart because here is an area where your creativity can shine. Did you realize that as someone with ADD, you are an enormously creative person who can use your quirky personality to help you meet your goals?

One of today's popular singers who listens to his inner voice is Clay Aiken, the 2003 runner up in the TV program *American Idol*. His debut album, *Measure of a Man*, hit number one on the Billboard Music Awards for best-selling single.

In his book *Learning to Sing: Hearing the Music in Your life*, Clay reveals how he learned to overcome his fear and embrace his talent. He explains how he developed his voice in middle school and stayed on target to reach his goal: "I'd practice every time I had to sing in church—I'd sing in front of the mirror first. I'd pretend I had a microphone and I would act big. I'd sing looking up, imagining there were rafters or that people were in the stands. This wasn't the case, of course. My church was about the size of this tour bus. But I'd always look skyward and move my arms and tilt my head."[5]

Two authors give insight into this kind of learning challenge. Edward M. Hallowell and John J. Ratey, MD, have written several books on the subject, including *Delivered from Distraction: Getting the Most out of Life with Attention Deficit Disorder* and *Answers to Distraction*.[6]

"As Hallowell and Ratey point out, 'attention deficit disorder' is a highly misleading description of an intriguing kind of mind. Original, charismatic, energetic, often brilliant, people with ADD have extraordinary talents and gifts embedded in their highly charged but easily distracted minds."[7]

Still not convinced that you may have a special creative edge with ADD? Here are the words of someone who can accept his challenges and see them as a gift.

> To those who think ADD/ADHD is not real . . . your [*sic*] wrong. That being said, I wish to state here that it is not a defect. It is simply another brain/mind type. It is NORMAL, but it does not fit in with the majority. That is why we with ADD/ADHD struggle. We have to fit into a world set up for the majority. Once one learns that this is a GIFT rather than a disadvantage, it is incredibly freeing and even life saving.
>
> I know what I am talking about. I learned I had ADD when I was 37. I thank God every time I think about it that He made me this way. My advantages are far too numerous to list here, but suffice it to say, I can do what others only dream of because of this

Did you know there are many styles of learning (and showing your creativity)? The term often used to describe this phenomenon is multiple intelligence, or MI. Seven specific learning styles have been identified, but the most commonly referred to are visual learners (those who learn through seeing), auditory learners (those who learn through listening), or tactile/kinesthetic learners (those who learn by moving, doing, and touching). Perhaps your creativity reveals which kind of learner you might be. You can even take a self-help quiz online to determine which way you learn and express yourself best.[8]

> GIFT! My suggestion to all who are like me? Rejoice in it, and make it work FOR YOU. We are the dreamers of big dreams and we can make them HAPPEN.[9]

Maybe you're more of a visual person and show your creative side through seeing things rather than hearing them. Are you someone who thinks in 3-D? Do you like to construct art from paper? Are you good at folding complex origami forms that you can turn into mobiles, or can you make paper sculptures? Would you like to know more about designing pop-up books?[10] This art form has become very popular through the inventive work of paper sculptor Robert Sabuda, an award-winning artist who constructs entire books in 3-D.[11]

Maybe you like to build Iraqi-war models[12] or collect *Star Wars* vehicles.[13] Dr. Steven Fratt, chair of the History Department at Trinity International University, in Deerfield, Illinois, employs his talents as a well-known military buff to make his classes come alive. How? He uses miniature soldiers and military models as teaching aids and encourages teens to contribute their models as part of the exercises. His students can often be found huddled over tables or zoned into their computers as they reenact historical military battles or play modern war games such as the Battle of Helm's Deep.

Dr. Fratt further encourages teens to expand their creative hobbies and show their hand-painted models through Little Wars, a competition of the Historical Miniatures Gaming Society.[14]

Many teens show off their creative skills at computer club meetings at their local library. Is your passion to wage video battles between Orc forces and the Riders of Rohan? At the Grayslake Public Library near Chicago, Illinois, teens haul in their laptops or use the designated library computers. Then they are patched together through the library's server so they can battle each other in games like Warcraft III through local area network, or LAN, parties.

"I'm majoring in Graphics Art in college. I started out drawing and painting anime and little by little I've expanded into other styles. Sure, I'm still polishing my drawing techniques and creating my art, but that's just the basics.

"Now, I've decided to go for animation—it's art in motion. It's fun but a lot of work. I've learned a lot of technical things and I've moved into more composite graphics programs. I still have a lot of foundation classes to take, but luckily there is little math and science. My goal is to do an independent film. Then I'll move on from there.

"The big deal I'm working on now is an Internship with one of my professors. We're creating an animated film and I'm developing one of the characters. It could go on for another semester. But who cares? I'm lovin' it."—Victor, age 19

Check your local library for various other teen activities. Many have anime clubs where you can display your art. If anime is your artistic passion, there are good books available full of illustration tips to help you to develop your art skills.[15] It's important to realize that whatever your hobby may be, it shows your creativity.

Perhaps filmmaking may be the perfect way to express your creativity. Today, many colleges and universities offer a bachelor of arts degree with majors in graphics and animation. Although many American film studios have cut back on staff artists, there is still a buzz over the manga art style of the graphic novel, which is a fast-growing portion of the U.S. book industry. This has become popular through the works of the Japanese artist Osamu Tezuka and his *Adolf* fiction series for teens.[16] Tezuka is credited with introducing anime into the United States through his cartoon character Astro Boy, and this art trend remains very popular.

Victor's anime.
Art by Victor Courtright.

You can find many opportunities to show your creative work. How can you make this happen? Become proactive and constantly check on upcoming art shows at school, the local library, the county fair, or local art clubs, where new talent is always welcome.

In the Chicago area, teens from twenty-eight city and suburban high schools compete annually to show their work in the Great Frame Up art galleries. Since 1995, the gallery owners, David and Marlowe Klitzky, have held the Lisa (Life Is Simply Art) Show in memory of their daughter, a graphic artist, who lost her struggle with cancer. The show has five categories that include painting, drawing, graphic design, sculpture, and 3-D design. The awards range from two-week scholarships at the American Academy of Art to cash prizes from one to two thousand dollars. The first place winners are then selected for the Best of the Best art show held in downtown Chicago at the Thompson Center, which has a permanent gallery displaying more than 150 works, the largest single collection of contemporary Illinois art.[17]

Here is one teen's modest explanation that shows her winning style:

"Last year when I won Best of Show I was really surprised. Even though the drawing was complex, I finished it in two days and I didn't feel like it would win anything because I'm used to putting in very long hours for all of my pieces.

"Around 42 high schools from our area were represented in this art show. Our school has always done really well there because we have such wonderful art teachers. The show awards one Best of Show award in addition to the eight different categories that award first through third place and honorable mentions. I was surprised that the judges picked my piece as the Best of Show because I kept thinking how hard it is for them to decide since there are hundreds more pieces and many of which were well done."—Natalia, age 18

Kate and Natalia's award-winning art.
Art by Kate Leaver and Natalia Bulsza.

You can show your creative spirit in the way you keep your art space, in the way you decorate your room, or even in the way you color your hair. Even if you're a complete slob who leaves your clothes (or paints) all over, you're still making a statement about yourself.

CRAZY WAYS I SHOW MY CREATIVITY

How do you reveal the real you? You'll find you're using creative imagery in all kinds of ways in your everyday life. When you link

EXAMPLE: NO SWEAT EXERCISE 16—CRAZY WAYS I SHOW MY CREATIVITY

I doodle when I'm talking on the phone.

I create new words to describe my weird ideas in a different way.

I go into an anime frenzy as I draw all over my bedroom wall.

I pour on makeup to help me blast through a dreaded quiz.

I layer two different shirt patterns to be obviously un-cool.

I plaster sarcastic decals on the rear bumper of my car.

I write e-mails to magazine editors and rant on about my favorite cause.

I draw cartoon characters on my shoes that make outrageous statements.

NO SWEAT EXERCISE 16—CRAZY WAYS I SHOW MY CREATIVITY

Directions: Put the title on the top line, then number eight lines. Remember to be creative and go wild with your own list.

____

1. ______________________________________
2. ______________________________________
3. ______________________________________
4. ______________________________________
5. ______________________________________
6. ______________________________________
7. ______________________________________
8. ______________________________________

your creativity with imaging, you'll find your talents. To bring your talents into focus we'll use another No Sweat Exercise. Need a kick start? To put yourself in the picture, try this list for a brainteaser.

HOW MY FRIENDS SEE THE CREATIVE ME

When you finish exercise 16, share your creative list with a friend and see if he or she agrees it shows the real creative side of you. Next take two of your friend's ideas about your creativity, and add them to your list. Next, in No Sweat Exercise 17 you'll expand one idea to unveil a hidden talent.

Jay is in touch with his creative side. He's a guy who likes to wear his hemp necklace and laugh at people's reaction when he explains he made it himself.

Jay's hemp necklace.

Do you find you love to doodle? Doodle art can show amazing creativity. Even though it's an unconscious act, it can reveal reasons you are not meeting your goals.

USING CREATIVE IMAGERY

Creative imagery is the art of using your talents and visualizing the end results you wish to actualize or achieve. Now that you

EXAMPLE: NO SWEAT EXERCISE 17—HOW MY FRIENDS SEE THE CREATIVE ME

An example of expanding a creative idea would be the following: Your friend points out that you're great with braiding hair. To expand on that idea, try the following:

Learn different braiding techniques by going to beauty school.
Look into creating your own hemp chokers with beads or pendants.
Create a website that features your beaded jewelry.
Explore weaving on a loom.

Suddenly you have four new creative outlets to explore from one small suggestion.

NO SWEAT EXERCISE 17—HOW MY FRIENDS SEE THE CREATIVE ME

Directions: Since your Goals Notebook is probably still open, turn to the next empty page for No Sweat Exercise 17—How My Friends See the Creative Me and write out the title. On the second line copy one of your friend's suggestions. Next, open your mind to new possibilities. How? Go crazy expanding the new idea into two, three, four, or even more creative opportunities. The point is, look everywhere for your creative side.

According to the teen magazine *Quizfest*, you can "Decode Your Doodles" to "uncover the secret meaning behind all of your notebook scribbles."[18] Anything from doodled geometric shapes or faces, to hearts and flowers all have a deeper meaning.

You can "change your mood just by doodling in four different categories."[19]

Check which one could be right for you!

	Yes	No
For Confidence: Write your name over and over for a quick confidence boost. It tells your brain you're sure of who you are.	☐	☐
For Energy: If you start zoning out in class, try drawing a bunch of zigzags. It ups the brain activity and makes you more alert.	☐	☐
To beat Stress: If you're totally tense, try drawing lots of ocean waves. It lowers your heart rate and makes you feel relaxed.	☐	☐
To get Creative: If you want to feel more creative, try drawing circles. The looping motion helps thoughts flow freely.	☐	☐

Sukruthi doodling.

"I created a new twist to my biography report by building a show-and-tell 3-D Roller Coaster with Legos. I used little red flags to mark the significant events in my life. I figured, why not? My life's been a roller-coaster ride and I'm not getting off any time soon."—Mark, age 17

know you're creative and you've drafted a list of creative possibilities (or dreams) for your future, it's time to use the "image" part of creative imagery to make one or more of those possibilities come true.

For years I have used Shakti Gawain's principles from her book titled *Creative Visualization: Use the Power of Your Imagination to Create What You Want in Your Life*. Considered a pioneer in the field of personal growth, Ms. Gawain lists four basic steps for effective creative visualization:

1. **Set your goal.**
2. **Create a clear idea or picture.**
3. **Focus on it often.**
4. **Give it positive energy.**

Since we've already looked at setting goals, let's focus on the many ways creative imagery can help you create a clear idea or picture to meet your goal.

"I like to think of myself as an artist and my life is my greatest work of art. Every moment is a moment of creation, and each moment of creation contains infinite possibilities. I can do things the way I've always done them, or I can look at all the different alternatives and try something new and different and potentially more rewarding. Every moment presents a new opportunity and a new decision."—Shakti Gawain, author[20]

One of the first modern thinkers to focus on the concept of creative visualization was Dr. Norman Vincent Peale. He wrote over forty-six books during his career as a motivational speaker and pastor of the Marble Collegiate Church in New York City. He was best known for his book *The Power of Positive Thinking*, first released in 1952. It "immediately became a best seller and stayed on the *New York Times* best-seller list for 186 consecutive weeks."[21] Peale's philosophy was that life holds both good and bad events for everyone, but it is better to always focus on the good. By deliberately filling one's mind with positive ideas and affirmations, negative thoughts can be crowded out. This was considered revolutionary thinking at that time.

THE POWER OF POSITIVE THINKING

From the example of Dr. Peale, you can learn how to win when failure comes into your life, how to turn things around with positive thoughts and attitude so the images in your mind reflect your goals.

One example of turning your life around came to the public's attention in June 2005 through an article in *Seventeen* magazine. "Heather's Story" is a great revelation of how you can meet your goal, even when it means overcoming a lifetime obstacle. In the story, Heather (last name withheld) proved that reversing childhood obesity can become a reality with positive thinking and determination. She revealed the pain and rejection she felt when by the seventh grade she weighed 267 pounds, and then how her life changed when she decided to set her goal: "Today, after five years of eating right and exercising, I weigh 151 pounds. I'm still the same person, but being fit has boosted my confidence, so I'm more outgoing now. That's helped me to make friends—I even have a boyfriend! . . . Maintaining my weight is still a struggle. . . .

But then I remember that being healthy—and feeling happy about who I am—makes it all worth it."[22]

Positive thinking is the core of Dr. Norman Vincent Peale's message; it is a useful tool to help you meet your goals when, like Heather, you come up against obstacles. Positive thinking is one of the underlying principles found in *Guideposts Sweet 16*, a magazine where an optimistic spin is given on tough teen topics—anything from being a foster kid, to losing your boyfriend, to dealing with unhealthy diet trends. If you have days when you are failing to meet your goals, you can check out the magazine's website where you'll find a chat room. (Be sure to check with your parents before going there.) The magazine accepts personal stories from people of all ages so, if you've got a writing bug, check out how to make an online manuscript submission.[23] This is a great way to spotlight your creative writing talents and show how you've met your goals.

CHANGE YOUR SUBCONSCIOUS WITH POSITIVE IMAGING

In *Positive Imaging: The Powerful Way to Change Your Life*, released in 1982, Dr. Peale proposes that there is a deep tendency in the human psyche to become that which we can imagine ourselves being. He felt that if one held an idea in the conscious mind and reviewed it over and over, eventually it would sink into the subconscious where it would be fully accepted. Dr. Peale also felt that with prayer and faith, one could bring him or herself to believe that the imagined wish had already been fulfilled through "divine assistance." Dr. Peale uses powerful examples throughout

"Imaging is positive thinking carried one step further. In imaging, one does not merely think about a hoped-for goal: one "sees" or visualizes the goal with tremendous intensity, reinforced by prayer. . . . This releases powerful internal forces that can bring about astonishing changes in the life of the person who is doing the imaging."—Dr. Norman Vincent Peale, author[24]

the book to show how to overcome a variety of problems ranging from family crisis to poverty to disease.

In one of the stories in the book, Dr. Peale describes how a patient battled cancer. She visualized an army of white blood cells flushing out her disease, rushing down the veins in her body, and actually attacking all the malignant cells, destroying them. She visualized this two to three hundred times a day for over six months while undergoing chemotherapy. At the end of her treatment she was declared "cured." Did visualizing help?

Imagine the faith and dedication that woman showed. You can use the same method to achieve your goals, and you can start right now. You'll need to go back and review the five steps on how to obtain your goal (chapter 1). For a moment, focus on the first step—you have to really want your goal. If that's a yes, you'll do whatever it takes; you'll visualize whatever you need to see in your mind's eye hundreds of times a day in order to make it happen. Do you want your goal enough to change your life?

Napoleon Hill was a contemporary of Dr. Norman Vincent Peale. With the revolutionary concepts presented in *Think and Grow Rich Action Pack*, Hill cautions his readers to distinguish between positive and negative thoughts and the law of autosuggestion.

Hill felt that the subconscious mind is driven by autosuggestion and cannot distinguish between positive (or constructive) impulses and negative (or destructive) ones, but works with the thoughts given to it. In other words, the subconscious mind will act upon fear-driven thoughts just as readily as thoughts driven by courage or faith. Furthermore, Hill believed that this kind of autosuggestive thinking leads you to prosperity, or failure, "according to your degree of understanding and application of it.

"If you fill your mind with fear, doubt, and unbelief in your ability to connect and use the forces of Infinite Intelligence, the law of autosuggestion will take the spirit of unbelief and use it as a pattern by which your subconscious mind will translate it into its physical equivalent."[25]

But what does "autosuggestion" mean? Hill defines it in the following way: "Autosuggestion is self-suggestion. It is the agency of communication between the part of the mind where conscious thought takes place and that which serves as the seat of action for the subconscious mind."[26]

You might be asking yourself, "Can this creative imagery idea be real? Can thinking in a new positive and visual way really work?" The answer is yes. The hardest question to ask yourself is, "Am I willing to create a new point of view where I am not bound by fear from my past viewpoints and disappointments?"

Positive thinking and creative imagery propel you to create a new reality. In short, positive thinking attracts more of its kind; negative thinking repels positive events. It is that simple.

I IMAGINE AND WRITE OUT THE FUTURE ME

Decide to reread your goals daily and let yourself feel as though they are already happening. The secret ingredient to make creative visualization real is to feel it being completed.

Picture your success. Feel the excitement and thrill of victory as if you've won a prize. Trick yourself. Feel your hands sweat. Let your heart race. Hear the audience clap. Feel butterflies in your stomach as you mount the stage to receive your reward.

In the stillness of a quiet moment when you are starting to fall asleep, hear your inner voice as it whispers, "Be all that you can become!"

A great example of a way to write out your imagined future can be found in a U.S. Air Force ad titled, "Girls dream often about the day they'll change their name." The ad displays a page in a girl's notebook where she doodles her name over and over, line upon line. However, before her signature on each line she gives herself a title as though she were rising through the ranks of the Air Force. What a powerful image to see your name start as an *airman basic* and rise through the ranks to become a *senior airman*, a *staff sergeant*, a *lieutenant colonel*, and finally a *general* in the U.S. Air Force.

NO SWEAT EXERCISE 18—I IMAGINE AND WRITE OUT THE FUTURE ME

Directions: When you combine creative imagery with written statements, you are writing your goals as though they were already happening and you begin to picture your goals as real. This is a tool you can use to condition your subconscious mind to accept the changes you are undergoing as you meet your goals.

Why not use this idea to bring changes in your life? Open your Goals Notebook to the first blank page and write out the title of the exercise. Select one of your previous goals and write it on the second line of the exercise. On the next line change it into a positive statement, as if you were achieving your goal in the present moment. Have fun with this exercise. Take the rest of the page and doodle all over it. Write your goal sideways, upside down or in flowery or funky print.

NOTES

1. Napoleon Hill, *Think and Grow Rich Action Pack* (New York: Hawthorn/Dutton, 1968), 85.
2. To showcase your creative writing, go to Teen Ink Magazine, www.teenink.com/ (accessed January 20, 2006). For information on art development, check out the following books:

    a. Mona Brookes, *Drawing for Older Children & Teens: The Internationally Acclaimed Method That Teaches You to Draw* (New York: Jeremy P. Tarcher, 1991).

b. Betty Edwards, *The New Drawing on the Right Side of the Brain: A Course in Enhancing Creativity and Artistic Confidence* (New York: Jeremy P. Tarcher, 1989).
c. Betty Edwards, *The New Drawing on the Right Side of the Brain Workbook: Guided Practice in the Five Basic Skills of Drawing* (New York: Jeremy P. Tarcher, 2004).

3. By Kids for Kids (BKFK) and Xerox Corporation launched the Invent-a-Toy World Games, which seeks new ideas for toys, games, or sporting goods. Winners will receive a licensing contract from BKFK, legal support for patents, professional marketing expertise, up to one thousand dollars of Xerox technology, and a five-thousand-dollar U.S. savings bond. To submit your ideas for a new game go to "By Kids For Kids 2007 Invent-A-Toy World Games," About.com: Toys, June 24, 2007, toys.about.com/b/2007/06/24/by-kids-for-kids-2007-invent-a-toy-world-games.htm (accessed November 14, 2008).

4. "Jammin Reggae Archives," niceup.com (accessed February 22, 2007).

5. Clay Aiken and Allison Glock, *Learning to Sing: Hearing the Music in Your Life* (New York: Random House, 2004), 181.

6. Edward M. Hallowell and John J. Ratey, *Delivered from Distraction: Getting the Most Out of Life with Attention Deficit Disorder* (New York: Random House, 2005); Edward M. Hallowell and John J. Ratey, *Answers to Distraction* (New York: Bantam Books, 1996).

7. Edward M. Hallowell and John J. Ratey, M.D., *Delivered from Distraction*, Random House, www.randomhouse.com/catalog/display.pperl?isbn=9780345442314 (accessed June 6, 2007).

8. LdPride.net, www.ldpride.net/learningstyles.MI.htm (accessed June 2, 2007)

9. Cascadegorge (Michael J. O'Malley; name as reviewer), "ADD/ADHD Is Real," Amazon.com, March 14, 2006, www.amazon.com/review/product/0679439730/ref=dp_top_cm_cr_acr_txt/102-1533538-2493722?%5Fencoding=UTF8&showViewpoints=1 (accessed June 6, 2007).

10. Joan Irvine. "How to Make a Pop-Up," Makers Gallery, www.makersgallery.com/joanirvine/howto.html (accessed January 7, 2006).

11. Robert Sabuda, www.robertsabuda.com (accessed January 7, 2006).

12. "Iraqi Model Military Tanks, Army Tanks from the Iraq War," YellowAirplane.com, www.yellowairplane.com/yellow_airplane_store/G_Models_Iraqi%20Military_Tanks.html (accessed June 2, 2007).

13. To learn the history of *Star Wars* models and their importance in filming the series read: Ryder Windham, *The Ultimate Visual Guide to "Star Wars"* (New York: D.K. Publishing, 2005).

14. "Stephen D. Fratt, PhD," Trinity International University, www.tiu.edu/college/people/fratt (accessed June 7, 2007). Learn about HMGS (Historical Miniatures Gaming Society) and its gaming event, Little Wars, at HMGS Midwest, www.hmgsmidwest.com/ (accessed June 7, 2007).

15. Check the teen services at your local library; here's the website for Grayslake Area Public Library to give you an idea of what your library might

offer: www.grayslake.info/teens.htm. To understand the difference between magna and anime, see "What Are Magna and Anime?" Massachusetts Institute of Technology, www.mit.edu/people/rei/Expl.html (accessed June 4, 2007). Books that explain anime, magna, and other art skills include the following:

a. Tezuka Productions, Osamu Tezuka, Jason D. Deangelis, *Tezuka School of Animation: Learning the Basics* (New York: Watson-Guptell Publications,1999).
b. Junji Kobayashi, *Let's Draw Manga: AstroBoy* (New York: Digital Manga Publications, 2004).
c. Richard Williams and Imogen Sutton, *The Animator's Survival Kit: A Manual of Methods, Principles, and Formulas for Classical, Computer, Games, Stop Motion, and Internet Animators* (New York: Farrar, Straus and Giroux, 2001).
d. Michael Burns, *Digital Sci-Fi Art: A Step-by-Step Guide to Creating Stunning, Futuristic Images* (New York: HarperCollins, 2004).

16. Osamu Tezuka's five-volume graphic novel *Adolf* includes the following titles:

a. *A Tale of Twentieth Century*
b. *An Exile in Japan*
c. *The Half-Aryan Prince*
d. *Days of Infamy*
e. *1945 and All That Remains.*

Hilary Goldstein, "Required Reading: Adolf," IGN Comics.com, May 2, 2005, comics.ign.com/articles/609/609520p1.html (accessed March 2, 2007).

17. Learn more about the annual metro-Chicago teen art show, the Lisa Show, at Life Is Simply Art, www.lifeissimplyart.com/lisashow.html (accessed November 7, 2007).

18. "Decode Your Doodles," *Quizfest*, November/December 2005, 42.

19. "Decode Your Doodles," 42.

20. Shakti Gawain, *Creative Visualization: Use the Power of Your Imagination to Create What You Want in Your Life* (Novato, CA: Nataraj Publishing, 2002), 170.

21. Dr. Norman Vincent Peale, *Positive Imaging: The Powerful Way to Change Your Life* (New York: Ballantine Books, 1985), 17. See also "Norman Vincent Peale," Wikipedia, en.wikipedia.org/wiki/Norman_Vincent_Peale (accessed June 6, 2007).

22. Whitney Joiner, "Real Life: Heather's Story," *Seventeen*, June 2005, 99–100.

23. "Guideposts Editorial Guidelines," Guideposts, www.guidepostsmag.com/writers-guidelines/ (accessed June 1, 2007).

24. Peale, *Positive Imaging*, 17.

25. Hill, *Think and Grow Rich*, 72.

26. Hill, *Think and Grow Rich*, 72.

7 Create Visual Goals with a Picture Map

Creating goals is more interesting when you learn to visualize. Artists create paintings, mathematicians solve formulas, and entrepreneurs envision new companies. What do they have in common? They all had a picture in their mind of what they wanted to create before they began. We call this process *visualization*.

Visualization isn't a phenomenon, but its importance can't be ignored. Dr. Darren Weissman believes we hold the power to picture our dreams when we visualize our goals: "One person's ability to believe in the power of his or her own imagination can, and indeed has, changed the course of the planet. Look up in the sky on any given day and you'll see airplanes and helicopters. Turn on the news and you'll receive your information via satellite and hear about spacecraft venturing in search of new

INVENTIONS IN MODERN HISTORY WHERE THE DESIGNER ENVISIONED THE GOAL

In 1865, Louis Pasteur created the formula for killing bacteria through pasteurization.[1]

In 1908, Henry Ford revolutionized mass production, creating the first assembly line to build the Model T.[2]

In 1955, Dr. Jonas Salk created the vaccine to halt the crippling disease of polio.[3]

In 1975, Bill Gates and Paul Allen founded Microsoft and licensed its first software program.[4]

In 1976, Steve Wozniak and Steve Jobs released the first Apple I computer, which they built in their garage.[5]

worlds. All of that is possible because people believed in themselves and their dreams."[6]

PLAN YOUR FUTURE IN PICTURES BY TREASURE MAPPING

Treasure mapping is a tool used to achieve a goal by looking at pictures of it. It is also referred to as a Wheel of Fortune, Picture Map, or a Dreamprint. It is a simple idea that's been used for eons—colorful paintings of men hunting the bison and antelope have been found in prehistoric caves, promising victory before the hunt began.

It doesn't matter what you call your map. What matters is that it is a tried-and-true method that works. I know because I have used it many times. The secret to its success is to be very clear about what you imagine your goal to be.

Once you have created your map, you'll look at it daily to study the details of every section. Then you'll close your eyes and visualize it as though it were real. This can become a practical way to meditate. It's as though you are watching an animated film of yourself, living out your dreams.

Let's look at how treasure mapping works. To start, you'll need the following supplies:

- **Two large colorful poster boards**
- **A selection of scissors, glue, ruler, pens, pencils, crayons or pastels**
- **A stack of various magazines, catalogues, and interesting printed material**

"A Dreamprint is a collage [a collection of pictures, words, images, and objects] of all the things you value and wish for. It allows you to think in pictures instead of words. It's your own personal work of art that represents all the things you'd like to do with your life."—Beverly K. Bachel, author[7]

"It is through writing, picturing and affirming prosperity that your thoughts, words and actions begin working for you in a happy, prosperous, productive way."—Catherine Ponder, author[8]

- **A pile of photographs of yourself, family, and friends**
- **A large pizza pie pan or any large circular tray, or a drawing tool for circles**

As you gather materials, sort through magazines and brochures to find pictures that appeal to you. Arrange your pictures into one of four piles as they relate to your physical, mental, emotional, or spiritual goals—the four sections that will comprise your Treasure Map. Then label four large manila envelopes or folders with the same titles, place your pictures inside, and set them aside.

Next, get a large circular tray and center it on the white poster board. Trace the tray and put it aside. I like to use two colors, saving the white for the main circle and accenting it with a dazzling color. If that's your choice, trace another circle on a separate colored poster board—then draw zigzag lines around the outside edge of the circle, creating a sunburst effect. Next cut out the colored zigzag border, and paste it around the circle on the white poster board. If you would rather use one color, make your circle all white.

Take a ruler and use it to find the center. Put a dot there, and divide the circle into four even quarters as if you were cutting a pizza. On the outside rim of each quarter section of the circle write or paste the words *Physical*, *Mental*, *Emotional*, and *Spiritual*.

Realize this is a unique visualization exercise to reach your goals with no set rules. It will simply become a Picture Map you'll look at every day to help remember your dreams. Allow yourself to make it very personal and meaningful by following the promptings of your heart.

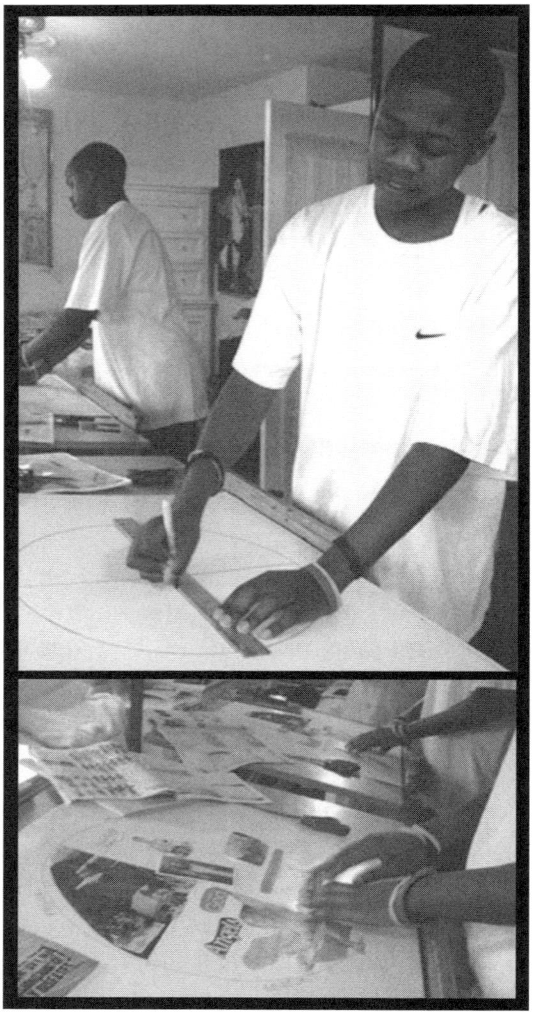

Sam's treasure map board.

Now you are ready to begin the pasting part of the exercise. I usually choose a symbol of something spiritual or meaningful, which I place in the center of the circle. You could choose any picture of a spiritual figure, such as Moses, Jesus, Mohammed, the Buddha, Lord Krishna, or whoever might be a reflection of your personal beliefs. Or perhaps you'd like to paste or draw a picture of something that holds significance, such as an angel, an open door, a crystal cup, or rays of sunlight. Once I have finished pasting this center image, I write under the picture, "All good flows from my Higher Power to help me fulfill my perfect plan." Feel free to choose different words that reflect your beliefs.

Turn your attention to the four sections, as each one will have a different purpose. The physical quadrant will reveal all of the "things" you long to have in your life. The mental quadrant will be for pictures of places and events that focus on your mental expertise, such as getting an education or completing some technical training. The emotional (or social) quadrant will focus on pictures of romantic relationships or events with your family and friends. The last is the spiritual section, where you will place pictures that have spiritual or religious value for you.

The Physical Quadrant

On my map, I start with placing word *Physical* to the right of the top center line. Here are some ideas to look for in the magazines you have assembled that might describe your physical goals:

- **A really buff person working out or performing some sport that appeals to you**
- **A model wearing a leather jacket or coat you've had your eye on**
- **A home you always hoped you might live in**
- **The new car or motorcycle you've always dreamed about**
- **Pictures of dollar bills, stacks of coins, or even the word *cash***
- **A check written out to yourself with a hint in the "memo" part of what you want to materialize**

I could list other things for the physical section here, but I think you get the idea. When looking for images for this section, be open and spontaneous——find pictures of your own ideas and dreams. You are trying to unlock your life's plan, which will reveal itself bit by bit as you materialize your goals.

Search through the photos you have collected of yourself, your family, and your friends. Keep them handy so you can cut them apart. Use either the original photo (if you don't care that it will get ruined) or run a copy on your printer. When you find the exact photo that expresses who you wish to become, such as a college graduate, someone driving a new car, or a person dressed up in a military uniform, rip it out of the magazine. Then cut your face out of your photograph and paste it over the face in the picture you have found. This can be hilarious if you let your creative juices flow and see what you learn about yourself.

"Last year I landed my first real job. Ever since I got my driver's license I've wanted a Honda convertible. I've had my eye on a cobalt-blue two-seater [car] with a roof that pops out and goes into the trunk, while the back window goes all the way down. It's been my dream car and I loved it!

"My job was an entry-level junior buyer in an advertising agency. What luck, as our client just happened to be Honda. Since we had to hang pictures of each model through out the office to please our client, I asked the manager if they would hang the convertible poster outside my office. He did, and I could see it while sitting at my desk everyday. It was such a huge motivation that the long hours and overtime I had to put in last year didn't bother me that much.

"Within five months' time I got the car. Granted I only leased it, but for the next two years it was all mine. The point is, I wanted something and was willing to work hard for it. The daily visualization on that poster really helped to motivate me and make my goal seem much more attainable."—Tina, age 20

Picture Good Health

If you suffer from a physical ailment or someone you care about is ill, try some positive imaging on the situation. You can picture a healthier, more active you by pasting your face on a photo of an athlete. Remember the third step to creating your goal and let yourself feel the excitement of becoming well again.

To read further information on teens with disabilities and how they view their victories, or to get other upbeat ideas on how to deal with health issues, turn to authors such as Denise Thornton and Louise Hay. In her book *You Can Heal Your Life*, which also has a companion study guide, Ms. Hay shares creative methods of healing, and she also encourages creative meditation through her CD *Meditations for Personal Healing*.[9]

Dr. Darren Weissman also suggests you can take positive steps to improve your health. How? Simply by being grateful for

"Create in your mind a picture of yourself in perfect health. Explore all the aspects of this; visualize how you will look when you possess abundant energy, a positive mood, a relaxed and supple body, and so on. Go into as much detail as possible."—Gerry Maguire Thompson, author[10]

everything that happens in you life. He feels that instead of being negative or resentful, you can embrace your physical condition through affirming "infinite love and gratitude." Weissmann states, "You are your own healer. Once you awaken to how your subconscious mind impacts your life, as well as to the Five Basic Steps for Optimal Health, your body will be able to create balance and naturally mend itself. The process of healing is a spiritual journey, the evolutionary voyage to awakening your spirit. And the first step begins with choosing to own your power and to feel."[11]

Dr. Weissman's "Lifeline Technique" provides the tools necessary to restore the body's balance and facilitate good health. His five basic elements for "Optimal Health" consist of water, food, rest, exercise, and owning your power. He feels it is important to stay in the "Present Time Consciousness," pay attention to what your body is telling you, set goals, and take steps to achieve them.[12]

The Secret Gift Test

Maybe you have doubts about using this Treasure Map experiment to help visualize your goals, and you find yourself thinking, "Can this really work?" I can only tell you what happened to me when I thought this was a lot of bunk. I decided to test it out. How? Check out my method in No Sweat Exercise 19.

The Mental Section

Move to the mental section. Cut out pictures of the college you hope to attend and place a photo of you in a cap and gown

EXAMPLE: NO SWEAT EXERCISE 19—THE SECRET GIFT TEST

One time when I was seriously broke and needed guidance I decided to test this whole Treasure Map idea on something I thought was an impossible thing to achieve. We lived in Colorado and went hiking every weekend. I only had sneakers, so I struggled along the mountain trails wearing those.

I found a picture of an expensive pair of hiking boots I knew I couldn't afford, and I pasted it on the Treasure Map in the physical section. Within one month a friend offered to trade me her new hiking boots (that were exactly my size) for a pair of my new heels that I had never worn. That's when I realized I could create my own dreams through treasure mapping.

NO SWEAT EXERCISE 19—THE SECRET GIFT TEST

Directions: When you experiment with this secret gift idea, remember step 1 in creating goals—you have to really want your goal. This works for goals you visualize as well. Find a picture of something personal you want that only you will know about. It could be a baseball cap, a watch, a ring, or whatever moves you. Go ahead—be brave and try it.

To begin, write the exercise title on the first line. Then take the next four lines to write down your secret gift in detail so when you reread this in several months, you can see how long it took for you to reach your specific secret goal. Remember to paste the picture of your secret gift onto your Treasure Map.

"When my school counselor asked me if I wanted to take a workshop on visualizing goals, I thought it might be a bunch of magical stuff. But the one thing I found I could really get into was this wheel collage. So, I confess, I went a little nuts over it. I shut myself up for an entire weekend and cut and pasted myself right out of one of the worst depressions I had ever been in since I broke up with my boyfriend last summer. Yeah, I thought it was strange, but what did I have to lose?"—Ellie, age 16

standing on the campus. My niece did that when she finally got up the guts to go back to college and finish her degree. Before she started the classes, she took a brochure from the college and found a picture of one of the instructors who was congratulating a student. She cut a photo of her face and put it over the other student's face. In one year her goal was completed. The day she was awarded her degree, her instructor congratulated her just like

Chef.
Illustration by Peg Raasch.

she envisioned, and a friend took her photo of that exact moment she had envisioned!

Do you dream of being an exchange student and studying abroad? How can you make that become a reality? Google a travel site and find your dream country. Print out photos of people having fun there. Get brochures from a travel agency, and make a collage of all of the sights you would see if you lived there. Paste yourself in the photo riding on planes, trains, and ships. That's how you make things start to happen.

Do you dream of being a chef? Get a catalog from a cooking school and put yourself into a chef's hat. If you're short on money for tuition (one of problems that keep us from believing our dreams will come true), take a blank check and write it to the school for the amount of the tuition. Date it and in the memo on the bottom left of the check, write, "tuition for . . ." and insert your name. Then practice by watching Food Network and making all of Rachael Ray's famous recipes.

View photos to demonstrate to your subconscious mind you have already completed the schooling you'll need for your success. If you dream of becoming a teacher, find a classroom full of little kids all sitting at their desks, smiling at you. If you want to fly a plane, find a photo of a pilot strapped into the cockpit; give him your face. If you want to be a scientist or a PhD, write out those credentials after your signature (similar to the exercise in No Sweat Exercise 18, where you doodled how you envisioned yourself in the future).

Maybe your destiny is to be the scientist who will create a vaccine that will end the AIDS epidemic some day!

Brainstorm on Your Life Goal

Do you have a dream to help AIDS victims in Africa? We'll create an example using this as a topic. First you write your dream in a brief statement. Next you feed your passion and go on a creative frenzy and brainstorm—write down whatever comes to mind to accomplish your goal.

If you take the following brainstorming exercise, you can use it for ideas on other parts of your Picture Map. Maybe this could help you to define what you want in a college. Here are some ideas to help you get started.

EXAMPLE: NO SWEAT EXERCISE 20—BRAINSTORM ON YOUR LIFE GOAL

Ideas to help defeat AIDS in Africa:

- Take a trip to Africa and do a photo shoot of AIDS victims.
- Create a blog to track your progress and start a chat room about your AIDS project.
- Get Peace Corp volunteers to help with the distribution of medical supplies.
- Send exchange students to Africa to educate teens on stopping the spread of AIDS.
- Start a marathon in your hometown to raise money for the cure of AIDS.
- Get a coffee company to sponsor you and print your AIDS projects on java cups.
- Start a pen-pal group between school kids in Africa and kids in the United States.
- Get your town municipal office to adopt an African village and post AIDS victims monthly.

If you want to major in theater, brainstorm to find a location for your potential college. Try clustering to keep your search to a particular geographical area, such as the Midwest. So you would scribble down Iowa, Missouri, Nebraska, Ohio, Illinois, Indiana, and Michigan. Then jot down other words, like touring with a summer theater, marquis (where you'll see your name in lights for top billing) audition, rehearsals, orchestra, and dance. Write down other things that would help you to make up your mind, like the school must have a gym, fitness equipment, a trainer, a swimming pool, a track, and so on. Then you could go online and search for the perfect college, putting in both the state and your desired major.

Get excited about this whole mental-visual way of thinking. It makes you feel so free and it is amazing to see what pictures you'll find for your Treasure Map.

NO SWEAT EXERCISE 20— BRAINSTORM ON YOUR LIFE GOAL

Directions: Ready to clarify your vision? Pull out your Goals Notebook and print the title on the top line of a clean sheet. Write out your statement on the next line. Next number eight lines where you can describe different ways to could accomplish your life goal.

____

____

1. ____
2. ____
3. ____
4. ____
5. ____
6. ____
7. ____
8. ____

It is important to learn different creative techniques to use in achieving your goals. Clustering is one of these tools. It is a writing tool developed in the 1970s to help you find and develop ideas through brainstorming.

Do not confuse this idea with the technical term *clustering*, which refers to the connecting of two or more computers so they function like a single unit.

As John Crystal and Richard Bolles point out, "You cluster according to your own preferences. There are no categories that you have to fit into, no system that you must embrace. . . .

"Part of [your] uniqueness is expressed not only in the skills and personal traits that you possess, but also in the way that you blend them together. How you perceive them, how you cluster them, is a part of your uniqueness."[13]

Recently, a friend told me that her high school daughter shared this dream of helping fight the AIDS epidemic in Africa. She plans to major in world health to prepare herself to reach her goal. Here are her words.

"I think I've wanted to be a doctor for almost six years now. My dream is the type that's changed around a lot. When I was younger, my goal was to be in gory fields like working in an emergency room or being an open-heart surgeon. But now I'm hoping to do something that has an even broader impact. That's why my goal is to get involved with international health, like become a doctor for the World Health Organization.

"I'll be starting college this year and I'm already planning all the "pre-med" courses I'll need to take as prerequisites, starting with chemistry this fall. I'm really looking forward to these science-related courses, but I'm also planning to take courses in completely unrelated fields. I'd like to major in biochemistry and maybe anthropology.

"As ready as I am to dive into getting into a good medical school, I want to use college as a time to explore other options too. Honestly, I could see myself being anything from a math teacher to a film director. But for now I'm doing what's involved in really educating myself."—K.J., age 18

Emotional Shock Therapy

Let's play Emotional Shock Therapy. How? In the emotional, or social, segment of your circle you can really go wild. Find photos of a happy family. Look at magazine ads by pharmaceutical or life insurance companies that show happy families doing things together, something everyone craves.

Once you have found the right family picture, go to your own photos and cut out the faces of your siblings and parents. Paste them on kids smiling with their arms around each other.

"When I got accepted as an extra in a Jennifer Anniston film last year, I realized that I wanted to major in theater. So I looked at several colleges in the Midwest that offered that.

"When I visited this campus, it just felt right. But there was one glitch—it wasn't that I just needed to get accepted into the college—I had to audition to get accepted into the theater program, too.

"On the day of the audition, my mom came with me for that and it was an all-day event. I had to sing two songs, one slow and another a little more contemporary. I got a call back within the hour that I had passed and I would be going on to audition for dance. I aced that and got a second call back for the third event of the audition, which was a monologue. I had to do a comedy and a dramatic skit.

"The judging panel was made up of the head of the theater department, as well as the heads of the music and dance department. I was so elated when I got accepted on that day!

"Fifteen of us got chosen out of a hundred in our group.

"Now we are rehearsing for our first production of the 'Pajama Game' and I'm loving every minute of it. Broadway—here I come."—Carreen, age 19

As long as you are dreaming in pictures, place your whole family in Hawaii or—where else?— Disney World. How's that for an emotional shock?

In the example of No Sweat Exercise 1—Crazy Things I Want to Do Someday (back in chapter 1) one of the suggested activities was "Learn fly-fishing—then go to Alaska and fish with my dad." If that sounds like fun, paste you and your dad in a tent by a river near an icy mountain. Get courageous and put both of you into a kayak, or plaster your faces on skydiving figures. The possibilities are endless. You can get into a twisted humor and use this to vent a little, which might open the door for you and your parent to become closer.

Why Spiritual Goals?

The last section is the spiritual part of your circle. You might think this is way off for you, but you are planning things for your

Broadway, here comes Ivy!

entire life. Now is the only time you have, so take the few minutes to look inside and find out what is important to you. You might find yourself wondering, "I can hardly think of goals in the physical, and now I should look at them in the spiritual. Isn't this stretching it a bit?"

Don't shy away from your innate spiritual side. Throughout history humans have shown their spiritual yearnings in all cultures. Today, Native Americans still honor the spirit in the earth, the moon, and all of nature through meditation, prayer, and dance.

If you were raised in a particular religious belief and you have mixed emotions about it, now could be the time to bring that back into focus. Find a photo of a religious book that appeals to you, like the Bible, the Koran, the Torah, the Bhagavad Gita, or any

Some entertainers don't hide their religious side. Clay Aiken, runner up of the 2003 TV program *American Idol*, is one of those stars. He states this opinion: "Some people have argued that I am too religious and that I talk about my faith too much. My response to them is that I'm not going to hide how I feel, but I do my best not to cram it down anybody's throat. I'm not trying to change anybody's beliefs, but if someone asks me about it, I'm happy to share it. I want to be here for that."[15]

Native American or other indigenous symbol, and paste it into your map.[14]

Do you like to sing for the sheer joy of it? Kelly Clarkson did. Her joy and enthusiasm spilled over into her act when she became the first *American Idol* winner in 2002. Today she makes it very clear that she is open to reaching out and helping others. She gives the credit to her teenage church experiences: "I grew up in a really active youth group. I know in order for me to help others in their situations, I've got to be open about mine. I'm probably one of the

Many successful entertainers started singing with their church choirs. Here are a few:

- **Clay Aiken**
- **Toni Braxton**
- **Mariah Carey**
- **Whitney Houston**
- **Avril Lavigne**
- **Aaron Neville**
- **LeeAnn Rimes**

"I've a good voice and have always done well in theater in high school. I was interested in the college I chose because it has a sixty-five-year tradition in a cappella singing. I was pretty tense when it was time for the auditions, but it was fun, too. They went on for two days, and of course, there were callbacks on the final day. Since this kind of singing involves several skills, you get tested on all of them. So, it was no surprise when I was first asked to do my scales. Then they asked me to sing a solo, and I was okay with that. Other things they look for is your ability to blend in with the other twelve guys, so you sing with several guys during the audition.

"Fortunately, we were given a heads up, so I also had a joke ready to tell the group, too. I think my favorite is the vocal percussion. We just jam on and on with that.

"So far we've given twenty-two performances, so I also have to plan way ahead with my studies, and, of course, I can take some of my work along to do on the trips. I hope I can keep this up for all four years of my college."—Steve, age 19

most open people. . . . I will tell you anything about myself if I think it's going to help [you]."[16]

Singing is a huge trend in fraternities and sororities these days, especially if you can sing a cappella.[17] If singing is your passion, find a photo of a choir and paste yourself into it. You can even do research to find out which colleges have an active singing program. One teen did just that.

Maybe you want to find some new spiritually minded friends. Many synagogues have youth social clubs. Why not find out when the next meeting is in your area and just show up?

If you've really had it with trashy social events and you long to have some uncomplicated fun, find pictures of kids doing healthy things like hiking or swimming or gardening. Summer is a great time to meet new friends and explore the great outdoors. Whether you want to learn ecological skills or meditate in the Rockies, be proactive, as many camps offer scholarships.[18]

Maybe you've wanted to study for the ministry but you couldn't admit it before. Cut out a photo of a college with a ministry program. If you are considering teaching as a profession, why not earn a certificate there? Religious-based colleges often have excellent teaching curriculums, and credentials from a school with a good reputation can open many doors when you want to practice teach. [19]

Meditate to Hear Your Inner Voice

At some point in a person's life the idea of meditation seems interesting. Get rid of the idea that meditation is "way out there" because it could be a new tool to help clarify your goal. If this rings true to you, find a picture of a person sitting in the yoga position, meditating, and paste it with your face into your spiritual section.

There are many kinds of meditation including "sensory awareness meditation, loving, kindness meditation, mediation of sound, visual meditation, healing meditation and charka mediation," to mention a few.[20]

You can even do "active meditation," which brings increased awareness of any routine activity you are doing. You can be more in sync with your life by making each aspect of your meditation significant. When you take a walk, become aware of your breathing as you listen to the sounds of nature. When you listen to music, let the rhythm engulf you; or if you go to a quiet place, let the silence free up your mind. You can even try Soduku as a form of mental meditation.[21]

"The principles of meditation can be applied even more broadly on a moment to moment basis, across the whole spectrum of daily life. Doing a job with full awareness and being in the present moment, rather than with absent-mindedness, can be applied to almost any task in your day."—Gerry Maguire Thompson, author[22]

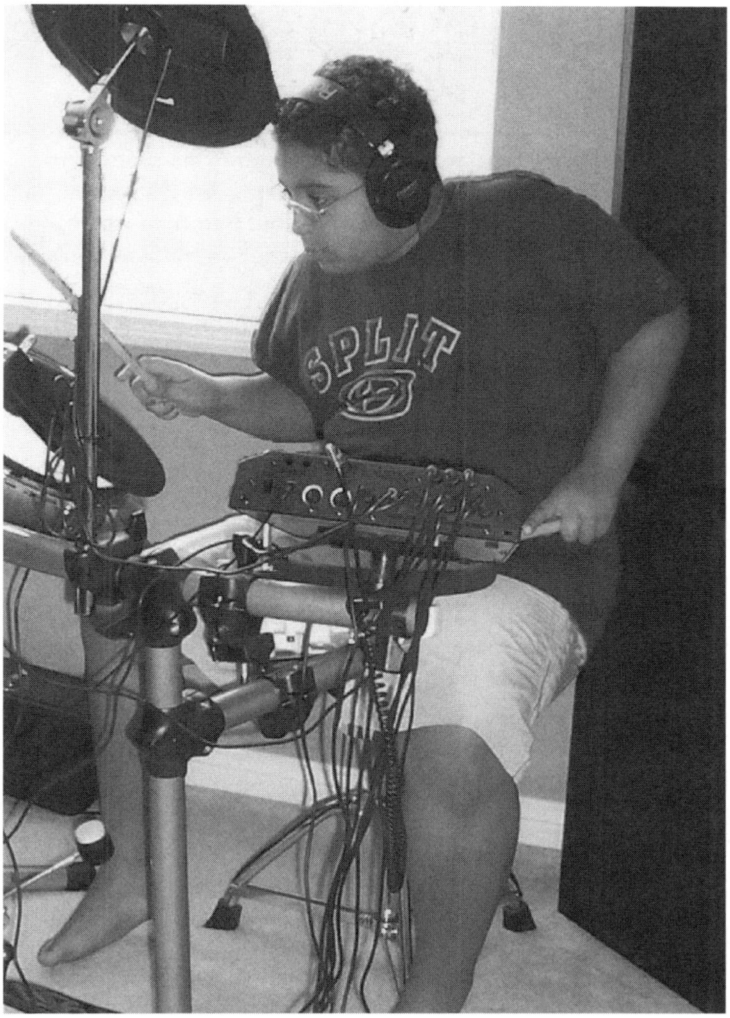

Evon dreams of drumming.

I find that music is helpful to unearth my goals. When I need to analyze my writing, I often exercise because working out is very calming and repetitious. Afterward, I cool down with a long walk on the track. I plug in my iPod and tune out the world. Soon I'm in a meditative state, where changes in my manuscript become crystal clear.

When you are doing something repetitious, your mind goes into a space where you can get in touch with your intuition and listen to your inner voice. Then, little by little, your goals and dreams will surface for you.

Maybe you find yourself thinking, "Why would I want to meditate? The idea gives me the creeps." Honor your feelings, but

PAULO COELHO

Paulo Coelho is a Brazilian author who inspires his readers to pursue their goals in life. His first best seller, *The Alchemist*,[23] is a simple but moving story about a boy named Santiago who follows his inner voice to pursue his dream. Another significant book, *The Warrior of the Light*, introduces the reader to a different boy whose quest leads him to become the person he wants to be.

Coelho believes it is important to use your intuition to find your way in life.

> **The Warrior of the Light knows the importance of intuition. In the midst of battle, he does not have time to think about the enemy's blows, so he uses his instinct and obeys his angel. In times of peace, he deciphers the signs that God send him.**
>
> **People say, "He's mad."**
>
> **Or, "He lives in a fantasy world."**
>
> **Or even, "How can he possible believe in such illogical things?"**
>
> **But the warrior knows that intuition is God's language and he continues listening to the wind and talking to the stars.[24]**

also realize your viewpoint may have shifted since you have been setting goals.

Meditation is a form of mental clearing that will help you to figure out answers to pressing problems. Once you quiet your thoughts, you can hear your inner voice. How can you pick a college, break up with a girlfriend, or make the decision to join the military when thoughts are racing through your mind 24/7?

To find information on local meditation classes, skim through free magazines at your local health food store. If you want a more in-depth analysis of the physiological changes that the brain goes through during meditation, google *Time* magazine. Bring up the archives to find the issue dated August 4, 2003, which dedicates the cover to "The Science of Meditation" and reviews a variety of different Americans who are getting hooked on meditating, including students, lawyers, and even inmates. You can even find whole classrooms of teens doing, what else, meditating![25]

To conclude your Treasure Map, cut out words like *meditate*—or find other words like *patience*, *courage*, or *winner*—and paste them around photos of yourself in the four different sections. Since this is a visual map, paste gold stars in every section. Add

You—the soccer star of your dreams.
Art by Anne Courtright.

colorful words that describe yourself as the star you want to be, with titles such as "star soccer champion" or "first place Merit Scholarship winner."

Congratulations for having the courage to try treasure mapping! Review your map often until the visual pictures of your dreams become a reality. Once you feel you have reached the goals on your Treasure Map, you can start a new one.

Realize in completing this exercise you have shown your creativity and have uncovered your hopes and dreams. Don't be afraid to explore new opportunities that will reveal additional goals. Reach for new ways to unlock the potential you have realized through self-discovery. Believe in yourself and that you are molding your life to reflect your inner beliefs. Know you are becoming a winner, achieving your goals using creative visualization!

NOTES

1. "Louis Pasteur," Wikipedia, en.wikipedia.org/wiki/Louis_Pasteur (accessed December 28, 2006).

2. "Henry Ford (1863–1947)," About.com, inventors.about.com/library/inventors/blford.htm (accessed September 8, 2006).

3. "About Us," March of Dimes, www.marchofdimes.com/aboutus/14458_15363.asp (accessed June 8, 2007).

4. In 1975, Bill Gates and Paul Allen founded Microsoft by licensing BASIC (the first computer language program written for a personal computer) to MITS, the manufacturer of the Altair 8800 personal computer. "History of Microsoft," The History of Computing Project, www.thocp.net/companies/microsoft/microsoft_company.htm (accessed February 7, 2006).

5. Mary Bellis, "The History of Apple Computers," About.com: Inventors, inventors.about.com/library/inventors/blapplecomputer.htm (accessed February 7, 2006).

6. Darren R. Weissman, *The Power of Infinite Love and Gratitude* (Carlsbad, CA: Hay House, 2007), 11.

7. Beverly K. Bachel, *What Do You Really Want? How to Set a Goal and Go for It: A Guide For Teens* (Minneapolis: Free Spirit Publishing, 2001), 29.

8. Catherine Ponder, *Open Your Mind to Prosperity* (Marina Del Rey, CA: DeVorss & Company, 1983), 73.

9. Louise Hay, *You Can Heal Your Life* (Carlsbad, CA: Hay House, 2005); Louise Hay, *Meditations for Personal Healing* (Carlsbad, CA: Hay House, 2005), audio CD; Denise Thornton, *Teens with Disabilities: The Ultimate Teen Guide* (Lanham, MD: Scarecrow Press, 2007). All three of these sources will inspire you to picture good health.

10. Gerry Maguire Thompson, *Meditation Made Easy: An Introduction to the Basics of the Ancient Art of Meditation* (New York: Sterling, 1999), 54. This is the best (and smallest) book I've found on meditating.

11. Weissman, *Infinite Love*, 10, 135–36.

12. Weissman, *Infinite Love*, 135–36.

13. For more on clustering as a prewriting technique, see John C. Crystal and Richard Nelson Bolles, *Where Do I Go from Here with My Life?* (New York: Seabury Press, 1974), 75; "Pre-writing Strategies," Resources for Writers, www.english.udel.edu/dbaer/prewriting.html (accessed June 19, 2007).

14. The Holy Bible is the name used by Jews and Christians for their differing canons of sacred texts; see "Bible," Wikipedia, en.wikipedia.org/wiki/Bible (accessed September 9, 2006). The Koran contains God's words to Muhammad through the Angel Gabriel; see "Islam: The Koran," ThinkQuest, library.thinkquest.org/28505/islam/koran.htm (accessed September 9, 2006). Torah refers to the Tanak, the first five books of the Hebrew Bible; see "The Written Law (The Torah)," Jewish Virtual Library, www.jewishvirtuallibrary.org/jsource/Judaism/The_Written_Law.html (accessed December 11, 2008). The Bhagavad Gita was spoken by Lord Krishna to Arjuna during battle around 3135 BC and is revered by most Hindis as Vedic scripture; see

"Srimad Bhagavad-Gita," Bhagavad-Gita, www.bhagavad-gita.org/ (accessed February 23, 2008). For American Indian symbols, see Takatoka, "Symbols of Indigenous Peoples," Manataka American Indian Council, www.manataka.org/page29.html (accessed December 2, 2007).

15. Clay Aiken and Allison Glock, *Learning to Sing: Hearing the Music in Your Life* (New York: Random House, 2004), 226.

16. Meredith Milstein, "Kelly Clarkson," *Seventeen* 65, no. 1 (January 2006): 86–90.

17. a cappella: choral music unaccompanied instrumentally. *The New Lexicon Webster's Dictionary of the English Language* (New York: Lexicon Publications, 1988), 4.

18. For unique summer camps, check out the following websites:

a. Omega Teen Camp, omegateencamp.org/dates-fees-register.htm (accessed January 2, 2008)
b. Allen's Guide, www.allensguide.com/religious-camps/jewish-summer-camps/ (accessed October 10, 2007)
c. Awake, www.humanityinunity.org/SYMPLE/AudioVideoFiles/index.cfm (accessed December 18, 2007)
d. Higher Ground, www.carolinacamp.com/camp%20videos.htm (accessed October 10, 2007)

19. If you want to be a ministry college sleuth, try these sites to get you started:

a. Washington Post.com, education.washingtonpost.com/site/16192458001 (accessed June 12, 2007)
b. University Ministry, studentaffairs.depaul.edu/ministry/jewish.html. (accessed June 12, 2007)

20. Thompson, *Meditation Made Easy*, 72.

21. Thompson, *Meditation Made Easy*, 72.

22. Thompson, *Meditation Made Easy*, 20–22.

23. Paulo Coelho, *The Alchemist* (San Francisco: HarperCollins, 1993).

24. Paulo Coelho, *Warrior of the Light* (New York: HarperCollins, 2003), 45.

25. Joel Stein, "Just Say Om," *Time* 162, no. 5 (August 4, 2003): 48–56.

8 More Tools for Self-Discovery

Sometimes events happen that change your picture of life and it's hard to see through the maze of confusion. That's the time you will need to reach for your new tools of self-discovery and positive thinking. These tools can include a variety of different things, such as keeping a daily journal, learning to relax through doing contour drawing, creating the perfect place for your spirit to flourish, and learning to accept all of life's gifts, especially that it's okay to be yourself. Finally, think about honoring your music and favorite books by putting your own library list together.

GETTING BACK ON TRACK

Achieving your goals can come to a screeching halt when unpredictable events happen. Maybe your parents announce they are getting a divorce, or a relative dies, or your family moves to a new city. With little warning to adjust, you find you're in a tailspin, changing your school or home. Hidden in the chaos could lie the key to discovering your next goal. This may seem bittersweet, but often the person or situation you resist the most will hold a key for your success.

So, after crying and arguing, or becoming depressed, you wake up one morning and remember, "Hey, what about my goal to become the doctor who specializes in cancer research—what happened to that?" Maybe in trying to fit in to a new family situation, you've been overwhelmed by helping your mom. You've forgotten about yourself. Suddenly you realize it's time to think about yourself and your own goals.

"Crazymakers" is Julia Cameron's name for people who have huge amounts of drama in their lives: "Crazymakers are those personalities that create storm centers. They are often charismatic, frequently charming, highly inventive, and powerfully persuasive. And for the creative person in their vicinity, they are enormously destructive.

Crazymakers are . . . people who can take over your whole life. [They] like drama. If they can swing it, they are the star. Everyone around them functions as a supporting cast, picking up their cues, their entrances and exits, from the crazymaker's whims.[1]

If you let the new situation take over your life, you could go nuts with all of the drama. You might find yourself wondering, "How can anyone think straight when other people cause all this confusion?"

When you are living in a tumultuous situation, you cannot always see what is causing you to go off course in meeting your goal. This is the time to start to record what you are going through. When you read it back to yourself, you will see events more clearly.

KEEP A DAILY JOURNAL

Now that you are becoming aware of how important it is to stay on track, it's time to add a few more tools to help you succeed. Did you know that daily journaling helps you focus on your life and find new ways to meet your goals? You could call it an "eye-opener."

Although we have been using your Goals Notebook to record your No Sweat Exercises, daily journaling is slightly different because it is not tied to one particular activity. If you wish to experiment with the art of journaling, set aside some loose-leaf pages and keep them in a separate notebook, or buy a small diary for starters. If you're the kind of person who finds it hard to write in longhand, journaling directly on your computer might work better for you.

Journaling is nothing new or revolutionary. To "journal" you simply find a quiet place such as your school library or your

Sandra and Harry Choron, whose expert advice can be found in *The Book of Lists for Teens*, believe that you can be successful in keeping a journal if you follow three rules: "Write freely and honestly, and don't worry if your entry doesn't make any sense. Make it a habit to write something every single day, even if you think nothing happened that day. Finally make sure [your journal] is kept as private as you want it to be, so you always feel safe saying *anything*."

Here are some additional benefits the Chorons feel you can experience from journaling:

1. **You can express your feelings without feeling judged by anyone.**
2. **By keeping a daily journal of your activities you're creating a living part of history.**
3. **Journaling helps you to solve problems.**
4. **Your journal becomes a place to store your best memories.**
5. **Journaling teaches you things about yourself you never knew before.**
6. **Journaling gives you a time and place to write about your favorite people.**
7. **You can take turns writing a journal with a friend and share your secrets together.**
8. **A journal is a great place to illustrate your new creative writing and poetry.**
9. **You can use it to leave people messages (and leave it around for them to read it!)[2]**

bedroom at home, and you start to write about what's happening in your life.

I write everyday in *The Artist's Way Morning Pages Journal*.[3] It is a companion journal for *The Artist's Way: A Spiritual Path to Higher Creativity*. The journal is a large paperback book. Most of each page is blank except for a particular quote that corresponds to the original text. Once in a while I'll grab that book and read the quote in its entire context, but most of the time I just let my thoughts flow onto the page.

You can find a variety of similar journals for teens. Most have all blank pages for writing. *Through My Eyes: A Journal for Teens* by Linda Kranz, mixes blank sheets with others that contain quotes such as "What are things that matter most to you in your life?"[4] Begin to write any way you wish. You could turn the quote

Kayla's journal.

into a fuzzy cloud by doodling around it to get you started; then color in the cloud or draw all over the page. A lot of the time I try and write something about the quote for the day and see how it relates to my life. In this case, you call that kind of quote a "prompt" because it causes, or prompts, you to think about that subject in a new way.

You might wonder, "Won't people laugh at me if I do this in my dorm every morning?" You might be uneasy and self-conscious at first, but you'll gain a lot of respect—first from yourself, for being disciplined to follow your goal, and then from others.

The journal I use is aimed at helping me to overcome writer's block, so it organizes the blank pages into weeks. Right now I am beginning week 4, entitled, "Recovering a Sense of Integrity." The quotes I'll address tomorrow are page 1, "Growth is an erratic forward movement: two steps forward, one step back"; page 2, "Be alert for support and encouragement form unexpected quarters"; page 3, "Experiment with solitude."

Respect and value your journaling time. It will help you to dump information out of your brain that is clogging it up. That will help you to see important things you need to remember. You can also reread your old journals. You will find they are

As Piero Ferrucci tells us in his book *Inevitable Grace*,

> **We all have moments of inspiration—a sudden flash of understanding, the solution to a problem, a state of grace, a brilliant thought about a future project, a witty remark. These are the moments in which we experience original thoughts.**
>
> **Inspiration comes . . . at the most unlikely times and in the most inappropriate situations . . . [and] it must be anchored . . . this is where a most valuable item makes its appearance: the notebook.[5]**

comforting because they help you to see how much you have changed to meet your goals. Some successful authors refer to the journals and diaries they kept as kids to find excellent stories with vivid details.

Here is an example of how I journal. It seems important to share this so you can see how valuable the entire process can be. These are some of my thoughts on how the opinions of teens should be respected:

> Teens have something important to say. It's just that no one older, or in any position of authority wants to listen to them or take them seriously. (Then I doodled a bit in the margin as I thought more on the subject.) I think this is true, because it is hard for adults to see the difference in what kids feel truly passionate about versus what they are reacting to that is simply a fad. Sure kids have something to say. But another problem is that peer pressure is so great and they don't want to be alienated for their different ideas. Both fads and the idea of being popular take over a kid's life. It's almost as though there's only a tiny stream of light for their real ideas to climb to the surface through. They are so bombarded all the time. Kids need down time, quiet time, time to think—to feel alive—to know they are real and that their opinion matters.

Those were my thoughts on a day when I was deep into the writing of this book.

Journaling has universal appeal. It has even proven to be helpful to inmates trying to reconstruct their lives by looking back at their past. As part of an outreach program for men and women,

ANNE FRANK

Did you realize that your diaries could make you famous? One of the most famous teens remembered for her diaries is Anne Frank. She got her first diary for her thirteenth birthday, in April 1942. For the next two years she filled page upon page with her thoughts, concerns, and creative fiction stories. For the first three months, Anne wrote about her normal life as a teen, but over the next two years she documented how she spent her time in hiding with her family in a secret apartment in Amsterdam because they were Jews.

Anne wrote three full diaries, most in the form of letters to an imaginary friend named Kitty. Anne had started on her fourth diary when her entire family was arrested on August 4, 1944. Because Anne left in a hurry, she couldn't take her diaries with her. They were found the next day scattered on the floor of the secret annex, by two trusted friends, Miep Gies and Bep Voskuijl. Meip returned them to Anne's father, Otto Frank, after the war was over.

In March of 1944, before the arrest, Anne heard a radio address that spoke of publishing diaries after the war. Then she rewrote and edited a large portion of her original diaries to prepare them for publication.[6] When Otto read Anne's diary, he realized her goal was to publish the story of the two years her family spent hiding in the secret annex. Although it made Mr. Frank very sad to read about the hardships his family endured, he agreed to fulfill his daughter's wish.

Anne Frank is a great example of a teen dedicated to achieving her goals, because through daily journaling, she met her goal to become a writer.

Tracy Emsun, a youth counselor with Lake County Health Department in Waukegan, Illinois, introduces the finer points of journaling to inmates. She advises that a great way to start to journal is to write the title of a song that describes your life in the past (pick any age), the present, and the future (what you want your life to be). You can also write song titles that describe each stage in your life or major events. Finally, allow yourself to write verses for your own new tunes.

Still holding back? Take a look at the list of books on journaling for teens Ms. Emsun has put together. These books will give you more ideas on journaling and show how to blend several creative activities together.[7]

Since this isn't a real No Sweat Exercise, but something to try as an experiment, give yourself ten minutes and start to journal on loose-leaf paper or in the back of your Goals Notebook. Let everything or anything tumble out onto the page. Fill an entire blank page, if possible. Journaling can give you a renewed sense of dedication to achieve your goals because you will write down new ideas to keep yourself on track.

When you journal, if your pen stops for a minute, try and listen inside for a thought. Right now my inner voice is telling me, "It's time to move on to another subject," so I will.

TRY CONTOUR DRAWING

There is a similar exercise to journaling that you can do with your art. It's called contour drawing. You approach this kind of exercise by looking at an object and translating everything you see from your eye to your hand in a smooth, running line that acts like an outline. You can also use this as a meditation.

If you look down occasionally to see if your hand has run off the page the drawing is called a modified contour. Then you adjust your hand slightly until your drawing meets with the flow of the original line. This is also a great way to improve your drawing ability because it forces you to "see" the entire object with all of its crannies and crevices and then translate what you see to the page. If the spirit moves you and you get engrossed in being creative—don't stop. Instead, draw all over your journal when you run out of ideas to write about.

On the next page are two contour drawings from Georgia, one of my art students in 2007. Her first contour drawing was the simple outline of her shoe. The second illustration of a cricket shows how rapidly her drawing skills improved. Like her art, Georgia's goal grew to find a college where she could use her drawing skills to pursue fashion design. This kind of progress reveals how effective contour drawing can be for you, too.

Why not draw all over your journal when you run out of ideas to write about? If you make contour drawing part of your daily routine, you'll have more fun journaling.

Here is another idea to do in your journal. Since most of us keep our innermost secrets hidden away, let's try to uncover one or two. How? Since you've learned to visualize with pictures by treasure

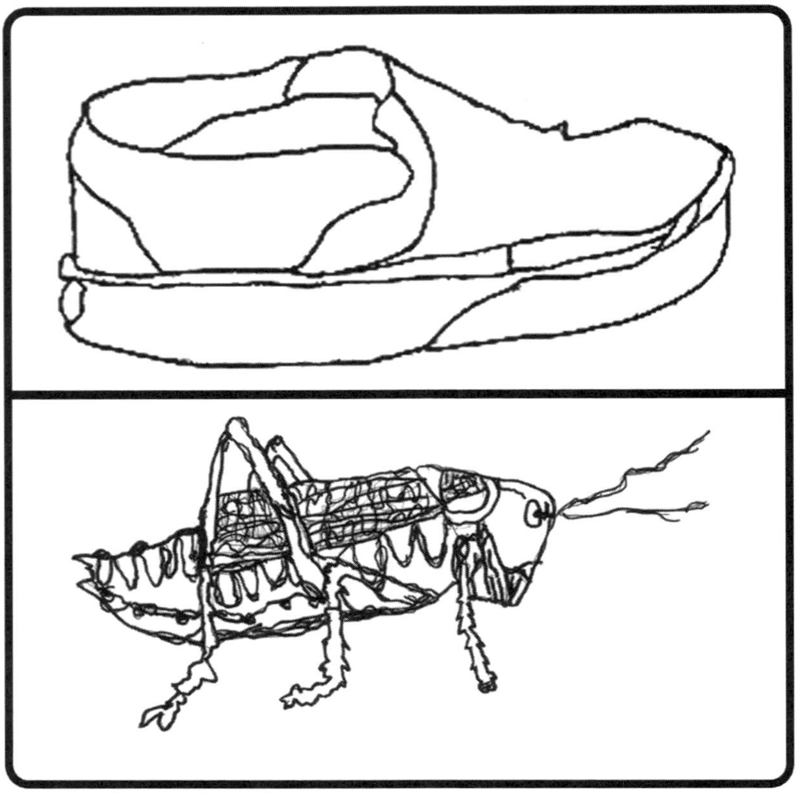

Georgia's shoe and cricket.
Art by Georgia Metz.

mapping, why not use that idea to experiment with your hidden life goal? If you dream of becoming a fashion designer, adapt contour drawing to the game of cut-out paper dolls. You can use contour drawing to design outfits. You can also adapt this drawing method to help you to create small graphic patterns you can transfer into some of your fashion designs. Tear photos from fashion magazines

"I like contour drawing because it's like a maze where you have to get to the end and finish the picture without stopping and starting again. It's also cool to look at it when you're done and realize you drew your picture in just one time! It's a challenge and it feels good once you've created a whole picture without lifting your hand."—Georgia, age 16

to create your model. Next, cut paste and designer clothes to fit the model in your journal. You can even get brave and put your face over the models and voila! You're an instant celebrity!

You can also use contour drawing to design futuristic cars, or even planes or spaceships. Then all your visual ideas can be found in one place—your private journal.

If you're willing to try a contour drawing now, turn to a blank page in your Goals Notebook. Don't see this drawing phase as a No Sweat Exercise—simply give yourself a time and place to experiment visually. If this becomes your thing, you can get a separate notebook or journal. To begin, focus on any object within your view and draw the outline of it. Try to get as detailed as possible. Keep yourself from looking at the paper as you draw, but you can peek and reposition your hand if you find you are going off the page. It doesn't matter if your drawing doesn't look at all like the object, either. This is a great way to start the flow for any creative project. You can "doodle-draw" in your journal as often as you wish to start the creative flow for yourself. Use markers and you will be pleased at how quickly your work can evolve from a small sketch to an amazing drawing. Here is a creative doodle drawing, so you will feel inspired to do more of your own.

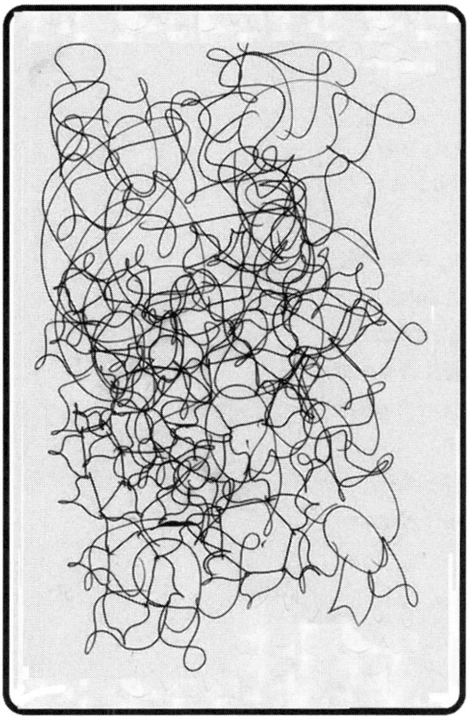

Panjri's doodle drawing.
Art by Panjri Shukla.

CREATE A SACRED PLACE FOR SPIRIT

You can honor your inner spirit in all phases of your life. How? Maybe you're attached to several trinkets that have some inner meaning to you. Try and group them together in a special place. If you're wondering how this relates to meeting your goals, go back to the ideas you used for treasure mapping. Then you'll realize this is another way to picture your goals and convince your mind you are achieving them. Here's an example.

There's a computer desk in my bedroom. Near it is a narrow shelf with objects that represent my goals. One of the trinkets on it is a gold wooden star I found by the side of a country road. When I glance up from my desk, it reminds me of my goal to become a star author and illustrator.

Find other unique ways to remind yourself of your goals. You could glue a green troll or a Bobble Head figure on your dashboard that is always reminding you, "Yes, you are achieving your goal." Or hang a first place ribbon from your dresser to remind you of your goal that someday you'll make the U.S. Olympic Soccer Team. You can even create a theme song for yourself and envision yourself as you win your goal (like in the

Create a space where you honor spirit as your creative force within. It doesn't need to be a glitzy or cluttered space.

"This haven can be a corner of a room, a nook under the stairs, even a window ledge. It is a reminder and an acknowledgement of the fact that our creator unfolds our creativity. Fill it with things that make you happy. Remember that your artist is fed by images. We are meant to celebrate the good things of this earth. Pretty leaves, rocks, candles, sea treasures—all these remind us of our creator."[8]

Rocky Balboa movies).[9] You'll be surprised how often you'll hear your song of victory!

As you strive to reach your goals, you are beginning to be yourself and discovering it's okay to be you.

IT'S OKAY TO BE YOU

Maybe you don't like all the conditions in your world right now. Pressure might be put on you that makes it hard for you to be the real you. You might be in school (at least part time) where many people expect different things from you. Your coach might be counting on you to become a star runner so the team will look good at the state finals next month; your math teacher might be expecting you to turn in that trig calculation so she can give you extra credit; your parents might be pushing you to get honors

"I used to be so embarrassed because I was always the tallest girl in my class. When I was younger, I'd try a shrinking act, but that never really worked. Kids would tease me and call me names because they could see I was self-conscious. The funny part was I was the shortest kid in my family!

"But last year this tall guy John, asked me out to one of the school dances and I went and had a great time. We saw each other for a while but broke up over the summer because he moved away. But he helped me feel good about myself and I still do."—Jane, age 15

"I like to do Soduku because it relaxes me and I go into a zone where I can't think of anything but my puzzle."—Neha, age 16

(which cuts into social life); and your girlfriend might expect you to take her to the dance next week. Even your dog expects food, some play time, and a daily walk.

The real question is, What do you expect of you? It's your life and you can express yourself in so many different ways and have so many interests. Maybe math is one of your secret passions. Why not pamper yourself with a Soduku magazine just to play with numbers?[10]

Take a look at the music that reflects you, because music helps bring clarity, especially for goal setting.

Do you relate to events in terms of a musical experience? That's what motivated Confucius as a teen, some 2,500 years ago in China. He believed that music and tradition held the key to national peace. He made the blending of these two traditions his life goal.

History records that when Confucius was a child, there was war between the states of China. At fifteen he made it his life goal to find a path for peace and restore social and moral excellence in society. He felt that through listening to music and tuning into their hearts, all men could live together in harmony, regardless of their class differences.[11]

Can you identify which recording artist has influenced you the most? When you listen to the music of recent pop-culture artists, such as Eminem, 50 Cent, and Kanye West, to mention only a few, you can see how they have influenced our society and how important rap music is in the expression of the ideas of today's youth.

If you love to write music or lyrics for tunes and your goal is to have one of your songs recorded by a famous entertainer, continue to feed your passion. To clarify your vision, create your own No

Sweat Exercise. Give it a catchy title such as, Five Steps to My Tune's Success. Next, apply the principles from Five Steps to Create a Goal. Comb through your stack of lyrics or poems, and pick out five. Reread them all and choose the best one. Next, flip back in your Goals Notebook to review your previous No Sweat Exercises to get ideas. Create action steps where you can move your lyrics from a dream into becoming a real song. Finally, envision it at the top of the Billboard Hot 100 list!

If your lyrics come and go in spurts and you classify yourself more as a poet, learn about other traditional poets who continue to influence our times, like Maya Angelou. Maybe your goal is to become the poet laureate of the twenty-first century.[12]

To clear your head and discover your goals, try to appreciate different kinds of music. Keep your Goals Notebook handy to jot down new ideas as you play soft music while journaling in your morning pages. Try this new idea—work in total silence.

When you are open to trying new ideas and discovering more about yourself, you will clearly see what identifies the new you.

As you continue to grow and reach more of your goals, you'll expand your tools for self-discovery. You will find that success is a

In *The Greatest Salesman in the World*, a man's life-long search for the true meaning of life is revealed. Skillfully written by Og Mandino, each chapter unveils a secret scroll that was hidden in an ancient chest. The story culminates when the wise master, Pathros, gives the scrolls to his faithful servant, Hafid.

Originally presented as chapter titles, Mandino's winning philosophy can still inspire you to reach your goals.

- **Today I begin a new life.**
- **I will form good habits.**
- **I will greet this day with love in my heart.**
- **I will persist until I succeed.**
- **I am nature's greatest miracle.**
- **I will live this day as if it were my last.**
- **Today I will be master of my emotions.**
- **I will laugh at the world.**
- **Today I will multiply my value a hundredfold.**
- **I will act now.**
- **I will pray for guidance.**[13]

self-generating force that will bring new opportunities for you to become all that you can be.

NOTES

1. Julia Cameron, *The Artist's Way: A Spiritual Path to Higher Creativity* (New York: Putnam, 2002), 44–45.

2. Sandra Choron and Harry Choron, *The Book of Lists for Teens* (New York: Houghton Mifflin, 2003), 38–40.

3. Julia Cameron, *The Artist's Way Morning Pages Journal* (New York: Putnam, 2002). This is a companion journal to the text. Its purpose is to "unblock" the creative artist within you through daily journaling.

4. Linda Kranz, *Through My Eyes: A Journal for Teens* (Flagstaff, AZ: Rising Moon, 1998), 1.

5. Piero Ferrucci, *Inevitable Grace* (Los Angeles, CA: Jeremy P. Torcher, Inc., 1990), 62.

6. "Anne Frank as a Writer," Anne Frank House, www.annefrank.org/content.asp?pid=122&lid=2 (accessed June 15, 2007).

7. For great books to get you started in journaling, explore the following:

   a. Lucia Capacchione, *The Creative Journal For Teens: Making Friends with Yourself* (Franklin Lakes, NJ: New Page/Career Press, 2001).
   b. Lucia Capacchione, *Visioning: Ten Steps to Designing the Life of Your Dreams* (New York: Putnam, 2000).
   c. Gabriele Rico, *Writing Your Way through Personal Crisis: Pain and Possibility* (New York: Putnam, 1991).

8. Julia Cameron, *The Artist's Way*, 189.

9. To find Rocky's theme song, "Gonna Fly Now" (which was composed and scored by Bill Conti for the 1976 Movie), go to YouTube, www.youtube.com/watch?v=bwpN_kGKj_Q (accessed November 29, 2008). This song popped up in a 2008 Super Bowl ad and is also available as a ringtone at AOL Mobile, mobile.aol.com/downloads/ringtones/artist-Rocky/ringtone-Gonna-Fly-Now-Theme/539394 (accessed November 29, 2008).

10. "Soduku Puzzle," Flash Game Codes, www.flashgamecodes.com/game/11340/SodukuPuzzle.html (accessed June 12, 2007).

11. Confucius is remembered as "the Supreme Sage," and his teachings are known as Confucianism; see ""Confucius," Standford Encyclopedia of Philosophy, plato.stanford.edu/entries/confucius (accessed December 28, 2006).

12. "Poet Laureate Timeline: 1953–1960," Library of Congress, www.loc.gov/poetry/laureate.html (accessed June 15, 2007).

13. Og Mandino, *The Greatest Salesman in the World* (New York: Bantam Paperbacks, 1983). For more on Mandino go to OgMandino.com, www.ogmandino.com/ (accessed June 9, 2007).

9 Creating Goals with Affirmations

To continue to explore new tools of creative visualization and to train your subconscious mind to accept your goal as a reality, we'll examine the power of affirmations.

REALIGN YOUR VISION

The idea of setting a goal and achieving it can be a life-changing experience. Are you at a stage where you need to realign what you want out of life, to reset your priorities and get a better picture of what's happening in your world? Take this time to become the success you've always dreamed you could be—through saying affirmations.

Learning affirmations is not difficult, and it can give you a boost in reaching your goals. Have you ever heard astronauts describe how making a small change of one or two degrees resulted in a huge difference in their trajectory, the path their space ship was traveling back to the earth? They could either hit their target right on the mark, or without an adjustment, they could go spinning off somewhere in space forever.

Tweaking your visualization through the use of affirmations can help you, too. Is a lack of focus holding you back from hitting your target? This new tool can help you to stay on track with your plan to realize your goals.

One of the greatest examples of someone who literally reached for the stars to realize her goal is Christa McAuliffe. She was the teacher-turned-astronaut who died in the Challenger explosion in 1986. She was passionate about teaching and felt she had a high

"We each have a significant contribution to make in this lifetime. I call this contribution our higher purpose. It always involves being yourself totally, completely, and naturally, and doing something or many things that you genuinely love to do, and that you have a natural gift for. As you use creative visualization, you will find that you become more and more attuned to and aware of your higher purpose."—Shakti Gawain, author[1]

calling to lead her students into the future. It took twenty-two years after her death for this goal to be accomplished.

Barbara Morgan (Christa's understudy for NASA's Teacher in Space program) went on to fulfill Christa's dream. How? In

Astro girl.
Illustration by Peg Raasch.

August of 2008, Barbara and several other crew members of the STS-118 Endeavor held two ham radio and video broadcasts from the International Space Station with students from North America in Idaho and Saskatchewan, Canada. They chatted together, answering a variety of science and space-related questions.

Today, through the Christa Corrigan McAuliffe Challenger Center in Framington, Massachusetts, the Teacher in Space program continues to inspire and reveal the exciting world of space travel to teachers and students.[2]

WHAT ARE CREATIVE AFFIRMATIONS?

You are exploring many different aspects of creative visualization to find your goals and the purpose of your life. When you combine creative imagery with affirmations, you keep yourself on track to meet your goals. Affirmations express a wish as if it has already come true. It is important that the statement be brief yet full of intention. You might wonder, "What are affirmations and how do they work?"

Let's see how today's pop culture spoofs ideas we hold to be meaningful, such as affirmations. Then we'll flip that idea to examine the correct way to use them to reach our goals.

Americans have always had a twisted sense of humor and make fun of the things that others hold sacred. *The Simpsons*, the longest-running sitcom in TV history, is a great example of this. People and events that range from Tom Cruise and his belief in Scientology to the news coverage of Hurricane Katrina in 2005 have been mocked on the show. As a glimpse into current American culture, the various Simpson episodes take on deeper

"Affirmations are one of the most powerful elements of creative visualization. To affirm means 'to make firm.' An affirmation is a strong, positive statement that something is already so. It is a way of 'making firm' that which you are imaging."—Shakti Gawain, author[3]

meaning when used as subject material for university courses and social discussions. For example, The Simpsons as Satirical Authors, a course taught at Columbia College, Chicago, Illinois, in 2006, examines how satire deals with social commentary. Some topics included "What's (Not) Wrong with America?" and "Homer's Body as a Vehicle of Postmodern Parody."[4]

Looking back further to the nineties, when positive thinking and creative affirmations emerged as elements of the self-help movement, they became the target of many jokes on *Saturday Night Live* (*SNL*). Jumping on the movement's popularity, Al Franken created a skit called "Daily Affirmations with Stuart Smalley." It was a spoof on people who were obsessed with twelve-step programs and needed therapy for their various addictions. In the skit, a guest celebrity was usually interviewed by Stuart Smalley, an effeminate self-proclaimed therapist played by Franken. He would project his own problem onto the guest so he could solve his dilemma using an affirmation. His conclusions were always hilarious. He ended each episode with a line that became the title of his hot-selling book *I'm Good Enough, I'm Smart Enough, and Doggone It, People Like Me!* Franken's other best-selling books, *Lies and the Wrong Lying Liars Who Tell*

Did you know that the idea of using a positive statement to change your life has been around for generations? In fact your great grandmother could have read the very words you are seeing today. How could that be possible? *The Game of Life and How to Play It* was self-published in 1925 by Florence Scovel Shinn. Her first book was considered revolutionary at that time, as it gave practical advice on how to change one's life through carefully choosing one's spoken words.

Here is her advice about the benefits of affirmations: "Speak these words aloud, with powerful conviction. 'I now erase and eliminate [by my spoken word] every untrue recording in my subconscious mind. They shall return to the dust heap of their native nothingness, for they came from my own vain imaginings. I now make my perfect recordings through the . . . [inner self] within—the recordings of Health, Wealth, Love and Perfect Self-Expression.' This is the square of life, the Game completed."[6]

Them: A Fair and Balanced Look at the Right and *The Truth (with jokes)*, keep him in demand as a guest speaker who mocks the current political events with his twisted humor.[5]

Although Franken's *SNL* skits were a satiric example of affirmations, his ideas were correct—you can change your negative thinking with positive statements.

An affirmation is a spoken statement to help you envision in your mind's eye what you wish to happen. You repeat it out loud to reinforce the idea so that your subconscious mind will accept it. Grab your Goals Notebook and flip back to No Sweat Exercise 18—I Imagine and Write Out the Future Me. As a new twist to that exercise, record yourself reading that goal out loud. Instantly, you've created an affirmation. Then play it back and repeat it as you drive, do chores, or fall asleep.

TRY AFFIRMATIONS ON FOR SIZE

What can you use affirmations for? Almost anything affecting your life. "Some suggested areas for using affirmations are success, health, self-esteem, self-expression, employment, integrity, and relationships, such as love, wealth and money."[7]

Affirmations can be fun, but they take a little getting used to. You can have a positive affirmation e-mailed to you every morning to get you into the habit of repeating affirmations. How? Once you register for this free service, Notes from the Universe will send you daily notes and affirmations that will encourage you to reach your goals.[8]

Like a new jacket, why not try one and see how it fits with your new way of positive thinking? Here are a few examples to use in your everyday life:

- **I, [your name], now have a great job selling shoes. It allows me to build my sales and marketing skills so I can become a marketing whiz with Nike by the time I'm thirty.**
- **I, [your name], am now prepared for my mid-semester exam in U.S. history. I will calmly remember all the important points I studied and ace this test to raise my grade.**
- **I, [your name], am in total harmony with the universe and I am open to learning new ways to successfully meet my goals.**
- **I, [your name], am in control of my life and I am achieving my daily goals.**

Can you feel one of those No Sweat creative waves flooding in? Why not grab your Goals Notebook and try your hand at this? Try to keep your first set of affirmations to one line each. At the bottom of the page is an example.

If you wonder, "When is the right time to use affirmations?" the answer might surprise you. You can use them anytime to help you meet your goal. You can write them over and over in your Goals Notebook, or say them over and over as you drive in your car.

"Write these feelings out into a statement as if you had already achieved the goals. For example, 'I am working in exactly the right place to use all my talents to the fullest, and I am working with people I have fun with. I make a wonderful living.'"—Carol Adrienne, author[9]

Affirming a good outcome can help you through unexpected life changes. Have you ever seen a "domino effect," where one change causes more? The world you knew falls apart, and you feel like you're spinning around in circles. Have faith that the event could bring the one thing you will need for your success.

Try to create an intention to reflect what you should do next.[10] How can you do that? Simple—write down the event and give it a positive ending. Even if it does not make any sense given the existing facts, take your mind through the exercise. Embrace the change that seems to interfere with your goal, and don't worry

EXAMPLE: NO SWEAT EXERCISE 21—TRY AFFIRMATIONS ON FOR SIZE

I, [your name], now have a clean bedroom without any clutter.

I, [your name], now own the car of my dreams.

We, [your name and your boyfriend's or girlfriend's name], are now enjoying the vacation of our dreams.

I, [your name], am now doing the job that I love and I am very happy.

These affirmations are almost too short and should usually have a lot more detail, but you can start small—then learn to think big.

NO SWEAT EXERCISE 21—TRY AFFIRMATIONS ON FOR SIZE

Directions: In your Goals Notebook, write the title on the top line of the next page. Follow that by numbering eight lines—number from one to four and then again from one to four. Then, be creative, but be practical. Take four of your identified goals and write them on the first four lines. Next, rewrite them into affirmations as though you were already experiencing your goal in reality. These can become templates, or patterns, you can use again as you change certain words within the affirmations to meet future goals.

____

1. ______________________________
2. ______________________________
3. ______________________________
4. ______________________________

1. ______________________________
2. ______________________________
3. ______________________________
4. ______________________________

how it will happen. Your intent is to write out a positive end result. With a little rewording, you will be able to mold your statement until it reflects your desired end goal. Then read it out loud until it sounds familiar.

Use affirmations when you see events and things are changing. Don't shrink from change, but try to understand it. With the help of affirmations you can regain your footing. That is how you stay on track to meet your goals.

When a crisis happened in my family, I learned to use affirmations for all my goals, big or small. Some affirmations were even silly, and those are the ones I'll always remember.

"After high school I decided to live at home. I felt I wanted to go into health care, perhaps nursing, so I'm taking both biology and chemistry as well as a couple of other classes at our local community college. I also have a part-time job one day a week, so I have a busy schedule. I wanted to see what it would be like to actually work in a hospital before I went into nursing full time. So I called a small hospital in our area and I met the head of the volunteer program. She agreed it was a good idea to try it out first and she put me into Physical Therapy as a volunteer. I pick up patients from their room and take them down for therapy and then bring them back when their session is over. I run other errands for the department as well. I really like it and I think it's interesting to learn what they do in my department. Before I leave the hospital, I'm going to volunteer in several other departments and see which part of nursing appeals to me most. Then next year, I'll transfer up to the four-year nursing program in the city. I'm glad I did it this way and I'll be ready to really go all out for it."—Ginny, age 18

LEARN TO THINK OUTSIDE THE BOX

To alter what you do and say is to learn to think outside the box. One of today's most successful advocates of this concept is Louise Hay. A metaphysical lecturer and teacher and the best-selling author of twenty-seven books, Ms. Hay is the founder of the influential publishing company Hay House, Inc., and the "I Can Do It" self-help movement. Her philosophy is that whatever we believe, we cause to come true and the power that is within us can transform our thoughts into experiences. Since she believes that affirmations and visualization go hand in hand, she has even created a fifty-card deck of affirmations as the perfect tool meant just for teens.[11]

It might be fun to try this new approach to thinking outside the box as we create our affirmations. *Affirmacise! 101 Affirmations*

In her book *I Can Do It: How to Use Affirmations to Change Your Life*, Louise Hay shows how you can change every aspect of your life "by understanding and using affirmations correctly." She explains, "Every thought you think and every word you speak is an affirmation. Even your self-talk, your internal dialogue, is a stream of affirmations. Your beliefs are merely habitual thinking patterns . . . and may be limiting your ability to create the very things you say you want. You must pay attention to your thoughts so that you can begin to eliminate the ones creating experiences that you don't want."[12]

for Daily Living, by Ona Mae Brown, is a great book to help you learn this.

To emphasize the importance of each affirmation, Mrs. Brown places only one to a page. The following are a few of her powerful affirmations:

1. **I am a Conqueror. No obstacle is too big for me to overcome.**
2. **I am unlimited wealth and love now.**
3. **I am Divine Action. I bring Ideas into existence by the Affirming words and work ethics I choose.[13]**

If you have an idea for an affirmation when you first wake up, grab your Goals Notebook and write it down because it could be a hidden goal that surfaced in your dreams. Early morning is the perfect time to review your goals, write down any new ideas, and say affirmations.

FOUR RIDICULOUS THINGS TO AFFIRM

Most of us have been trained by our parents, teachers, or society to follow the rules. Realize that when you affirm change to come so you can reach your goals, your outlook on life will expand. You will grow and begin to think differently about many things, including yourself and your choices. As you change and develop positive thinking, you might find you like following the rules. You might even create new rules to discipline yourself to reach your goal.

The following are Mrs. Brown's condensed directions on how to do affirmations from her book *Affirmacise!*:

"To affirm power, love, life and wisdom into your reality," follow these steps:

1. **Set aside quiet time.**
2. **Do your affirmations early in the morning and in the evening before bedtime.**
3. **Before you begin, take deep breaths, and clear your mind of any self-defeating, negative thoughts.**
4. **Relax and be receptive to reach the untapped potential within you.**
5. **Read each affirmation quietly then do the following:**
   a. **Visualize it becoming a part of you and your reality.**
   b. **Confess it out loud or softly with power and conviction.**
   c. **Know, believe, and feel that it is already done!**
6. **Focus on 1–2 affirmations for the entire week.**
7. **Do your affirmation workout everyday for at least 30 days."[14]**

There are many ways you can be yourself as you follow your goals. When you don't let friends or classmates intimidate you, you'll stay on course to choose your path and meet your goals. Tyler, whose story is on page 170, is a teen who decided to stick to his guns no matter what others thought about his unique lifestyle.

To loosen up your thoughts and shake your mind into seeing new possibilities, you can start with something ridiculous and try and turn it into a positive statement. In the example for No Sweat Exercise 22 are examples of some ridiculous ideas you might enjoy affirming.

"Choice produces results. Your mind constantly produces what you choose."—Catherine Ponder, author[15]

EXAMPLE: NO SWEAT EXERCISE 22—FOUR RIDICULOUS THINGS TO AFFIRM

1. I, [your name], now have a perfect score on my credit report and I receive offers to open a new credit card every month.
2. I, [your name], now have a fabulous exercise room in my Malibu beach house. It has the latest workout equipment plus heated floors, a sauna, and a steam room.
3. I, [your name], am now a popular video artist. My success has soared in the last six months due to my YouTube "Smartest Idiot on Earth," clip and I have to hustle to keep up to new demands.
4. I, [your name], am a successful entrepreneur. My Save-the-Planet carbon filter has broken all sales records, and I enjoy counting my money.

NO SWEAT EXERCISE 22—FOUR RIDICULOUS THINGS TO AFFIRM

Directions: There are three things to remember when you think outside the box:

1. You are brainstorming, so write whatever comes to your mind.
2. Write each sentence in the present tense, as if your goal was already happening now.
3. If you get on a roll, write another list of ridiculous affirmations.

Now it's your turn to have a go at this. Get out your Goals Notebook and copy the title on the first line. Next, number four lines and be ridiculous as you brainstorm.

____

1. ______________________________________
2. ______________________________________
3. ______________________________________
4. ______________________________________

"When I first started high school my mom would pack me a 'vegetarian' lunch everyday comprising of anything from tofu sandwiches to home made nori rolls or sushi, with sides of squash and carrots.

"I was so embarrassed in the beginning I would either throw it out and buy school-made crap, or I would hide my food under the table in the cafeteria, sneaking a bite when I thought no one was watching. Due to my own internal fears of being made fun of, and trying to hide it, it only made the other kids make fun of me more when they found out, or saw my food.

"It was not until my senior year of high school that I really started to understand why the other kids would make fun of me. It was because I was embarrassed and afraid to be myself. As soon as I stopped letting them get to me, and was confident in myself being a vegetarian and was up front about it, people just stopped.

"My advice for any vegetarians out there is when others make fun of you, don't worry about it. Rather, if you choose not to eat meat, face the ridicule and be proud of who you are. Make that your ultimate goal."—Tyler, age 19

LIFE IS MEANT TO BE HAPPY

No Sweat Exercises can be more fun and interesting when you get into the swing of being ridiculous. Exactly how can you get this wacky attitude? Simple—put on a smile! Really! Then remind yourself, "Life is meant to be happy—even your life." Using this as a core theme, you could personalize that sentence and make it into an affirmation. It would read this way: "Life is meant to be happy—even my life." Or you could simply repeat over and over "My life is happy." If you've become an affirmation fanatic, brainstorm to see how many ways you can change this statement. Give it a little twist each time until you can settle on your perfect "happy mantra." Challenge yourself to say it, sing it, write it, drum it, walk it, or even e-mail it to yourself until you convince your subconscious that you expect a happy outcome for your life.

If you still can't buy into an affirmation to make you happy, look within and dig a little. Ask yourself, "What's wrong with empowering myself?" Ask a bigger question, "What is it I truly want out of life? Do I want to be happy?"

If you find you are not happy, here is one thing to ask yourself—"Am I sincere?" This is a big question to ponder because many teens look to their friends and peers to find out what they like. Is it the newest iPod nano or some other techy gismo? Or is fashion your main interest? Teens can change their mind as quickly as a new phase hits the market.

To be sincere means to be "utterly honest and genuine."[16] Try and catch yourself when you are being insincere. Why? Because being insincere creates an uneasy rumbling in your heart. When you gave your word you would show up at your friend's party and something better came along so you ditched your commitment, you are being insincere. The best way to handle the situation is to text your friend a message that something came up. Insincerity can also pull you away from meeting your goals, so don't be afraid to stand up for what you want and be sincere about your wishes.

MY DAILY AFFIRMATION FOR CHANGE

Since affirmations help you focus on your goals, remember this is done through changing your previous mind-set. Since you are gaining a new skill through affirming your goals and intentions,

EXAMPLE: NO SWEAT EXERCISE 23—MY DAILY AFFIRMATION FOR CHANGE

As an example we'll choose the fourth statement from the previous exercise: "I am a successful entrepreneur. My Save-the-Planet carbon filter has broken all sales records, and I enjoy counting my money."

You can substitute your main interest for the words "successful entrepreneur" and adjust the rest of the sentence to describe a victory for your venture. Try this simple scenario to describe your picture: I have a daily pet-walking service called "Beau's Buddies." My dog and I have so much fun on our walks that we added a second shift so all the neighbors' dogs can join us for doggy treats. Next month we're expanding our business to "Beau's Baths and Babes."

NO SWEAT EXERCISE 23—MY DAILY AFFIRMATION FOR CHANGE

Directions: To begin, place the title on the top line and number the next three lines. Next, pick one ridiculous affirmation (from No Sweat Exercise 22—Four Ridiculous Things to Affirm) and copy it onto the first numbered line of the exercise. Next, flip your ridiculous statement into a serious affirmation, and on the bottom line restructure it—play with the words so it is catchy.

To help you memorize your new affirmation, repeat your statement ten times every day. Be determined to do this exercise for one week in your morning affirmation workout.

____

1. ______________________________________
2. ______________________________________
3. ______________________________________

why not make this a planned habit? How? Play with the idea of affirming positive thoughts every morning for three weeks and see if you can notice a change in your attitude.

Make this commitment to yourself. Now is the time—today is the day to reach your goal. Now you see why change is necessary to achieve your goal. You realize how focused you must become to affirm your goals. Are you are ready to do whatever is necessary to achieve your end? Dig deeper and find the real treasure—you, living a happy life with purpose!

NOTES

1. Shakti Gawain, *Creative Visualization: Use the Power of Your Imagination to Create What You Want in Your Life* (Novato, CA: Nataraj Publishing, 2002), 168–69.
2. Check out the following sites to learn more about NASA's Teacher in Space program: The Christa McAuliffe Center, www.christa.org/main_page.htm (accessed December 10, 2006); "Barbara Morgan Talks with Students on Ham Radio," NASA, www.nasa.gov/multimedia/podcasting/STS118_morgan_radio.html (accessed August 20, 2007).
3. Gawain, *Creative Visualization*, 27.

4. "Now Homer Shows Class," from "The Redeye" section of *Chicago Tribune*, December 7, 2006.

5. Al Franken, *I'm Good Enough, I'm Smart Enough, and Doggone It, People Like Me! Daily Affirmations with Stuart Smalley* (New York: Dell, 1992); "Stuart Smalley," Wikipedia, en.wikipedia.org/wiki/Stuart_Smalley (accessed December 10, 2006); *Lies and the Wrong Lying Liars Who Tell Them: A Fair and Balanced Look at the Right* (New York: Dutton Books, 2003); and *The Truth (with jokes)* (New York: Dutton Books, 2005).

6. Florence Scovel Shinn, *The Game of Life and How to Play it* (Carlsbad, CA: Hay House, Inc. 2005), 115. Excerpts can be found from the original book at Self-Improvement-Ebooks.com, florencescovelshinn.wwwhubs.com/game.htm (accessed July 3, 2007).

7. Diane Sukiennik, Bill Bendant, and Lisa Raufman, *The Career Fitness Program: Exercising Your Options* (Scottsdale, AZ: Gorsuch Scarisbrick, 1986), 33.

8. You can receive free daily affirmations from Notes from the Universe to give yourself a positive boost. Register at Tut's Adventure Club, http://www.tut.com/mmm.shtml (accessed December 10, 2006).

9. Carol Adrienne, *The Purpose of Your Life: Finding Your Place in the World Using Synchronicity, Intuition, and Uncommon Sense* (New York: HarperCollins, 1998), 133.

10. The Power of Intention will be more thoroughly examined in chapter 10, "Being In Sync with Life."

11. Louise Hay, *Power Thoughts for Teens: A 50-Card Deck* (Carlsbad, CA: Hay House Inc., 2001). This can be ordered from the Hay House website: Hay House, www.hayhouse.com/details.php?id=292 (accessed November 15, 2007).

12. Louise Hay, *I Can Do It: How to Use Affirmations to Change Your Life* (Carlsbad, CA: Hay House, 2003), 158–59.

13. Ona Mae Brown, *Affirmacise! 101 Affirmations For Daily Living* (Chicago: Divine Order Communications, 1998), 82, 40, 7. To learn more about Ms. Brown's positive philosophy and further books on affirmations, go to Ona Brown, www.onabrown.com (accessed October 10, 2007).

14. Brown, *Affirmacise!*, 4–6.

15. Catherine Ponder, *Open Your Mind to Prosperity* (Marina Del Rey, CA: DeVorss & Company, 1983), 49.

16. *The New Lexicon Webster's Dictionary of the English Language* (New York: Lexicon Publications, 1988), 928.

Part 3: GOALS!

In the first part of this book, "Get Ready," we examined goals—what they are and the five steps necessary to achieve them. In the second section, "Get Set," we analyzed the various elements of creative imagery and how they can become tools for your goal-setting.

In this third part, "Goals!," you will find answers to the question, Where do I go from here? You will discover what it means to be in sync with your desires and intentions and the importance of listening to your inner voice. You'll ponder your family's values versus your ideas on life. You'll explore the step-by-step process of placing goals into your daily routine. As you integrate this goal-setting process, you'll begin to see which past events have been signposts on your path.

The most important point to understand is that a master plan for your life is unfolding as you reach one goal after another. During this process you are becoming your real self, confident and whole, reaching your life goal. Are you ready to play this game of your life?

Let's GOAL!

10 Being In Sync with Life

We will explore two principles to help you become even more successful in reaching your goals. We will look at them separately—then show how they become one. The two principles are *being in sync* and *listening to the voice within*.

These are the most challenging principles of goal setting, but when you understand them you'll be light-years ahead of your peers in reaching your goals.

BEING IN SYNC

A common term for living in the now moment is called synchronicity, or being "in sync." It is similar to what some call déjà vu. It can be explained as the eerie feeling you get when you think something you are doing right now has happened before. In reality, you've simply anticipated the event because your awareness was heightened at that exact moment.

You may think that this idea is weird, or at least not ordinary. That's what makes it so interesting. It's the feeling you get when everything points to a moment in time, which is now. Realize that all you can count on is what's happening right now.

Maybe you've heard the expression of being in sync. This occurs when you become aware of something you never focused on before, and you notice other events that seem connected to it. It's not a coincidence but the result of using your sixth sense. At that instant, you are tuned in to living your life to the fullest possible experience.

In his best-selling book *Change Your Thoughts—Change Your Life: Living the Wisdom of the Tao*, Dr. Wayne W. Dyer searches the Tao (written by the great Chinese sage, Lao-tzu, 2,500 years ago) for answers to the problems that confront us today.

In his chapter titled "Living without Difficulties," Dr. Dyer analyzes the sixty-third verse of the Tao. Lao-tzu "counsels that we learn to think in moments, rather than in days, weeks, months, years, decades, or a lifetime. All we ever get is right now—that's it. So we must avoid the inclination to magnify tiny events or worry about a future that may never arrive. . . . As Lao-tzu reminds us, 'See simplicity in the complicated . . . do great things while they are still small.'" Dr. Dyer concludes, "This then, is the wisdom of this verse: There's no such thing as difficulty when you live in the present moment, doing only what you can right now."[1]

Being in sync is a terrific feeling. See it as a magical sign meant only for you. Imagine it as the many prisms of a crystal all shining a different color on your wall at the same instant.

In her book entitled *The Purpose of Your Life: Finding Your Place in the World Using Synchronicity, Intuition, and Uncommon Sense*, Carol Adrienne examines synchronicity.[2] She explains that when you start to focus on a particular goal, you should pay attention when other ideas on the same subject pop up and other contacts come into focus, because your positive thoughts in creating a goal can become a magnet. That's the moment to grab your Goals Notebook and brainstorm.

Now is the only time you have, so pay attention to what you are doing in this exact moment, or now. Experiment with this idea. Say to yourself, "Right now I am in perfect shape to win the 800 meter butterfly in the state swim competition tomorrow." Or, when you are cramming for a midterm, tell yourself, "Right now, I am learning everything I need to ace the trig exam next Monday." When you are waiting for the SAT exams to be passed out, tell yourself, "I am realizing my goal to go to Stanford University by acing this test right now!"

Maybe you find yourself wondering, "If I simply pay attention to what's happening and then take the next obvious step—is that the secret to winning my goal? Can it really be that simple?" The

The term *being in sync* can have different meanings. Here are a few of them:

- **On TV, it's called "synch views," or adjusting the sound with the action.**
- **In the movies, the term means to adjust (the shutters of the camera) so that the flash bulb goes off when the shutter opens.**
- **Your camera is said to be in sync when a built-in digital radio transceiver triggers an auto-relay mode between your camera and flash.**
- **To synchronize time requires several people to regulate their watches so they all agree.**
- **In-sync swimming (synchronized) is an Olympic sport where teams perform gymnastics, underwater summersaults, circular swimming, and ballet in unison.**
- **You can be in sync when you use a data management system to access your remote computer files.[3]**

answer lies in the intensity and passion with which you experience each moment. It may seem too easy, but being in sync is what can make the difference.

Here is an example of how a sequence of events can bring about your goal.

You have a burning desire to become a doctor, let's say, an oncologist in cancer research; you write down that goal. You cut out photos of a physician wearing scrubs, and you paste your face over his or hers to help you "see" your goal. You say affirmations and visualize this goal is already happening in the present tense, or now.

What have you done in that moment? You have put that goal that will happen fifteen years from today into the present. Right now you are putting out the intention to become a doctor, and right now you are accepting it into your subconscious as though it has already happened. You have set up many situations that will occur in the future to bring this moment into the present. If that sounds impossible, consider this possibility.

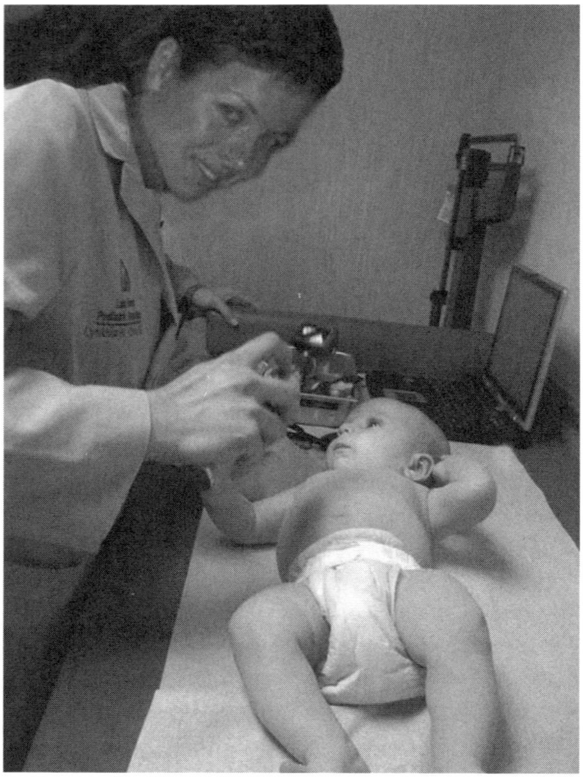

A doctor with Olga's face.

You will get a high score on your SAT, which will allow you to be admitted into a university with a good pre-med curriculum; you will study, you will pass, you will graduate; you will ace the required courses to get accepted into the pre-med program; you will be awarded a bachelor of science degree; you will get admitted into medical school where you can begin to study your specialty; you will earn a scholarship to pay for your tuition; you will meet the right professors who will recommend you to the right research hospital where you can join a team that specializes in new cancer immunizations.

All these people, places, and events will come to pass because you have already dreamed it, said it, written it, visualized it, expected it, and allowed it to come into the present moment. You have created your own goal through experiencing your burning desire as though your goal were already happening. In short, you are attaining your goal now because you have used your power of intention.

"At school, I like to get involved in a lot of activities, like our science club, where I'm president this year. I won an award for a science fair project I did on stock selection. I got interested in stocks when my parents bought me some in the eighth grade, and I still follow them.

"I'm waiting to see where I'll go to college next fall. I'm pretty sure I want to major in economics or political science or something that'll put me into the financial world. At least that's my intention. But right now it's a wait and see game."—Rahul, age 17

Up to this point you have learned how positive thinking and creative imagery are important tools to reach your goals. Now shift gears to examine the underlying forces that give you the power to be successful. First you'll examine some scientific findings brought to light through the advancement of computers. Whereas the Internet reveals global connectivity through invisible pulsing electronic bits, Global Positioning Systems, or GPS

What is meant by *connectivity*? Here are a few of the basic principles:

Connectivity is a perception related to using computer networks that link people and resources. You can link to the Internet and access worldwide information resources just by clicking on your computer.

In mathematics and computer science, connectivity is one of the basic concepts of graph theory. It is closely related to the theory of network flow problems. The connectivity of a graph is an important measure in its "robustness" as a network.[4]

tracking systems, can visually pinpoint any locality on the earth's grid. The invisible links of the Internet and the visible tracking of GPS systems have one key thing in common: "connectivity."

If we can realize that we are all connected electronically, can we make the jump to the findings of quantum physics that we are interconnected? In the movie *What the Bleep Do We Know!?* released in 2004, and its sequel, *What the Bleep!? Down the Rabbit Hole*, physicists explain how we connect to waves of energy through our thoughts and feelings.[5]

As the Bleep films have escalated interest, the wave structure of matter, or WSM[6] has become a hot topic for high school and college physics clubs. These concepts reveal the core of how to reach your goals using creative visualization—through understanding interconnectivity and the power of intention.

This intangible force that will assist you in meeting your goals has been discussed by various well-known authors. Carol Adrienne describes it in *The Purpose of Your Life* as follows: "Intention is that activity of the mind, energized by the passion of the heart, that wills something to happen. It is the wish or purpose behind the initiation of the action."[7]

In *The Seven Spiritual Laws of Success*, Deepak Chopra further elaborates: "One pointed intention means holding your attention to the intended outcome with such unbending purpose that you . . . [exclude] all obstacles from your consciousness. . . .

"Learn to harness the power of intention, and you can create anything you desire."[8]

THE POWER OF INTENTION

What is the power of intention? It is the underlying force that acts to fulfill your goals. In his book *The Power of Intention: Learning to Co-create Your World Your Way*, Dr. Wayne Dyer describes intention as an invisible energy field that is found in all physical things but is also part of the nonmaterial world of spirit. He takes us back to the idea of listening to our inner voice. He feels that you can access this invisible field simply by feeling inspired through a silent knowing that comes from within.

Dr. Wayne Dyer suggests that to create our intentions and mold them into goals, we can try an experiment to experience our nonphysical selves.

How? It's amazingly easy.

"First close your eyes and empty your mind of rational thoughts and the . . . ever-changing chatter that goes on. Next, hit the delete button every time doubt appears. Finally, open to the emptiness. Then you can begin to discover how to silently know the power of intention."[9]

You can really do it, but first you must have enough courage to change and no longer listen to doubts that accept failure and confusion. Instead, listen to your voice within to hear a plan of action. This is your "higher power,"[10] the part of you that already knows what must be done to take you from the senior in high school who is reading this book right now, to that doctor who, fifteen years from now, will save a patient's life from cancer.

Many authors and philosophers have tried to describe our higher power. In his book *The Way of the Wizard: Twenty Spiritual Lessons for Creating the Life You Want*, Deepak Chopra calls this higher power our inner wizard. He describes how it exists in every man and sees and knows everything about each person. He even suggests where to find this power. Mr. Chopra feels that the inner wizard resides in the crystal cave that is "a privileged place inside the human heart. It is a refuge of safety where a wise voice knows no fear, where the turmoil of the outside world cannot enter. In the crystal cave there has always been a wizard and always will be—you only have to enter and listen. . . . The way of the wizard doesn't exist in time—it is everywhere and nowhere. It belongs to everyone and no one."[11]

Since we show our inner thoughts through creative expression, it should be no surprise when a rock star catches the wave of "being interconnected." Billy Corgan, the former lead singer in the rock band Smashing Pumpkins, confessed that when he found himself at the pinnacle of his success, he realized he was unhappy. It wasn't until after the Pumpkins dissolved and his second band, Zwan, went defunct that Billy took time off to see where his life was headed.

When he reemerged with his music video *The Future Embrace*,[12] Billy's fans realized that his personal philosophy was different from his angry past. In an interview, Billy said his new mission is "to raise the collective consciousness of society" and through his music to "motivate the people he touches through his heart to bring about positive change in their perspective areas of strength."[13]

Everything we experience in life can't always be seen in a positive light. Sometimes things happen that can temporarily change your outlook. This happened to Bethany Hamilton as she swam in the surf of Hawaii and lost her arm in a shark attack. Since that day on October 31, 2003, Bethany has seen the good in what happened to her. She has gone on to make a positive change in the world for other teens by writing several books, including *Soul Surfer: A True Story of Faith, Family, and Fighting to Get Back on the Board*, and *Devotions for the Soul Surfer: Daily Thoughts to Charge Your Life*. She became the spokesperson for World Vision International in 2004, making TV appearances on *Oprah*, *The Tonight Show*, *20/20*, and *Ellen*, and has been quoted in *People* and *Time*.

"When we work toward a goal, we center ourselves on the goal and not on some small difficulties we encounter as we work toward that goal. Do the same. As you know, rosebushes have thorns, but you also know that close to the rose there are no thorns; therefore, focus and center on the rose and not on the thorns."—Sai Maa, author[14]

"My mom used to tell me when I was little, 'Listen to your little voice.' When I got older, I thought that was stupid and I'd test it out. So, last year I played a game with my 'little voice' to let him know I was grown up.

"To test it, I lit a match and held it. 'Put it out,' the voice told me, but I didn't. The match burned down to my fingers, but I held on. It was stupid. I burned my fingers and put a hole in the rug because I refused to listen. Who was I fooling?"
—Chuck, age 15

The best way to see Bethany is on MySpace, where her website reveals her positive philosophy toward life: "I guess [people] see me as a symbol of courage and inspiration. One thing hasn't changed—and that's how I feel when I'm riding a wave. It's like, here I am. I'm still here. It's still me and my board—in God's ocean. . . .

"I know I have something important to say. Something that people need to hear—but sometimes they get so caught up in my story part, that they miss the meaning."[15]

When you realize that a teen such as Bethany Hamilton can put a positive spin on her life, your success can seem possible to attain, too.

Learning to reverse negative thinking and to incorporate new ideas can be life changing. Sometimes you might wonder how attaining your goal can seem so difficult. You can remind yourself that you are learning different ways to use creative visualization one idea at a time. Finally, when everything has meshed together, you will find you have reached your goal.

When you're living in the now moment, when you've relaxed and abandoned your insecurities, you feel more open and you experience a shift in consciousness. This creates a "gap" that allows you to open your mind to new possibilities where you can grow to meet your goals.

WEIRD HABITS THAT BLOCK MY INNER VOICE

Many ideas in this book may seem like deep thoughts, but you're beginning to understand this stuff in ways you would hardly believe. Take the No Sweat Exercises as an example—they let you laugh at yourself and feel free, and that's important. Because the second you see how silly the things are that worry you, in that instant when you have an Aha! moment, you can see what you do to block your inner voice.

To prove this point is true, it's time for another No Sweat Exercise. As an example, here are some questions to ask yourself.

WHAT THE VOICE WITHIN MIGHT SAY

The question remains, Will you take time to listen right now? Here are a few subjects you might recognize as familiar.

- **Don't drink and drive.**
- **This sounds like trash talk. Turn around and walk away.**
- **You can't go to the mall tomorrow because you promised Aunt Ruthie you would help her.**
- **Don't gossip about your best friend when she's not here.**
- **Don't take a ride home alone from Jim. Not even this one time!**
- **Don't go to the party tonight. Something bad is going down.**

EXAMPLE: NO SWEAT EXERCISE 24—WEIRD HABITS THAT BLOCK MY INNER VOICE

- My hands—Do I pick at my fingernails constantly?
- My coffee—Am I addicted to it and always carry a "to go" cup?
- My friends—Do I feel left out if they do anything without me?
- My cell phone—Do I feel like a loser if I don't get many calls at home?
- My music—Is something missing in my day when I can't plug into it?
- My dog—Have I made him a substitute for a real best friend?
- My workout—Do I go into a blocked mental zone where I can only focus on one thing?
- My e-mail—If I don't sign in, am I afraid I will sign off to life as I know it?

NO SWEAT EXERCISE 24—WEIRD HABITS THAT BLOCK MY INNER VOICE

Directions: Okay, now it's your turn again. Write the title on the first line. Next, number eight lines and laugh at all the weird things that hang you up sometimes. Could these habits keep you from hearing your inner voice? Keep your time to three minutes. Ready? Go for it!

____

1. ______________________________
2. ______________________________
3. ______________________________
4. ______________________________
5. ______________________________
6. ______________________________
7. ______________________________
8. ______________________________

- **Don't cheat on your history exam. You'll regret it for the rest of your life.**
- **Stay and talk to your dad tonight. There will be no time tomorrow.**

But the voice within also tells you things you actually want to hear. Why be afraid to listen? They could be things like this:

- **I know you can do this. Look deep inside and I'll show you each step to take.**
- **You are a good person.**
- **Don't let it bother you if your brother is lying to mom.**
- **I believe in you even if your friends don't.**
- **There is something very special that only you can do in this life.**
- **I am with you until the end and even beyond that.**

- **The only moment that is real is right now. Grab it!**
- **Don't give up on your dream. It could be the purpose of your life.**

EMBRACE YOUR INNER SELF

We've done so many different things in this book that you have accepted, so here's one more for you to try. Stand up and wrap your arms around yourself and give yourself a big bear hug. Stay there for a minute or two, then sit down, close your eyes, and be silent. Unlike the previous chapters, this one will end on a very quiet note. Without talking, simply close your book, pack up your stuff, and go off by yourself to be alone and listen to your inner voice.

MY "WHAT IF?" LIST

As an experiment, we're going to write down a "What If?" List. Ask yourself, "What if I didn't do that limiting habit for one day?" The results might surprise you.

EXAMPLE: NO SWEAT EXERCISE 25—MY "WHAT IF?" LIST

- My fingernails—What if I didn't pick at them? Wouldn't I feel better about myself?
- My coffee—What if I cut down to two cups a day? Wouldn't I be less hyper?
- My cell phone—What if I didn't charge it or check my messages for a day? Peace!
- My music—What if I went unplugged? Couldn't I discover new music in my head?
- My dog—What if I took him for a walk with my friend? Couldn't that improve two friendships?
- My workout—What if I skipped it for one day? Couldn't I sleep in and be deliciously lazy?
- My e-mail—What if I gave trivial e-chatter a rest? Wouldn't this help to de-clutter my brain?
- My friends—What if I spent a night without them? Wouldn't that give me time to think and write in my journal?

NO SWEAT EXERCISE 25— MY "WHAT IF?" LIST

Directions: Start by writing the title on the top line and number another eight lines. Next copy your previous eight answers on each line. Then, vent a little and tease yourself with a truthful rebuttal. Be loose and open as you have a go at it.

____

1. ____
2. ____
3. ____
4. ____
5. ____
6. ____
7. ____
8. ____

To find out more, put yourself into the picture as you review an example of how this reveals your inner voice.

Take a hard look at this exercise because it will reveal what keeps you from tapping into your inner source. Can you handle it?

You might feel uncomfortable living so spontaneously and find yourself wondering, "What's the point of this?" The point is to get real and ask yourself why you are afraid to hear your inner voice. Even when you are trying to ignore it, this voice is always true to you.

NOTES

1. Dr. Wayne W. Dyer, *Change Your Thoughts—Change Your Life: Living the Wisdom of the Tao* (Carlsbad, CA: Hay House, 2007), 299.

2. Carol Adrienne, *The Purpose of Your Life: Finding Your Place in the World Using Synchronicity, Intuition, and Uncommon Sense* (New York: Eagle Brook-William Morrow, 1998), 133. Go to Carol Adrienne's website to learn

more on the purpose of your life: The Purpose of Your Life, www.caroladrienne.com/ (accessed June 28, 2007).

3. BeInSync, www.beinsync.com/ (accessed June 28, 2007).

4. "Connectivity (graph theory)," Wikipedia, en.wikipedia.org/wiki/Connectivity_(graph_theory) (accessed June 27, 2007).

5. *What the Bleep Do We Know!?* www.whatthebleep.com/whatthebleep/ (accessed March 2, 2007); *What the Bleep!?, Down the Rabbit Hole*, www.whatthebleep.com/rabbithole/ (accessed March 2, 2007).

6. "The Wave Structure of Matter (WSM) explains Positrons (antimatter) of Quantum Physics, as Opposite Phase Spherical Standing Waves to the Electron Wave Structure. . . . In a synopsis, if you wonder, why is this important? . . . it tells us what we really are as humans, how we exist as matter in space, (and) how we are subtly interconnected to all other matter in the universe." "Quantum Physics: Paul Dirac," On Truth and Reality, www.spaceandmotion.com/physics-paul-dirac.htm (accessed September 6, 2006).

7. Adrienne, *The Purpose of Your Life*, 131.

8. Deepak Chopra, *The Seven Spiritual Laws of Success: A Practical Guide to the Fulfillment of Your Dreams* (Novato, CA: Amber-Allen, 1994), 74–75.

9. Dr. Wayne Dyer, *The Power of Intention: Learning to Co-create Your World Your Way* (Carlsbad, CA: Hay House, 2004), 24.

10. As found in Families Anonymous (and many other twelve-step programs), the term *the voice within* refers to the voice from your "higher power"; Families Anonymous, Inc., *The Twelve Steps and Twelve Traditions* (Van Nuys, CA: 1980), 5; Families Anonymous, www.familiesanonymous.org/ (accessed December 2, 2008).

11. Deepak Chopra, *The Way of the Wizard: Twenty Spiritual Lessons for Creating the Life You Want* (New York: Harmony Books, 1995), 5.

12. Billy Corgan, *The Future Embrace*, Spike, www.ifilm.com/video/2674472 (accessed June 26, 2007).

13. Bettina Kozlowski, "Billy Corgan Comes Out of the Dark," *Conscious Choice* 18, no. 6 (June 2005): 26–29.

14. Bethany, www.bethanyhamilton.com (accessed April 15, 2007).

15. Sai Maa, *Petals of Grace: Essential Teachings for Self-Mastery* (Crestone, CO: HIU Press, 2005), 132.

11 The Long and Short of Goals

By now you might consider yourself a pro on goal setting. Maybe you have developed little ways to keep yourself on track to reach your goals. Do you stick Post-it notes on your bathroom mirror or by your light switch, so you can read your goals first thing in the morning and last thing at night? Think of other quirky ways to have fun while you move closer to reaching your goals every day.

In this chapter we will begin to dissect the various aspects of goals. You'll learn that there are different levels of goals, how to adjust your goal as you change, why it is beneficial to excavate your authentic self, and how to allow your life goals to surface through playing with your hidden kid talents. Finally, you'll learn to expand one of your talents in a practical way and affirm your life goal.

DIFFERENT LEVELS OF GOALS

Everyone feels more confident when they become good at a particular subject or skill. Learning to set and achieve goals can hold the same kind of satisfaction.

To become an expert in goal setting, you'll need to learn the different levels of goals you can achieve. There are short-term goals, intermediate goals, long-term goals, and life goals. Let's examine the difference.

- **Short-term goals, or objectives, are activities that can be quickly attained.**
- **Intermediate goals are goals that can be attained within six months and beyond.**

- **Long-term goals are career goals.**
- **Life goals are what you want to accomplish before you die.**

For a moment, we'll pretend your life goal is like mine—to become an author/illustrator. On your way to becoming a writer, you would reach many different goals. At first, the short-term goals could be small creative-writing assignments. Then those goals could become larger. An example of the short-term goal could be writing an essay for school on a topic you are passionate about, such as overcoming toxic waste.

Then you could expand your goal. How? You could adjust your essay to become the text for a video documentary with clips of local industries dumping chemical waste into your neighborhood creeks. In that case you would have created both the written text and the corresponding visual picture. Both of those events would be examples of meeting an intermediate goal.

Short-term goals are referred to as objectives. "These are specific, practical visible and measurable. They are short-term baby steps. They are signposts that indicate where we are relative to reaching our goal. . . . If you incorporate baby steps into your timeline you are more likely to meet your goals."—Dr. Diane Sukiennik, Dr. Bill Bendant, and Lisa Raufman, authors[1]

You would be meeting a career goal when you submitted your documentary to a professional studio that would help you to release it to a national audience.

Finally, you could say you were meeting your life goal when you received a nomination for an Oscar for the Best Documentary Short Subject category. This was a dream realized by Leslie Iwerks and Mike Glad in 2006 for the film *Recycled Life*. Their documentary recorded life in the vast, toxic Guatemala City garbage dump, where generations of families live and pick through the trash in search of items they can recycle.[2]

You won't always accomplish every goal you write down, but writing each goal down actually helps you to see what you really want. Some of the old goals I set several years ago were not very realistic. But it's exciting to see that a lot of them have become part of my life.

You will find that some goals expand from your original idea. Since my first goal was to write a middle-grade novel, when it was completed, I realized my vision was not big enough. My picture had to be changed. To put this idea into concrete terms, your goal expands as your talents grow.

GOALS ARE NOT SET IN STONE

Maybe you've found that you didn't want your goal after you achieved it. That happens sometimes because you couldn't see the outcome of your goal until you experienced it. You change and grow as you reach your goal, and things seem different from what you imagined.

I experienced that scenario when I was a junior in high school. My goal was to become a nurse. A nine-month training course to become a certified nurse's aide was the first requirement. After the first month of the training, floor time was required at the hospital once a week, so my Saturday free time went down the tubes. But I still remained passionate about my training and helping others in need.

My goal seemed within reach when the school year was over, as the hospital hired me full time. My workload included seven or eight patients of my own every day. Some were easy to care for, but others were the hopeless cases.

That summer, three patients died in my arms! That put a whole new spin on what it meant to reach my goal because it made me realize that I wasn't ready to take on a life-and-death situation as part of my job. I learned that disappointment can become a turning point. It can lead you back to a different goal or something you are more passionate about.

"It's surprising how often we allow goals to become carved in stone. That's because, even as the value of certain goals diminishes, the urgency and yearning associated with them may remain. Emotional resources can be squandered by holding onto goals that are no longer meaningful or counter productive to the life you actually lead.

". . . To set goals that are achievable, discard those that no longer apply to your life and narrow down new ones."
—Joy Browne, journalist[3]

Clay Aiken had conflicting goals. One revolved around his love for music; the other was his passion for children with special needs.

In 2003, prior to his musical success on American Idol, Aiken was a college student pursuing a degree in special education. He joined forces with Diane Bubel while tutoring her autistic son, Michael. Together they founded the Bubel/Aiken Foundation, a nonprofit organization that sponsors educational integration known today as inclusion. Their goal was to create a movement that would help children with disabilities fit into the normal activities and environment of their nondisabled peers.[4]

Before Aiken could pursue a master's degree, his gift as a singer took over his life. Almost miraculously, from February to May 2003, Aiken ended up wooing over 21 million American Idol fans each week with his sensational singing voice. Although he did not win the competition (he finished second to Ruben Stoddard), Aiken became an overnight success. He rose to instant stardom by landing a deal with RCA through Simon Fuller's "19 Recording Limited."[5]

The reason all goals are not set in stone is because the very nature of achieving a goal requires you to grow and change in the process. Therefore choice is the important thing to remember. Sometimes you'll realize that reaching one goal was only a side path on the long journey you must take to reach your final destination.

Becoming a nurse's aide at sixteen gave me a feeling of confidence and let me see that I could reach my goal. In college, nursing was not my main interest, but art and creative writing

"Last year when I was planning on moving into the city to begin classes at a four-year university, at the last minute it didn't feel like it was the right thing to do. I had gone through all of the steps to get accepted, to check out the classes I wanted, even to see my dorm room. But in the end, I know I did the right thing.

"So, I did reach my goal but the timing wasn't right. Now, two years later, I feel I'm ready, and guess what? I have to start the whole process of getting accepted all over again. That's life, and I'm okay with my decision both times." Gina, age 19

Setting goals and creating ways to achieve them is a lifelong process. Rod Moore, an international motivator and goal setter, has created an e-class program, titled Design Your Life, to show you how to determine and implement your life goals. His philosophy is simple and something every teen should consider: "Setting Lifetime Goals gives you the perspective that shapes all other aspects of your decision making. . . . Goals are set on a number of different levels: First you create your 'big picture' of what you want to do with your life, and what large-scale goals you want to achieve. Second, you break these down into the smaller and smaller targets that you must hit so that you reach your lifetime goals. Finally, once you have your plan, you start working to achieve it."[6]

were much more compelling. My love for the medical sciences resurfaced later when I combined them with my art. Since I couldn't see what to do with my interest in medical illustrations at eighteen, I simply made another choice to concentrate on creative writing classes, which seemed right at that time.

ALLOW LIFE GOALS TO SURFACE

Recently, my old medical interest surfaced when I did some illustrations of human organs for a writer-friend, Tina Schwartz. They can be found in her book *Organ Transplants: A Survival Guide for the Entire Family*.[7] The experience of drawing human organs helped me to get some of my art published and to fulfill my goal to become an illustrator.

"I got involved in my school's debate team four years ago when some of my friends joined. Since then, I've grown to really enjoy it. We have regional tournaments once a month where you debate the topics submitted by the participating schools. You're judged on how well you know the subject and how well you explain your opinion.

"Debating has opened a lot of doors for me as it has built my confidence, both socially and academically. I've won awards at the regional, state, and national level. Who knows? Maybe I'll end up as a TV commentator!"—Rob, age 17

When you write out the statement for a new goal, consider these points. Can you answer "yes" to the following questions about this goal?[8]

	YES	NO
1. Did I actually choose it personally?	☐	☐
2. Am I ready to make a written commitment to this goal?	☐	☐
3. Am I setting a deadline?	☐	☐
4. Is it within my control?	☐	☐
5. Have I thought through the consequences?	☐	☐
6. Is the goal based on my values?	☐	☐
7. Can I visualize it in considerable detail?	☐	☐
8. Will I work toward it?	☐	☐
9. Am I taking responsibility for this goal?	☐	☐

This brings up a vital point about discovering what you want to do with your life. Take a look back and remember what you did between the ages of eleven and fourteen. That is the period when some of your real talents began to surface. Realize that what seemed like a minor victory at the time might actually be the tip of the iceberg for your life goals.

FIND YOUR AUTHENTIC SELF

In *Something More: Excavating Your Authentic Self*, Sarah Ban Breathnach suggests new ways to discover your life goals through looking back into the past. The author compares the search for your inner self to an authentic archeological dig. She suggests you "search for the moments that have made a difference in the trajectory [path] of your life." Then, revisit these events by creating a Dream Collage, a project similar to treasure mapping.[9]

If you find yourself thinking, "I'm not Tiger Woods, and this is way too serious stuff for me," ask yourself, "Am I willing to zoom in on my life goals?" Maybe it's time to see what your silly kid talents show you about yourself and what ultimate goal you will pursue. Here's a hint—it's something you've always enjoyed doing, even when you were a kid.

A life goal never stops calling until you achieve it. You can see this in Tiger Woods' determination to surpass Jack Nicklaus' record for victories in professional majors (golf tournaments). Tiger's simple formula for success? He focuses on "one stroke at a time" to meet his goals: "This is a great example of short-term goal setting and goal accomplishment. Each stroke is a short-term goal. With the completion of each short-term goal, Tiger is that much closer to completing the long-term goal of winning the game. Each completed game then reverts to a short term goal allowing him to work towards his long term [life] goal or dream of being the very best in the game of golf—past, present and future."[10]

Josh the golfer.

Believe it or not, you might already know what your life goals are, even if you aren't consciously aware of them; your goals lie beneath your conscious level of awareness.

What you want to do in your life becomes clear over time. At seventeen, you're not expected to know if you want to become a physicist or a coach or even an actor. But you might get a feeling now and then that you are interested in some part of a particular field or occupation.

CRAZY KID TALENTS THAT REVEAL HIDDEN GOALS

Sometimes, when you journal or listen to your music, you feel the pull of some deep desire that seems a little hazy in your mind. We'll use an exercise to unearth your crazy kid talents to find a hidden life goal. It's a two-step process. Ask yourself if these scenarios could hold a truth for you. Then you see how each could develop into a life goal.

Examples of other kids doing this kind of crazy stuff can be seen from time to time on *The Tonight Show with Jay Leno*. In a

EXAMPLE: NO SWEAT EXERCISE 26—CRAZY KID TALENTS THAT REVEAL HIDDEN GOALS

Did you draw on the dining room wall?	Life goal: to create cool screensaver designs
Did you love to make mud pies?	Life goal: to design your own line of pottery
Did you break up your sibling's arguments?	Life goal: to help bring about world peace
Did you dress up your cat in doll clothes?	Life goal: to sew trendy pet clothes
Did you spend money on allowance day?	Life goal: to give money to charity, like Bill Gates
Did you build Lincoln Log houses?	Life goal: to help others in Habitat for Humanity
Did you swim several miles every morning?	Life goal: to win an Olympic Gold medal
Did you save box top codes for prizes?	Life goal: to become a recycling expert

Neha's pottery.
Art by Neha Manchanda.

segment called "Teenage Wasteland," Jay features various teens who do crazy things like drink a whole soda through their nose, perform double-jointed twists or display how they "stomp" their amazing wheel barrows.[11] Although this may seem weird, it allows these individuals to showcase their act on national TV. Maybe their goal will be to become stand-up comedians!

Crazy talents get noticed, even when you're no longer a teen. An amusing talent was important enough to win Jamie Foxx the Favorite Celebrity Hidden Talent in the 2005 Nickelodeon Kids' Choice Awards. His amazing talent? He "can roll his eyes in opposite directions."[12] In the case of Sanjaya Malakar (*American Idol*'s sixth season teen phenomenon), his crazy kid talent could help his singing career—as he confessed, "I can independently raise both corners of my upper lip."[13]

EXPAND A TALENT

When you carry your Goals Notebook with you all the time, and feel you are in sync, pay attention to what's going on in the back of your mind. You could be driving in your car or riding on a bus,

NO SWEAT EXERCISE 26—CRAZY KID TALENTS THAT REVEAL HIDDEN GOALS

Directions: Now, you need to identify a talent (even if it's trivial) and see if you can unearth a life goal. You know the drill. Pull out your Goals Notebook and write the title for the exercise on the next clean sheet. Then number lines one through eight. On the left of each line, write down a crazy kid memory. On the right of the same line, dig out your hidden dreams and talents—describe where this could take you as an adult. There are only two important concepts to remember: (1) this is supposed to be crazy; (2) the event is something a kid would do.

---

1. ____________________
2. ____________________
3. ____________________
4. ____________________
5. ____________________
6. ____________________
7. ____________________
8. ____________________

and see something that triggers a thought. Or you could start humming a tune that turns into an entire song or a verse that could be the start of a poem. If possible, see how much of your idea you can get down. Then try and identify it as a potential life goal to become a songwriter or a poet. In short, learn to identify and expand your talents.

AFFIRM YOUR LIFE GOAL

Next you'll take one idea that you're passionate about and expand it into a serious life goal. Selecting one of your goals

EXAMPLE: NO SWEAT EXERCISE 27—EXPAND A TALENT

Take a look at the second part of your list from No Sweat Exercise 26—Crazy Kid Talents That Reveal Hidden Goals, and select one of your eight crazy talents. Next you will expand that talent into the four different levels of goals. Here are some ideas to clarify this exercise.

If one of your crazy kid talents was, "I rescued bugs I found inside our house," your expanded talent could be to become an entomologist, a scientist who is fascinated with insects. To expand that into a serious life goal, you could start the process by writing a science essay, "How Bugs Can Save the Earth."

The essay could lead to a short-term goal, to write a monthly column for your school newspaper that describes helpful insects in your neighborhood. Your intermediate goal could be to join the Junior Sierra Club, where you could go on hikes and journal about the habitat of insects or how you witnessed a butterfly migration.[14] You could even create a blog about your adventures.[15] Next you could expand this to find two more ideas that show you are serious about pursuing your goal.

NO SWEAT EXERCISE 27—EXPAND A TALENT

Directions: Open your Goals Notebook and write the title on the first line. Select one of your eight crazy talents and write it on the second line. Number four more lines to expand your talent into the following categories: short-term goal, intermediate goal, long-term goal, and life goal. Remember, "no sweat" means don't take this too seriously.

____

____

1. ______________________________________
2. ______________________________________
3. ______________________________________
4. ______________________________________

EXAMPLE: NO SWEAT EXERCISE 28— AFFIRM YOUR LIFE GOAL

I am a passionate entomologist creating a global matrix of friends who will save the earth from harmful changes through my organization SEEB, "Save Earth's Environment with Bugs."

from No Sweat Exercise 27—Expand a Talent, write an affirmation to clarify your life goal. The example for No Sweat Exercise 27 contains some thoughts to start the ball rolling.

If you are serious about succeeding in goal setting, write out your new affirmation ten times in your Goals Notebook before you go to bed tonight. Try and do it for an entire week!

Now that you are feeling very focused, let's review the five steps to create a goal:

NO SWEAT EXERCISE 28— AFFIRM YOUR LIFE-GOAL

Directions: Open your Goals Notebook and write the title on the top line. The point of this exercise is to become very clear on your life goal. How? Follow these simple steps. Copy your goal from the previous exercise on the second line. Then number three lines and take two lines of those lines to describe your goal in more detail. This helps you see what you are trying to "say." Next, cut out the extra words and rewrite the final version of your life goal in one statement on the bottom line.

____

____

1. ____________________________

2. ____________________________

3. ____________________________

> **"Successful people have clearly defined plans and objectives that they refer to daily to keep in mind their lifetime goals and to order their daily priorities. Clearly defined, written goals help to move us to completion."— Dr. Diane Sukiennik, Dr. Bill Bendat, and Lisa Raufman, authors[16]**

FIVE STEPS TO CREATE A GOAL

1. **Desire the end result—you've got to really, really want it.**
2. **Write out action steps and a time they will be completed.**
3. **See the goal completed—every day act as if it's already happened.**
4. **Feel the excitement—how will you feel when you meet your goal?**
5. **Track your progress—grade yourself on completing each step.**

At this stage of setting and achieving a goal, you begin to realize that goals are more than a statement—they are an extension of you. That is the reason to examine the long and the short of goals and all their different aspects.

NOTES

1. Diane Sukiennik, Bill Bendat, and Lisa Raufman, *The Career Fitness Program: Exercising Your Options* (Scottsdale, AZ: Gorsuch Scarisbrick, 1986), 94.

2. *Recycled Life*, www.recycledlifedoc.com/ (accessed November 17, 2007).

3. Joy Browne, "How to Set Goals and Keep Them," *Parade Magazine*, March 18, 2007, 8–9.

4. Diane Bubel's autistic son, Michael, was tutored by Aiken. Later, as this friendship continued, Diane and Clay founded the Bubel/Aiken Foundation (BAF). The BAF runs summer camps that reflect the mission of "educational inclusion" and also presents Able to Serve awards to support the volunteer efforts of children with physical and mental disabilities. In 2005, the BAF was presented with a $500,000 grant from the U.S. government to develop a curriculum for inclusion to be used in schools across the country. The

Buble/Aiken Foundation, www.bubelaiken.org/default.aspx?tabid=104 (accessed December 5, 2008).

5. “Clay Aiken,” Wikipedia, en.wikipedia.org/wiki/Clay_Aiken# American_Idol (accessed December 5, 2008).

6. Rod Moore, “Personal Goal Setting,” Mind Tools, www.mindtools .com/page6.html (accessed November 17, 2007)

7. Tina Schwartz, *Organ Transplant: A Survival Guide for the Entire Family* (Lanham, MD: Scarecrow Press, 2005). Turn to the introduction, page ix, for the listing of Anne Courtright’s illustrations.

8. Quiz questions taken from Sukiennik, Bendat, and Raufman, *Career Fitness*, 98.

9. Sarah Ban Breathnach, *Something More: Excavating Your Authentic Self* (New York: Warner Books, 1998), 19–21, 60–66. When featured on Oprah’s Book Club, this became a best seller in 2003. Focusing on women’s issues, the author helps to define life’s talents and goals. An exercise called the Dream Collage uses pictures to bring out “small things forgotten” and decode messages of things that brought happiness in the past.

10. To find out more about Tiger Woods’ goals, go to the following sites: ”At 30, Tiger becomes Youngest to 50 PGA Wins,” ESPN Golf, sports.espn.go .com/golf/news/story?id=2541607 (accessed July 2, 2007); Leanne Hoagland-Smith, “A Lesson—One Stroke at a Time!” ZeroMillion.com, www.zeromillion .com/personaldev/one-stroke-lesson.html (accessed April 19, 2007).

11. To be featured on the show, go to the NBC website and find the segment called “Be on the Show.” Then scroll down to “Teenage Wasteland” where teens are encouraged to send in their personal videos. NBC.com, www.nbc.com/The_ Tonight_Show_with_Jay_Leno/exclusives/be_on_the_show.shtml# (accessed December 1, 2008).

12. This fact was not common knowledge about Jamie Foxx. “2005 Kids’ Choice Award Winners,” Nickelodeon, www.nickkcapress.com/2005KCA/ index.php?option=com_content&task=view&id=33&Itemid=69 (accessed June 26, 2007).

13. “Sanjaya Malakar,” American Idol, www.americanidol.com/ contestants/season6/sanjaya_malakar/ (accessed June 25, 2007).

14. To learn about the Sierra Student Coalition, the national student chapter of the Sierra Club, go to Sierra Student Coalition, www.ssc.org/ (accessed April 20, 2007); for Monarch butterfly migration, go to “Monarchy,” Sierra Club, October 3, 2006, www.sierraclub.org/compass/2006/10/monarchy.asp (accessed November 17, 2007).

15. To master the art of blogging, go to “Blog,” Marketing Terms.com, www.marketingterms.com/dictionary/blog/ (accessed June 25, 2007).

16. Sukiennik, Bendat, and Raufman, *Career Fitness*, 29.

12 Reading the Signposts of Life

Since you are beginning to see your main passions in life, it's likely you will need more training or education to meet your desired goal. Your problem is to find out where you should go from here and what you should do to take the next step.

When you go on a trip, you usually take a map to show the route so you will arrive safely at your destination. The same is true of life. The purpose of this chapter is to help you plot out your course of action by learning to read the signposts in your life. This information includes what the advantages are in attending junior college, what you can expect from apprenticeships and careers without college, how military life can open doors to assist you in meeting your goals, and what to do if you encounter delays in reaching your goals. Several exercises will clarify these activities. In turn, these will show you the weird excuses you can invent to stay out of school, and four reasons to finish school. You will also explore the benefits of attending a four-year university. Finally, you will learn how to allow solutions to surface that will help you reach your goals.

WHAT ARE SIGNPOSTS?

Signposts can be people or events that point you in the right direction to meet your goals. They have also been referred to as guideposts. Once you identify them, you will need to figure out what message they hold for you, then act upon your prompting.

HEADS UP FOR JUNIOR COLLEGE

Many doors can open when you attend your local community college. Today almost every educational field is available there. Whether you need to take automotive classes to learn about diesel engines, so you can become a certified auto mechanic; study nutrition, so you can fulfill your dream to become a chef; or just strengthen your basic math skills, so you can go on to become a rocket scientist, you can reach your goals through attending your local junior college.

Typically junior colleges cover the first two years of required college courses necessary to earn a four-year degree. They offer a variety of other benefits, too, including counseling services and job placement guidance, as advisors are on hand to answer any

A signpost of life.
Illustration by Peg Raasch.

"I've gone through all of my schooling in elementary, junior high, and high school thinking I would go to my dream college, a private school in Nebraska. I was all set up to go there when I graduated from high school last May. I had even bought my plane ticket and everything was ready.

"Five days before I was to leave, the bank called with the bad news they didn't approve my student loan. I had no back-up money set aside so I had no choice but to cancel my application. I didn't want to be a freeloader off my parents until I could get the money to go back to the University the next year, so I applied at our local community college. I used to be against going to a community college and staying at home, but once I learned that the teachers are as high quality as those in the University, and how inexpensive it was, I was amazed.

"Going to private school would have put me over $40,000 in debt by the time I graduated in four years. I tell myself, by going to a community college for two years, I'll save up more for the University, get the equivalent in quality education, and also be able to pay for my junior college tuition in cash since it's so cheap."—Pearl, age 19

questions. These professionals can assist you in defining your educational needs, career planning, and personal development, and they can show you the requirements needed to transfer into a four-year university.

Counselors can do the following:

- Review transcripts and give credits for previous classes
- Assist you in selecting a four-year college or university
- Arrange for your transcripts to be forwarded
- Help in transitioning you from one major to another
- Create a step-by-step plan to complete certification before transferring
- Identify internships you may qualify for
- Refer you to open positions for employment within the junior college
- Arrange a leave-of-absence status for you if you have personal or family problems

Do you dream of attending a junior college when you are still in high school? Here is some information on how to accomplish this goal taken from our local high school's Premier *discoveragenda* in the suburbs of northern Chicago, Illinois.

In my district, "the Education Alternatives for Seniors [EAS] program [has been established] to broaden the student's background and experience, to offer enrichment, and to provide an opportunity for social services. This is a [credit] program offered to seniors with three alternatives: action education [such as volunteering], concurrent enrollment at [your local community college] and independent study via correspondence. In order to participate, students must pick up and complete an EAS packet from their guidance counselor. All programs are closely supervised through the Student Services department. Transcripts of coursework taken must be supplied upon completion of the course."[1]

Did you know that many community colleges hold classes that high school students are eligible to attend? If you're a senior in high school, get hold of the schedule of classes from your local junior college, then talk to your high school academic advisor so she or he can get you the necessary paperwork to apply. This opportunity may also apply to technical and nontraditional high schools so scour your handbooks for more information.

If you are a young adult who attends a technical or nontraditional school, you could be eligible to attend classes in your special interest at your local community college as well. Check with your school counselor to learn more.

APPRENTICESHIPS AND CAREERS WITHOUT COLLEGE

Maybe you have opted to get out of the entire school scene and focus on developing your dream career without pursuing your education. Although there are many statistics that show reaching your goal is more difficult by taking this path, many have won success without the classroom.

You will find a wide range of additional entry-level opportunities offered through internships in *The Intern Files:*

You'd be surprised how many people became famous without finishing school. Here are a few of them:

Richard Branson, billionaire British businessman
George Carlin, comedian
Jim Carrey, comedian and actor
Tom Cruise, actor
George Eastman, founder of the Kodak company
Albert Einstein, mathematician
Michael J. Fox, actor
George Gershwin, composer
Peter Jennings, news anchor and reporter
Billy Joel, singer
Keanu Reeves, actor
Thomas Sowell, economist, author, and political commentator
Quentin Tarantino, movie director
Dave Thomas, founder of Wendy's restaurant chain
Uma Thurman, actress
Randy Travis, country music singer
John Travolta, actor
the Wright brothers, inventors of the airplane[2]

Even the dynamic teen singer Sanjaya Malakar, who blasted into fame through the *American Idol* TV show in 2007, earned his GED to pursue his singing career. But after the *Idol* finale, his goal was still to go to college and pursue a degree in music.[3]

How to Get, Keep, and Make the Most of Your Internship, by Jamie Fedorko.[4]

For many young adults, going to college full time is really not possible. Your daily commitments might force you to attend nighttime classes while you hold down a day job. Maybe you'll have to postpone your goal to finish college until demands are not pulling you in every direction. I had to make this decision, but because I never gave up my goal eventually I did succeed in getting my degree.

Richard N. Bolles is considered a pioneer in the job counseling market, since he published the original book *What Color Is Your Parachute?* in 1972.[5] Since teens are entering the job market at a record-setting pace, he adapted many concepts and wrote a new book that he coauthored with Carol Christen, *What Color Is Your Parachute? for Teens*, to assist today's youth in their job quest.[6]

To explore a career that does not require a college education, check out the book *Apprenticeship: The Ultimate Teen Guide*, by Penny Hutchins Paquette. It is chock-full of information that will help you explore career options. The thirteenth addition to the critically acclaimed It Happened to Me series, the book is designed to help teens find jobs by providing specific details about apprenticeship programs in their desired field. It explains how various teens have found apprenticeships, how they enjoy the work, and how the classroom portion of the apprenticeship is handled. Chapters also include interviews with young people who are currently working in apprenticeship programs. When researching your particular field of interest, whether it be a dental assistant or a medical laboratory technician (or a variety of others), you might find the section titled "Job Outlook and Wages" the most helpful.

According to Penny, "There are currently over eight hundred apprenticeable occupations registered with the Department of Labor [in the United States]. . . . Although construction and production account for more than half of the apprenticeable occupations, there are still hundreds of other jobs that can be mastered through apprenticeship. Firefighters and police officers, stage technicians and wardrobe supervisors, funeral directors and embalmers, actors, artisans, avionic technicians, and animal trainers are among the jobs that may be trained through apprenticeship."[7]

Then the information was enhanced and placed into a workbook format titled *What Color Is Your Parachute Workbook: How to Create a Picture of Your Ideal Job or Next Career*.[8]

There are many excellent careers that do not require college. Here is a partial list you can explore that do not require a four-year college degree:[9]

Actor
Child care worker
Correction officer
Crime lab technician
Customer service representative
Dental hygienist
Emergency medical technician
Fire fighter
Food service manager
Hazardous waste technician
Heating and air conditioning technician
Home health aide
Makeup artist

Medical assistant
Medical record technician
Nurse assistant
Occupational therapy aide
Paralegal
Photographer
Physical therapy assistant
Private investigator
Radio announcer
Real estate sales agent
Retail salesperson
Security guard
Surgical technician
Television production assistant
Tractor-trailer truck driver

There are several ways you can get information on these careers to see if you have an interest and natural aptitude.

The most obvious way is to talk to people in that field and see what their experience has been. I do that all the time with teens, because I am interested in what they think about their jobs and I want to know what problems they have balancing both work and school.

When you are in the early stages of identifying your career interest, take time to gather the facts about the segment that interests you, then set a reachable goal. "Don't make the choosing of goals too complicated or significant. Start with simple obvious things. Remember you can always change and develop them as you go along."—Shakti Gawain, author[10]

A second way to become informed is to take vocational interest tests at your high school or community college. Here your skills

Many revolutionary ideas on the goal-seeking movement in the United States were first discussed in the book *Where Do I Go from Here with My Life?* by John C. Crystal and Richard N. Bolles. One of the main beliefs proposed is that a person's first job could hold the key to his or her entire career: "The single factor which seems to influence people's career or occupation more than any other, is their first job opportunity into which they glide or slide, without much conscious decision or examination. The first job opportunity then conditions the whole subsequent course of their progress in the world of work."[11]

are matched with the requirements of your career of interest. The school advisers and career planning offices can help you set up the tests or make computerized tests available. You'll find it interesting to watch your many talents surface.

Thirdly, you can do some online testing by yourself, which will help you identify your skill strengths and lead you toward choices in your career. Tests can also identify your personality traits and reveal your suitability for your career choice.[12]

Let's examine the field of health care as an example of a career you can follow up on your own, as explained by Penny Hutchins Paquette in *Apprenticeship: The Ultimate Teen Guide*.[13]

1. **Certified nursing assistant (CNA): Besides performing all of the basic patient comfort needs, other duties include taking temperatures, pulse rates, respiration rates, blood pressures and maintaining patient records and critical notes. (Some states require training certification.)**
2. **Dental assistant: Duties include assisting the dentist, handling the dental instruments, suctioning the patient's mouth, keeping instruments sterile, taking dental X-rays, and performing various lab and clerical duties.**
3. **Emergency medical technician (EMT): This course includes classroom instruction, practical demonstrations, testing, and clinical experiences in a hospital emergency department. Students learn CPR, patient assessment, stabilization, and initial pre-hospital medical treatment of injured and ill patients. (Some states require training certification.)**
4. **Licensed practical nurse (LPN): Under the supervision of a registered nurse, LPNs do the following: take vital signs, prepare and give injections, apply dressings, collect samples, perform routine lab tests, and maintain patient records and critical notes. LPNs must pass exams to be certified.**
5. **Medical appliance technician: Several specialties fall under this broader category that aims to help the disabled lead normal lives. Orthotic technicians fabricate arm and leg braces, and so forth; ocularist technicians mold, fabricate, and paint prosthetic eyes; while prosthetic technicians fabricate artificial limbs. All positions require a supervised hands-on training program and classroom study.**
6. **Medical lab technician: Under the supervision of a technologist, lab technicians may analyze body fluids looking for bacteria,**

"According to the Bureau of Labor Statistics, the number of people in older age groups with much greater than average health care needs will grow faster than the total population. New technologies and treatments will help severely ill or injured people survive, and they will need extensive therapy and care. The need [for medical assistants and home health care practitioners] will skyrocket in response."— Penny Hutchins Paquette, author[14]

"Two years ago I thought I could do anything. It didn't occur to me that I could fail because I felt invincible and that nothing bad could happen to me. I was a model and for my first big break I was sent to London by my New York agency.

"I was embarrassed to be the oldest girl out of seven who was sent there. We all shared a three-story modeling flat. I had castings all the time—about eight or nine 'go-sees' every day. It was hard work to find each place, to be on time, let alone look great.

"The one job I got was a terrible experience. It was a three-day shoot for a stockings ad. The makeup artist and the photographer didn't like me and they convinced the client I was wrong for the job because they wanted their friend instead. So I only worked one day.

"At the time, I didn't know I was taking such a risk. But now, I still say, go for the challenge or you'll never go anywhere because as they say, 'Nothing ventured, nothing gained.'

"Now, I'm back home getting my cosmetology license and I'll move on when I'm ready."—Chrissy, age 19

Heather's life goal—modeling.
Art by Anne Courtright.

parasites, microorganisms, or abnormalities; prepare specimens; and operate automated system analyzers.

7. **Pharmacy technician: Under a pharmacist's supervision, technicians may receive written prescriptions; weigh, measure, and mix medications; count tablets and label bottles; and price prescriptions. Technician must pass the National Pharmacy Technician Certificate Exam.**

WHAT ABOUT MILITARY LIFE?

Because the lure of travel is so overdone with TV commercials, many young adults feel the pull to live out of the country as an adventure. They find that military life offers this opportunity.

Perhaps you have been dreaming of joining the military or someone who you care about has enlisted. One thing is for sure—

this decision will bring change into your life. To see a broad picture on the ups and downs of what a teen might expect when entering military life, peruse *The Military and Teens: The Ultimate Teen Guide*, by Kathlyn Gay.[15]

One of the most publicized stories of injured soldiers in the Iraqi war came in April of 2003 when Private Jessica Lynch, a U.S. female army supply clerk with the West Virginia 507th Maintenance Company, was rescued from a hospital in Baghdad. She returned home to a heroine's welcome. Jessica's injuries included fractures in both legs, her right arm, and her spine, as well as a gunshot wound. She received more attention when a book, *I Am a Soldier, Too: The Jessica Lynch Story*, by Richard Bragg, described her ordeal and rescue.[16]

Thanks to the loving hands of friends and neighbors, Jessica's family home was retrofitted to handle a wheelchair, and after

"So, about how the military has affected my life. . . . In a direct way the military has affected my life when I got sent to Afghanistan where I am daily concerned about the continuation of said life. I have known people, good people, friends, who have been taken before their time because of this war. That is an experience I wish on no one.

"However, my experience here so far has forced me to look at myself and see what truly matters to me. Here are a few things I've considered:

"Friends; I am grateful to my military experience for giving me truly great friends.

"Myself; people get caught up in how we should look out for others all of the time and forget that if you don't look out for yourself as well, you are letting down the people who count on you.

"Family! My family is the most important thing to me in the whole world—I love nothing like I love my family.

"Politics and the mass media are two things that I have come to despise. I don't like to dump on things I have no solution for, but knowing that there's a problem is the first step, isn't it? Anyway, that's a tiny chip off the block of my military experience."—Joachim, age 20

Soldier boy.
Illustration by Peg Raasch.

many months of physical therapy, she stabilized her war injuries and merged back into life as a civilian.

Perhaps the most important lesson that can be learned from Jessica's story is that she adjusted to the changes in her life. Although she continued to wear a brace on her left foot due to her

Joe: "It's a soldier's life for me."

injuries, Jessica returned to a normal life, losing her fame by fitting into the American college scene. She went on to pursue her original goal to become a kindergarten teacher with a full scholarship at West Virginia University, which was paid through her military service benefits.[17]

DELAYED GOALS

You might wonder, if I take time out for work or my family, will I ever get back on track? Realize that there's something very rewarding about reaching a deferred goal. It seems to mean more than if you had reached it when you had originally planned.

Many students experience that scenario when they leave college to get married. Little do they imagine it might take years to go back and finish their degree. My experience was similar, but it had a positive ending. I earned a bachelor of arts degree in communications with a double major in art and creative writing—something I might not have tried to accomplish when I started my education.

If you are confronted with making a choice of delaying your goal to finish your education due to a family emergency, try and make a balanced decision. Don't go on an emotional flip-out and act like a little kid. Get counseling from someone you trust, perhaps an old teacher who has known you for many years. Accept the change with dignity and know you will grow because of it.

If you examine your situation armed with your many new visualization tools, you can have a much different outcome than you could have ever imagined. Why not create an affirmation to reinforce your positive outlook and broaden it to include all your

"For the last several months I've been working days, then taking high school classes at night. My mom is sick and, as the oldest girl, I thought I needed to do something to help out with our family's income.

"So far, I can handle my schedule. The only difficult part is I'm very busy and pretty exhausted. I hope by next September things can turn around for us and I can be back in school full time for my senior year."—Kathy, age 17

Shakti Gawain suggests that you become very specific in your goal setting and combine affirmations with your visualization. She explains how to create the "ideal scene": "Write down the goal as clearly as possible in one sentence. Underneath that write, 'Ideal Scene' and proceed to describe the situation exactly as you would like it to be when your goal is completely realized. Describe it in the present tense, as if it already exists, in as much detail as possible. . . .

"Then sit quietly, relax, visualize your ideal scene at your meditative level of mind, and do your affirmation."[18]

family members as well? Say it often as you go forward, expecting new and good things to come out of it.

WEIRD WAYS I DELAY MY GOAL TO FINISH SCHOOL

Since this book employs No Sweat Exercises to help you see your challenges and then laugh about them, let's do one now so you can see how you have let trivial things keep you from reaching your

EXAMPLE: NO SWEAT EXERCISE 29—WEIRD WAYS I DELAY MY GOAL TO FINISH SCHOOL

Scratching off the squares of lottery tickets is more fun than doing calculus.

If I take tech school classes one more year, I'll make the Guinness record book for shop.

Since I joined a volunteer group, I eat breakfast daily with my friends to save cereal box tops.

I'm training for the Olympics in four years, and school will mess up my workout schedule.

If I went away to college, my cat would die of being lonely.

I can't tear myself away from my significant other.

My grandma needs me. Who'll take out her trash if I'm in school 24/7?

I made a pact with three junior high friends we'd all go to the same college and one moved away.

NO SWEAT EXERCISE 29—WEIRD WAYS I DELAY MY GOAL TO FINISH SCHOOL

Directions: Open your Goals Notebook. To begin, write the title of the exercise on the top line of the next blank page and number eight more lines. If you haven't used this gimmick before, try doodling to unwind. Decorate your paper, write upside down, or print using your left hand (if you're right-handed). You can even write with different colored pens, change from script to printing in the same line, or write in code. Whatever way you choose, come up with eight weird excuses for not finishing school. If you have the beginning of a doodle masterpiece, give yourself extra time to finish this exercise.

____

1. ______________________________
2. ______________________________
3. ______________________________
4. ______________________________
5. ______________________________
6. ______________________________
7. ______________________________
8. ______________________________

goals. Use your sense of humor to create weird scenarios that will make you laugh at yourself. This might shed light on why you have not finished school. Put yourself in the picture with this example so you can laugh at a touchy subject.

FOUR REASONS TO FINISH SCHOOL

Everyone knows that finishing school is a huge issue in any young adult's world. But, life's day-to-day activities can rob you of necessary personal time to reach your goal. Plus there is always an underlying tension with the adults in your life that want you to

NO SWEAT EXERCISE 30—FOUR REASONS TO FINISH SCHOOL

Directions: Take the time now to take any negative idea you listed and reverse it in your subconscious mind. To accomplish this, turn to the next blank page in your Goals Notebook, place the title on the top line, and number eight lines. Copy four of your previous lame excuses on every other line. Next rewrite each one into a positive statement on the line beneath it. (If you really want to be proactive, write four more positive reasons to finish school as you dig deeper to target your success.)

____

1. ______________________________
2. ______________________________
3. ______________________________
4. ______________________________
5. ______________________________
6. ______________________________
7. ______________________________
8. ______________________________

focus on that dreaded concept of the "big picture." But there's good news. When you become proactive, you can focus on your goals and make sense of the feelings that compel you to seek a better life. Plus, becoming proactive always takes a little heat off your back from those authority figures worried you will do the right thing.

THE FOUR-YEAR UNIVERSITY

Many young adults want the experience of attending a four-year university away from home, where they can enjoy the illusion of total freedom from parental supervision. While it is exciting to begin your higher education this way, be warned that it can become a sink-or-swim situation with no adult backup if you make a mistake. Be aware of all the juggling you will need to do between scheduled classes, part-time work, midterm and final exams, and extracurricular events. Your planner can become your new best friend, constantly reminding you of overdue library books and pending assignments. So, remember to keep it close at hand and use it daily.

It's good to plan at least nine months ahead of time what school you will want to attend. Remember—don't overload your schedule during your first year away from home and allow yourself to adjust to your new daily routine.

You will need to budget your study time with your social time or else you'll turn into a *Saturday Night Live* comedy as portrayed in the Jimmy Fallon and Horatio Sanz skits of "Jarret's Room."[19] Who could forget that four-year-long satire about dorm life where Jarret and Gobi lived their college days as one giant party with guest stars ranging from Drew Barrymore, Britney Spears, and Ashton Kutcher to Al Gore? The skits exaggerated real college life when the characters bragged that Gobi had been enrolled in college for seven years without attending any classes! But the skits do raise some flags about balancing your time between education and socializing.

Another spoof on college life can be seen in *Fresh Prince of Bel Air*, the Will Smith TV adventures of the 1990s.[20] The point of both shows seems to be that college is the time and place to put goals into your life.

Living in a dorm can be a new experience. It can be challenging to share a cramped space with one or two roommates. You have to share so much stuff that sometimes you end up hating the idea. Why not look at the experience as another step toward independence?

One teen overcame the obstacle of sharing her stuff and furniture by creating her own dorm bed/study nook. She designed it for compact size and shipping, as she knew she would haul it around with her for at least four years. Her unit was so well planned that upon graduation, she included a photo of herself in it at the beach, as part of her application into architectural school.

Della's "bunk-me."

Realize that you, too, can find creative ways that could lead to your life goal!

When doors open for you that lead to different opportunities, remember to read the signposts around you. Dr. Norman Vincent Peale often referred to these signs as "guideposts." When you realize that these signs are clues that help you to be more in sync with your life, you can simplify your decisions by taking the next obvious step.

"Your individual vibrations are the key to understanding the art of allowing. The non-harmonious vibrations are largely in the form of your thoughts and feelings. Thoughts that emphasize what you don't believe you deserve set up a contradiction in energy. That contradiction puts a stop to hooking up of identical energies, and you've created a field of disallowing. Remember, it's always about being in harmony with your Source."—Dr. Wayne Dyer, author[21]

FIND GOALS THROUGH THE LAW OF ALLOWING

If you are uncomfortable with new terminologies and ideas presented in this book, remember—to reach your goal you must be willing to embrace change and discover new ideas that will help you believe in your goals. When you "allow" events to unfold that you might have resisted when you were younger, solutions become clear that you never could have imagined before. When you are moving toward your desired goal, you don't have to make things happen; you don't have to will or manipulate people. You'll find that answers and events emerge that point the way for you.

Even when you are trying to figure out what your next step should be in life or which college to apply to, when you remain calm, the right path will surface. You might even find unique ways to get your college application noticed, so why not try a different approach to get into the college of your dreams?

In the 2001 movie *Legally Blonde*,[22] Reese Witherspoon's character, Elle Woods, showed a winning attitude when she decided one day that she was going to Harvard Law School in order to win back her boyfriend, Warner Huntington III. With the help of her college adviser, Elle met the requirements to get into Harvard. How? She studied hard and scored over 175 on her LSAT (Law School Admission Test) and made a video-resume showing she was a "Beverly Hills shopping expert."

Of course Elle was accepted and moved into Harvard's dorms with her tiny Chihuahua pooch, Bruiser. She continued to set higher goals for herself, landing a summer internship with a prestigious law firm in New York. In a murder case handled by this firm, Elle exposed the lies of the star witness, Chutney, and went on to win the case even though she was only a student practicing law!

Elle's positive attitude became contagious and she changed the lives of all the characters in the story. The film ends as Elle addresses the students at graduation, telling them to always have faith in themselves and to remember that "passion is key to the study of law and in life."

You can argue that *Legally Blonde* is simply a make-believe story and you have real-life problems to cope with that a fantasy can't solve. But stop any negative thoughts from creeping in and

> **"Hold the image of yourself succeeding, visualizing it so vividly that when the desired success comes, it seems to be merely echoing a reality that has already existed in your mind."—Dr Norman Vincent Peale, author[23]**

realize that now you are better equipped to face life's problems because you've changed your attitude with positive thinking.

Don't make your life complicated. The way to reach your goals is simple when you recognize your guideposts. If your friends don't see your path but you do, follow your heart. Have faith in your life. Listen to your voice within. Speak up for yourself when things seem difficult and consider alternative changes. Then make decisions based on your own inner guidance. Following the signposts in your life is one of the many steps you can take to achieve your goals.

NOTES

1. Premier high school ***discover****agenda*, 2002/03 edition (Bellingham, WA: Premier Agendas, 2003), 24, www.premieragenda.com (accessed January 8, 2007). To find out what your school offers, search for headings such as "Educational Alternatives" in the back of your school handbook.

2. "Famous High School Dropouts," Increase Brain Power.com, www.increasebrainpower.com/high-school-dropouts.html (accessed June 28, 2007).

3. Malakar, who left high school early and earned his diploma through taking the General Education Development (or GED) exam said *American Idol* became his "junior and senior year in high school." "Sanjaya after 'Idol': Singer? Actor? Model?" MSNBC, April 19, 2007, www.msnbc.msn.com/id/18205910/ (accessed April 23, 2007).

4. Jamie Fedorko and Dwight Allott (illustrator), *The Intern Files: How to Get, Keep, and Make the Most of Your Internship* (New York: Simon Spotlight Entertainment, 2006).

5. Richard N. Bolles, *What Color Is Your Parachute? 2007: A Practical Manual for Job-Hunters and Career-Changers* (London: Parachute Library, 2006), based on the original book, *What Color Is Your Parachute? A Practical Manual for Job Hunters & Career Changers* (Berkeley, CA: Ten Speed Press, 1972).

6. Richard Nelson Bolles and Carol Christen, *What Color Is Your Parachute? for Teens: Discovering Yourself, Defining Your Future* (London: Parachute Library, 2006).

7. Penny Hutchins Paquette, *Apprenticeship: The Ultimate Teen Guide* (Lanham, MD: Scarecrow Press, 2005), 22.

8. Richard Nelson Bolles, *What Color Is Your Parachute Workbook: How to Create a Picture of Your Ideal Job or Next Career* (London: Parachute Library, 2005).

9. Capstone Press, www.capstonepress.com/ (accessed January 8, 2007). Below are three websites that will give you additional information on how to proceed into a particular career that does not require a four-year college degree.

a. Guidance Associates, www.guidanceassociates.com/50bejopracawi.html (accessed November 8, 2005).
b. BNET, www.findarticles.com (in the search box type *Careers without college*) (accessed November 8, 2005).
c. The Internet Public Library, www.ipl.org./div/teenpathways/ (in the search box type *Careers without college*. Watch for hidden fees!) (accessed November 8, 2005).

10. Shakti Gawain, *Creative Visualization: Use the Power of Your Imagination to Create What You Want in Your Life* (Novato, CA: Nataraj Publishing, 2002), 138.

11. John C. Crystal and Richard N. Bolles, *Where Do I Go from Here with My Life?* (Berkeley, CA: Ten Speed Press, 1974), x. When this ground-breaking book was originally published, the national unemployment had reached 10 percent (due to massive layoffs in the aerospace industry after the Apollo lunar expeditions were completed).

12. Check out these two websites for information on assessments that can help match you to a career:

a. Assessment.com, www.assessment.com/MAPPMembers?TakeMAPP.asp (accessed December 1, 2008). Seventy-one questions in this assessment reveal ten areas of career interest that match your personality profile.
b. Keirsey.com, www.keirsey.com/cgi-bin/keirsey/newkts.cgi (accessed November 8, 2005). This personality test is unique because it uses the Myers-Briggs system to analyze your score. Upon completion, you will receive your Jungian personality type with characteristics that reveal ten areas of career interest that match your personality profile.

13. Paquette, *Apprenticeship*, 134–53.

14. Paquette, *Apprenticeship*, 133.

15. Kathlyn Gay, *Teens and Military Life: The Ultimate Teen Guide* (Lanham, MD: Scarecrow Press, 2008).

16. Richard Bragg, *I Am a Soldier, Too: The Jessica Lynch Story* (New York: Knopf, 2003).

17. To learn more about paying for your education with military benefits, go to Military.com, edu.military.com/gibill/?ESRC=ggl_edu_miledu.kw&np=1 (accessed July 3, 2007).

18. Gawain, *Creative Visualization*, 146.

19. "Jarret's Room" was a *Saturday Night Live* sketch reoccurring between the years 2000 and 2004, www.answers.com/topic/saturday-night-live-tv-show-sketches (accessed December 4, 2006).

20. "*The Fresh Prince of Bel-Air*," Warner Brothers Studios, www.warnerbros.co.uk/television/freshprince/ (accessed November 19, 2008).

21. Dr. Wayne Dyer, *The Power of Intention: Learning to Co-create Your World Your Way* (Carlsbad, CA: Hay House, 2004), 177.

22. *Legally Blonde*, www.legallyblonde.com/ (accessed March 3, 2007).

23. Dr. Norman Vincent Peale, *Positive Imaging: The Powerful Way to Change Your Life* (New York: Ballantine Books, 1992), 29.

13 Moving Forward with Courage

The major event in the life of every young adult is attending school. Even if you're homeschooled, according to the structure of our Western society, school defines you. Where you go to high school, where you attend college, or whether you choose a career without college to meet your goals—these all seem like bigger-than-life decisions. But, great news—this is an area where you can create your own success.

Success is won in small steps. When you convert goals into activities in your daily schedule, you are achieving them in small but practical ways. It may seem like too simple a solution for your problems, but when planning becomes a daily habit, you'll have something to hold on to when your world begins to change. Life moves on, and it is easier to move with the current than to paddle your canoe upstream.

OUTGROWING THE HERDING INSTINCT

One of the hardest challenges to overcome is your need to fit in. This desire to be socially accepted underlies most activities in high school and college. You need to recognize this "herding" instinct. Love it or hate it—it's the glue that lets you feel safe as you move from being a kid to becoming an adult—from fitting in to emerging as the unique one-of-a-kind you.

When you identify and then attain your goals, you'll find you have a new sense of purpose. This will make you seem different to your friends, but you will still be the same you, and more! You will be confident, and this will draw even more success to you.

"A friend of mine convinced me to volunteer for our schools' annual art book called 'Creations.' We usually met every day for twenty-five minutes. In the beginning of my junior year I was shy because there were so many seniors in the group. But slowly I got to know them and found they were really friendly.

"My senior year I was art submissions manager and a member of the editorial committee. The book itself was amazing because we choose the theme of 'conflicts.' We selected two hundred works of art from five hundred submissions. There were all kinds, from paintings and drawings to photos, sculpture, and 3-D art. Other students submitted their essays and poetry that we would match up with the art. The part I enjoyed the most was talking with the other students as I scanned their work into the computer with Adobe Photoshop. It was like a dream come true.

"Since I see what great things have happened to me by picturing my goal, next time, when I get a chance to volunteer in college, I'll jump at it."—Preeti, age 18.

Whether you're chosen to lead a chemistry lab experiment, head up your school's environmental clean-up project, or find that you've been welcomed into a new cafeteria crowd, your self-confidence will begin to show itself in many ways.

"Having a vision for what you want to be is essential, but it's not enough. You need a plan for making that vision happen."—Stedman Graham, author[1]

Preeti, a volunteer for Art Year Book.

Did you know that goal setting has become trendy enough to make waves on the Web?

If you have become a dedicated goal setter and would like to share your new goals with your family, friends, or others, there is a website designed for people like you. It will help you organize your goals and it has a free membership.

"www.43things.com lets you create a list of goals and share them with others. You can write notes associated with specific goals to chart your progress and inspire others, or search through other people's goals and inspire yourself."[2]

"Last year I took an EMT course at our local tech school. That was really exciting. The program is for kids who want to work and go to school at the same time, which was perfect for me. We also got the chance to do what is called a 'ride along' with the local fire department. The firefighters were very helpful to me and let me see I could really do this. One of them gave me an EMT sticker that I've already pasted into my notebook. Now, the only thing standing in my way is a dreaded two-and-a-half hour EMT exam.

"My goal is to get my license before next year. That's why I'm thinking of going for that exam next month. Nothing can hold me back then."—Aurora, age 18

Sometime in the near future, you will be leaving the school and family you have known. Things like lunchroom mania, off-campus java runs, or the predawn swim team practices will gradually become faded memories.

But, take heart. Don't think because you're becoming an adult you'll need to shed your "can do" spirit. The most successful people in life always remain young at heart and their enthusiasm becomes contagious. So remember to hang on to your youthful personality and keep life fun and exhilarating.

RELEASING YOUR GOAL

There's a very unique way to be successful in reaching every goal. It's called releasing, or detaching. This is how it works—you do the best you can do in preparation for your goal. You go through

"The Law of Detachment says that in order to acquire anything in the physical universe, you have to relinquish your attachment to it. This doesn't mean you give up the intention to create your desire. You don't give up the intention and you don't give up the desire. You give up your attachment to the result."
—Deepak Chopra, author[3]

the five steps to complete your goal and turn it into smaller action steps. Once you've done that, you let it go. It's a hard thing to do in the beginning, but when you find out it works, you'll get better at becoming detached.

"I'm just finishing up my first semester at our local junior college, but I'm thinking of transferring to a four-year state college. I have a scholarship that'll pay 75 percent of my tuition there.

"But the reason I'm transferring is that I am following my passion. I love English Literature and Creative Writing. I've been working with a college advisor who had me take some aptitude tests to show where my greatest talents are. I'm not that great in science and math but the tests show that my favorite subjects are also my strong points.

"So, I'm considering working toward a degree in English and teaching. I think I'd like that because I enjoy my elementary child psych classes a lot, too. This way I could combine several of my passions at once and never get bored with my job.

"Just to make sure I meet my goal, I've already cut out a picture of a teacher smiling in her classroom. My next step is to make her look like me. Aside from that, I've released it and will wait for the next step to appear."—Liz, age 19

THE PINK BUBBLE

Certain ideas color our imagination when we are very young through watching childhood movies. Who can forget the time where Dorothy first encounters the wicked witch in *The Wizard of Oz*? But if you remember more clearly, the scene first opens with the appearance of the Good Witch of the North, Glenda, who travels to Oz in a beautiful pink bubble. Let's use this visual image—the pink bubble—in a unique exercise to experiment with releasing goals.

I have adapted this exercise in several ways. First, remembering a TV chewing gum ad where a teenager blew a pink bubble as big as herself, I envision myself blowing a big bubble. Then, I think of *The Wizard of Oz*, and I picture myself inside my shiny pink bubble, acting as though I have achieved my goal. Next, I envision myself floating over the rainbow in the bubble.

To practice this concept, here's a simple tool. The day before the exercise, buy a big pack of bubblegum. Maybe you can't live without the chocolate Hubba Bubba Glop (one of your middle school faves), but find pink gum if possible, for the fairy-like effect it will give. Next, have a "chew-fest" with anyone else who is reading this goals book with you and then release your goal into your pink (bubblegum) bubble.

Shakti Gawain, the master of creative visualization, calls the following exercise the "pink bubble technique." To begin, she suggests you relax, breathing comfortably, and imagine something you would like to achieve clearly as though it has already happened.

"Now, in your mind's eye, surround your fantasy with a pink bubble: Put your goal inside the bubble. Pink is the color associated with the heart, and if this color vibration surrounds whatever you visualize, it will bring to you that which is in perfect affinity with your being. [Next,] . . . let go of the bubble and imagine it floating off into the universe, still containing your vision. This symbolizes that you are emotionally 'letting go' of it. Now it is free to float around the universe, attracting and gathering energy for its manifestation."[4]

A pink bubble.
Art by Peg Raasch.

If you cannot use the bubblegum technique, substitute that exercise by creating a very large bubble with regular bubble solution. How? Get a gigantic outdoor bubble wand—so your visualization will be huge as well. To see a visual image of all that you can do with bubbles, go online to view the bubble-blowing videos of Fan Yang. A sensational entertainer, he tours the world in a magical show blowing all sizes of bubbles, some of which are life-size and can envelope an entire family![5]

Weather permitting, try and do your meditation outside, where you can see your bubble drift off into the clouds, and you can envision your goal floating over the rainbow. You can envision your bubble carrying away your problems, or even things that are concerns to you. Relating to this concept, one teen copied a magazine cover as a visual for her school art project.

If both these activities seem too foreign to your personality, there's another way to release your goals. How? Through a conscious/subconscious method, you release your goal, or intention, into "the gap" during a silent meditation.

The way this is accomplished is simple. You center yourself and go into silence. That means mentally, emotionally, and physically,

Bush in a bubble.
Art by Preetit Deshpande.

you are quiet and still. It is when your mind is between thoughts that a gap is accessible. At that exact instant you release your goal and you "relinquish your attachment to the outcome . . . and let the universe handle the details."[6]

See this as another tool for success in achieving your goals using creative visualization. Create a crazy reward for yourself (or for the person who blows the biggest bubblegum bubble) as a way to honor the many unique ways you can reach your goals throughout your life.

The flipping method used throughout this book—when you change one crazy idea into something more meaningful—allows you to see both sides of the coin. To make the law of detachment successful in releasing your goals, ask yourself these questions: If this exercise seems too silly, am I kidding myself about reaching my goals? Is my fear of trying something different holding me

NO SWEAT EXERCISE 31—THE PINK BUBBLE

Directions: The following exercise will incorporate the three previous visualizations and will only take five minutes. Reread the pink bubble technique explained by Shakti Gawain, then try to envision releasing your goal into a bubble. When you have finished your visualization, open your Goals Notebook to a blank page and write the title on the top line. Next, simply freewrite for five minutes about wafting bubbles or meditating on the gap, and record what you "saw" or felt. See how much of the entire page you can fill. If you're a gum chewer, chew and pop some bubbles while you write.

back from discovering who I am? Can I go beyond my boundaries of comfort and try something completely new?

SPIRIT—THE FORCE IN VISUALIZATION

When you visualize your goals intensely, you begin to feel a unique energy. Great thinkers and writers have felt this intangible spirit of visualization and have described it in different ways: Shakti Gawain describes it as "Magnetic energy,"[7] Napoleon Hill calls it "Positive Thought Forms,"[8] and Dr. Norman Vincent Peale calls it "Positive Imaging."[9] Even Oprah believes that spirit is the driving force in goal setting. "If you want to accomplish the goals of your life, you have to begin with the Spirit."[10]

Live your life with passion as if every second counts and leave a legacy to carry forward your message. A great example of this is

Stephen Covey, the U.S. goal-setting guru, believes that we all have a vision of ourselves and our future, and that unspoken vision affects the choices we make and how we spend our time.

Covey describes spirit in this way: "When we talk about the 'passion of vision,' we are talking about a deep sustained energy that comes from our deepest self. . . . It taps into the deep core of who we are and what we are about. It's fueled by the realization of the unique contribution we have the capacity to make—the legacy we can leave. It clarifies purpose, gives direction, and empowers us to perform beyond our resources."[11]

Steve Irwin, the Australian naturalist who followed his passion to protect wildlife, especially the unique wildlife of Australia.

MOVING INTO CONSCIOUS AWARENESS

We can witness people like Steve Irwin and others who are completely living the passion of their everyday lives with

Steve Irwin died in September 2006 during the filming of segment for his American TV show *The Crocodile Hunter*. Steve's life ended as he did what he loved best—swimming with wildlife off the coast of Australia. He would be the first person to apologize to the stingray who harpooned him in the heart, because he would realize that the great ray was defending his territory from Steve, the intruder.

Melanie Christiansen, reporter for *Australian Story,* recalled a previous time when Steve had discussed his passion for his work with her. "Steve Irwin regarded himself as a conservationist and an animal lover."

She quoted him: "I think I've actually got animals so genetically inside me, that there's no way I could . . . be anything else. I think my path would have always gone back to, or delivered me to, wildlife. I think wildlife is just like a magnet and something that I can't help."[12]

Steve's family turned down the offer of a state funeral because they wanted him to be remembered as a regular guy. During the first forty-eight hours after his death, Steve's supporters in the United States and Australia donated more than $400,000 to the Wildlife Warriors, the charity Steve and his wife, Terri, founded to support the Australian Zoo.[13]

"It's up to you to choose what to believe and what not to believe. You can choose to believe in anything, and that includes believing in yourself. . . . Only with awareness do you have the possibility of transforming your dream."—Don Miquel Ruiz, author[14]

conviction. Sometimes you might get a rush feeling yourself when you are completely absorbed in an event in your life. Perhaps you might wonder what is happening when this energy or "passion of vision" moves you.

When you become passionate about something or someone, your spirit within moves to your outer awareness and you begin to change and think differently. It seems that part of your subconscious mind moves into an active part of your day-to-day consciousness and you start to function in a more heightened state. You might know answers to questions that others ask or understand things without having to learn them.

Did you know that "conscious studies" has begun to emerge as an academic field of study within several educational institutions across the United States and abroad? As a leading professor in this field, Francis X. Charet, professor at Goddard College in Plainfield, Vermont, poses questions in the college journal to tickle the students' interest to join him: "What is Consciousness? That is, what is the part of us that experiences the world through the lens of I-self subjectively, and, along with that, what is its relationship to a world that exists seemingly independently of us 'out there'?"[15]

Becoming more aware of your world and developing a heightened consciousness to meet your goals may seem like a new trend, but people throughout history have turned to their inner spirit. One such figure was Siddhartha Gautauma. He was born about 500 BC in a small kingdom in the foothills of the Himalayas now called Nepal. His family was rich and powerful and assumed that Siddhartha would become ruler of the kingdom. But he had another plan—he wanted to follow his inner voice.

Siddhartha's story has been told and illustrated by Osamu Tezuka in eight graphic novels, comprising the Buddha series. The first two volumes, *Kapilavastu* and *The Four Encounters*, depict the prince's life within his kingdom; *Devadatta* (volume 3) and the remaining five books find the prince, a traveling monk, seeking his path of enlightenment.[16]

To some readers, his characters might look as though they come straight out of an *Astro Boy* cartoon (which was Tezuka's seminal work of anime). He portrays the people of ancient India just as they dressed—or didn't. According to Amazon, this series is for mature older teens who want a meaty, substantial biographical novel that also explains Buddhist thought.

Siddhartha's story still captivates us today. How could someone who was rich and famous leave it all behind to become homeless? And then just as he had turned away from family wealth, he turned away from asceticism. He chose instead to follow a new path, the middle way between the two extremes.

You might ask yourself, "Could anyone go that deeply within, even me?" Maybe you feel sometimes that part of your mind is

Gautauma was determined to achieve his goal and his time of deep meditation has fascinated people throughout history. "Siddhartha vowed he would sit beneath a tree and meditate without moving until he achieved awakening. . . . He looked deeply into himself and saw his desires and ignorance. He sat all night deepening his meditation and sharpening his insight. Finally, . . . his mind opened to the reality that no separate Siddhartha really existed. His desires and suffering vanished along with the illusion of his self. . . . He was enlightened, liberated. Siddhartha had become the Buddah."—Dr. Franz Metcalf, author[17]

accelerating—like when you stomp on the accelerator of your car—and you wonder, "How does it work?" Perhaps the simplest answer is to say that you're tricking your subconscious mind. But, in reality, it's not your subconscious mind you are changing, but your conscious mind.

When you tap into your deepest desires, you're moving into the awareness where your desires are already identified and accepted. Your subconscious mind has accepted your goal as a reality. Your desire is the motivation for your goal seeking. Remember step 1 of how to create your goals—you have to really want it.

Flip back in the beginning part of your Goals Notebook to No Sweat Exercise 3 and review Five Steps to Create a Goal. Notice how emotions fit into goal setting—they become the fuel that propels you forward to achieve your goal.

Emotions cause a stirring in your heart. This sends impulses to your brain, which in turn, sends impulses back to your heart, hands, and feet. Without realizing why, sometimes your hands tingle or sweat. That occurs because you've reacted on the spur of the moment to something or someone because "the spirit moved you."

In his book titled *Inspiration, Your Ultimate Calling*, Dr. Wayne Dyer describes these emotional flashes as inspiration in action. He suggests that you've got to act spontaneously on a desire to inspire others, which will help you to become a person of inspiring action yourself.[18] When you act on an impulse, you could say you become inspired. We'll look at this reaction to understand how it can lead us toward our goals.

CRAZY ACTS IN THE SPUR OF THE MOMENT

You might ask yourself sometimes, "Why did I do that?" We will look more closely at this impulsive thinking and the lessons we can learn from it. Since we all have done a lot of crazy things without thinking, here's a batch to reflect on. Put yourself in the picture and ask yourself, "Could this have been me?"

LESSONS LEARNED

If you think this last No Sweat Exercise takes you off course to meet your goals, think again! Remember your hidden desires reveal something you really want to do and—Bingo! That's the

EXAMPLE: NO SWEAT EXERCISE 32— CRAZY SPUR-OF-THE-MOMENT ACTS

1. I gave all my food to a homeless man who stood in the rain.
2. I comforted a friend when she cried at a sleepover.
3. I hugged my boyfriend's best buddy when his dog died.
4. I dove into the lake when a baby fell off our dock.
5. I slept in the hospital bed with my dying mother.
6. I turned myself in for lying after I smoked with friends on our high school campus.
7. I drove up a narrow mountain road by myself at dusk.
8. I ended an emotional relationship that was making me a wreck.

NO SWEAT EXERCISE 32— CRAZY SPUR-OF-THE-MOMENT ACTS

Directions: Can you think of eight crazy things you did on the spur of the moment? Remember it's time to let yourself be impulsive. To dive into this problem, open your Goals Notebook and write the title on the top line. Next number eight lines and describe memorable moments when you were impulsive and acted a little weird.

____

1. ____________________________________
2. ____________________________________
3. ____________________________________
4. ____________________________________
5. ____________________________________
6. ____________________________________
7. ____________________________________
8. ____________________________________

EXAMPLE: NO SWEAT EXERCISE 33— LESSONS LEARNED

Next we will pick four spontaneous acts for No Sweat Exercise 33, and try to uncover a hidden goal or personal characteristic each reveals. Try and identify with the scenario and ask yourself, "Could this have been me?" (The numbers chosen correspond to the list in the example for No Sweat Exercise 32.)

1. I gave a homeless man the special holiday bread I baked for my family. When I saw that 20 people had drowned in a flash flood on TV, I wondered if he was one of them.

   My hidden goal is to help the homeless.

5. While lying in bed with my dying mother, my love helped me to overcome my fear of death.

   My resolution is to face my fears during a crisis.

6. When I got suspended for smoking on campus, I learned to take responsibility for my actions.

   My intuition shows me to always tell the truth, no matter what the cost.

8. When I realized I was in an abusive relationship, I listened to my inner voice and decided to break up with my boyfriend [or girlfriend].

   I made a commitment to be true to myself.

first step to achieve your goal. To dig deeper, let's look at what you can learn from your actions.

When you've finished writing your answers to No Sweat Exercise 32—Crazy Spur-of-the-Moment Acts, reflect on your answers to find your inner desires and goals. These are the lessons you've learned about yourself. This is the point of the next exercise—to see what the consequences of your actions can teach you.

Maybe you find yourself questioning, "What's so important about things I did on the spur of the moment?" Those events show a heart-felt act because your instantaneous actions heighten your ability to identify with a situation. This, in turn, propels you to reach your goals faster.

Dr. Wayne Dyer explains what happens when we act on a spontaneous desire: "Everything else that we need [to accomplish our goal] will begin to arrive when we're in Spirit. The right people will show up, the financing will materialize, those around us will be attracted to our enthusiasm and commitment, and we'll be a source of inspiration to others . . . while becoming more inspired ourselves."[19]

If you are serious about moving forward into adulthood to fulfill your goals, you will you need to shed the outworn herding instinct and empower yourself to be the real you. Why is this important? Because the approval of your peers might never come. As you follow your inner guide to fulfill your goals, you will find your

NO SWEAT EXERCISE 33—LESSONS LEARNED

Directions: Turn to the next page in your Goals Notebook. To begin, write the title on the top line and number eight lines. Pick four scenarios from your previous exercise and copy one on every other line. Below each statement write the conclusion you can draw about yourself. If you reflect honestly on each circumstance, the lesson you learned will be staring you in the face. Jump into this one; time yourself for five minutes and have at it.

____

1. ______________________________
2. ______________________________
3. ______________________________
4. ______________________________
5. ______________________________
6. ______________________________
7. ______________________________
8. ______________________________

ultimate purpose. This is the simple message of how you can "move forward with courage."

You can start doing this today. Start in small ways—be the first to introduce yourself in a new group, or push yourself to help your peers in some way. Try volunteering to pick up the pizza some night, or do a java run for your study group before an all-night cramming session for final exams. Don't do these things to win the approval of others, but act to expand your self-awareness as you change to meet your goals.

NOTES

1. Stedman Graham, *Nine Steps to Success: Teens Can Make It Happen* (New York: Simon & Schuster, 2000), 66.
2. Information on 43Things can be found from two sources:

   a. David Boyer, "Computersmarts," *BottomLine/Personal*, February 1, 2006, 11.
   b. 43Things, www.43things.com (accessed June 12, 2007). 43Things is a social networking site that is built on the principle of tagging rather than creating interpersonal links. Users create accounts (for free) and then list a number of goals or dreams; these goals are connected to other people's goals with similar words or ideas.

3. Deepak Chopra, *The Seven Spiritual Laws of Success: A Practical Guide to the Fulfillment of Your Dreams* (Novato, CA: Amber-Allen, 1994), 83.
4. Shakti Gawain, *Creative Visualization: Use the Power of Your Imagination to Create What You Want in Your Life* (Novato, CA: Nataraj Publishing, 2002), 98–99.
5. Large wands have been popularized by Fan Yang's bubble shows. You can find large wands in the toy department of most retail stores or at the following Internet sites:

   a. Flea Market 1000.com, www.fleamarket1000.com/bubblewand.htm (accessed May 11, 2007).
   b. Gazillion Bubble Show, www.gazillionbubbleshownyc.com/index.htm (accessed November 23, 2008).
   c. David Stein, *How to Make Monstrous, Huge, Unbelievably Big Bubbles* (Palo Alto, CA: Klutz, 2005).

6. Chopra, *Seven Spiritual Laws*, 78.
7. Gawain, *Creative Visualization*, 9.
8. Napoleon Hill, *Think and Grow Rich Action Pack* (New York: Penguin, 1990), 197.
9. Dr. Norman Vincent Peale, *Positive Imaging: The Powerful Way to Change Your Life* (New York: Ballantine Books, 1992), 17.

10. "Oprah Winfrey," Cybernation.com, www.cybernation.com/quotation center/quoteshow.php?type=author&id=9608 (accessed November 10, 2007).

11. Franklin Covey, *Sense of Purpose: Discovering Your Personal Mission Statement* (Salt Lake City, UT: Franklin Covey, 1999), 15.

12. Melanie Christiansen, "A Look Back at Steve Irwin's Life," PM, September 4, 2006, www.abc.net.au/pm/content/2006/s1732722.htm (accessed September 9, 2006).

13. Wildlife Warriors Worldwide, www.wildlifewarriors.org.au/ (accessed March 3, 2007).

14. Don Miquel Ruiz, *The Four Agreements* (San Rafael, CA: Amber-Allen, 1997), 106.

15. Francis X. Charet and Hillary S. Webb, "Approaching Consciousness Studies," *New Perspectives*, no. 20 (Spring 2007): 50. To find more information about attending Goddard College, which offers students independent studies and low residency requirements, go to Goddard College, www.goddard.edu/bachelorarts_individualizedstudies (accessed January 29, 2008).

16. The popular Buddha series by Osamu Tezuka includes the following eight paperback graphic novels, all of which can be found at Amazon.com, www.amazon.com (accessed March 1, 2007):

a. *Buddha*, volume 1: *Kapilavastu* (New York: Vertical, 2003).
b. *Buddha*, volume 2: *The Four Encounters* (New York: Vertical, 2003).
c. *Buddha*, volume 3: *Devadatta* (New York: Vertical, 2004).
d. *Buddha*, volume 4: *The Forest of Uruvela* (New York: Vertical, 2004).
e. *Buddha*, volume 5: *Deer Park* (New York: Vertical, 2004).
f. *Buddha*, volume 6: *Ananda* (New York: Vertical, 2004).
g. *Buddha*, volume 7: *Prince Ajatasattu* (New York: Vertical, 2005).
h. *Buddha*, volume 8: *Jetavana* (New York: Vertical, 2005).

17. Dr. Franz Metcalf, *Buddha in Your Backpack: Everyday Buddhism for Teens* (Berkeley, CA: Seastone, 2002), 17–18. To learn about the eightfold path of Buddha, go to About.com: Buddhism, buddhism.about.com/od/theravada/ss/BuddhismSS.htm (accessed April 24, 2007).

18. Dr. Wayne W. Dyer, *Inspiration: Your Ultimate Calling* (Carlsbad, CA: Hay House, 2006), 175–87.

19. Dyer, *Inspiration*, 185.

Part 4: THE AWARD GOES TO YOU

You have accomplished a lot in part 3, "Goals!"

You have understood the importance of planning and how goals are attained by writing action steps into your day planner and completing them at the given time and place. You have also learned to be in sync with your inner voice, use affirmations as part of your planning, and visualize and accept the completion of your goal.

This section will help you further clarify your vision. You'll focus on your ideas about life in general and create a strategy to become the new, mature you! This will help you to see your goals from a different viewpoint and plan ways to keep focused. In short, as you weave these new elements together, you'll begin to see the "big picture" about yourself and your destiny.

This is the section that can empower you for life. You made it through that eye of the needle from childhood into your teens; now you're growing naturally into adulthood where you will fulfill your goals. The door stands open before you. What do you do next?

Simple! Take a deep breath, clutch your day planner, and walk through the gate of opportunity.

14 A New You with Mission and Vision

There are several pieces of the puzzle still missing to put together your life goals. They are your vision statement and your mission statement. But before you analyze these final categories of goal setting, let's briefly look at what makes you happy. Why? Because when you are happy you are on course to complete your goals.

SMOLDERING DESIRES—A SIGN OF HOPE

Do you feel good when you make someone else smile? This can give you a feeling of self-confidence and make you proud of yourself, even though you may not like to brag about it.

If you did some serious thinking in the last two No Sweat Exercises to find out why you act impulsively and what lessons you could learn from your past, it might have left you with an unusual feeling of hope. The sensation could feel like a smoldering ember within.

You can't be expected to jump up and announce to everyone in the room that you felt a stirring in your heart and now you think there's new hope for you. But hope for what? you might wonder. Perhaps you can be more genuine and stop pretending to be somebody you are not, but act like your real self instead.

How's this for a new idea? Pull out your Goals Notebook and illustrate how you feel. Draw a picture of your heart opening up, or draw a cartoon of yourself surrounded by zigzag action lines becoming the hero figure of your own comic book. You can give yourself a title, or write a dynamic affirmation for yourself such as, "I am an inspired ___ [fill in the blank]." Then repeat your affirmation to convince yourself you are becoming that new person.

If this kind of expression is too awkward for your personality, choose to mentally recognize that something good is happening within. It could be the sign of an inner calling, pointing the way toward your ultimate goal.

Dr. Wayne W. Dyer addresses this feeling in *Inspiration: Your Ultimate Calling*, one of his best-selling books. He suggests that we pay attention to our moments of inspired action and realize they are inseparable, "like two sides of the same coin, giving and receiving are inseparable." Dr. Dyer feels we should become a person of inspiring actions who responds to his or her inner desires and goals if we wish to become a role model and inspire others.[1]

FEEL INSPIRED TO VOLUNTEER

One of the ways to feel inspired is to help others less fortunate than you. When you're at a crossroad and wondering what to do next, look around you and find a cause where you can start to give. Your temple, church, or local community center can be great places to seek out volunteer opportunities.

If you don't want to volunteer at church, you can find many other ways to safely volunteer.[2] *Volunteering: The Ultimate Teen Guide*, by Kathlyn Gay, addresses this question.

Kathlyn suggests that one of the first steps is to determine what motivates you, then you should focus on your personal interests: "Would you like to volunteer with a local group that provides services for seniors? Do you want to help the ill, abused, disabled, homeless, or hungry? Do you like to protect animals? Are you an environmentalist? Are you artistic and able to design posters,

"I was a volunteer helping other kids from my school with their homework and writing assignments. The program was called the Write Place and I did it for a couple of hours a week.

"At the time I was trying to figure out if I wanted to be a teacher, but after two years I decided it didn't seem like the perfect fit for me. But, it was fun, plus I got school credit for doing it."—Carreen, age 19

"I help out at our church every other week with the three-to-five year olds. We've made it a family effort, so I feel fine assisting with the crafts. Each time I get to work with two or three other kids my age.

"The little kids sit in small groups at tables and we help them do the cutting or coloring to go with their lesson that's part of the sermon for that day. Then we sing simple bible songs from CD's that they have memorized. That's followed by a snack and, of course, a sticker!

"Anyway, I really look forward to our turn twice a month and so do the other volunteers because we really have a lot of fun together."
—Shelby, age 16

brochures, or other graphics for fund-raising campaigns? Do you have computer skills to help set up or maintain websites for other volunteer groups?"[3] Maybe you have a talent for teaching, coaching, or mentoring.

You can volunteer to do some casual things, such as take out your elderly neighbor's trash, while other activities can involve a more serious commitment. This is not meant to suggest you should become a "disposal engineer" or "trash man," but helping others gives you insight into what you want to do with your life.

When the pressure of choosing the right college became too stressful, Whitney decided to take twelve months out of her life and volunteer with Mission Year.[4] Her volunteering efforts came at a crucial time for more than a dozen women who were residents of a twelve-step recovery program in Chicago. When they found their project was canceled and their supporting agency was

"Last summer I volunteered in Philly at the New Hope for Women Shelter while I lived at home. The program was in an inner-city neighborhood and it went from September until August.

"Then as the school year came I told my parents I didn't want to go to college right away and they thought, 'OK, that's our free-spirited daughter. We'll give her some space.'

"Now fast-forward nine months and I'm here in Chicago volunteering for a program that helps women get off the streets and I love what I'm doing here.

"I looked at the Peace Corps, but it wasn't right for me. But Mission Year is more what I wanted because it's like living life with people like Rachael [one of the residents], who I love."—Whitney, age 18

Whitney, a volunteer from Mission Year.

"The opportunities to reach into the lives of others in an inspiring way arises in countless ways, every single day. We can act on these momentary impulses and feel inspired, or we can ignore them and stay in our ego-dominated world. I choose to act for it makes me feel creatively alive, connected to good and everyone else in the world.

"If we're heeding our ultimate calling, we must be willing to act."—Dr. Wayne W. Dyer, author[5]

closing, all of the residents had to move to another halfway house for women in the city. Whitney was one of the few staff members who stayed on to help them through this stressful time because she wasn't salaried, but functioned as a volunteer. This was extremely important to everyone, as the residents went through great emotional turmoil. As all of their belongings were packed and trucked to the new location, the ladies found hope to start again through Whitney's calming manner.

One of the most inspiring young adults of our time was Mattie Stepanek. Although he only lived a short life of less than fourteen years, he published several best-selling books of poetry, including *Journey through Heartsongs*, *Hope through Heartsongs*, *Celebrate through Heartsongs*, *Loving through Heartsongs*, and *Heartsongs*.[6]

If you are inspired by the works of Mattie Stepanek and are looking for a way you can make a difference in the world as your life goal, you can find many ways to fulfill your dream. Making a difference in the world is the theme of a movie released by Warner Brothers in 2000 titled *Pay It Forward*.[7]

In the opening of the movie, a social studies teacher, Eugene, played by Kevin Spacey, tells his class to think of an idea to change the world for the better and create an action plan to accomplish that goal. On his way home from school, Trevor McKinney, played by Haley Joel Osmet, sees a homeless man and decides to make a difference in the man's life by bringing him home until he can "get on his feet." Trevor then comes up with the plan to "pay it forward" by doing a good deed for three people who must in turn each do good deeds for three other people.

Sometimes your dreams and goals can surface in unexpected ways.

In writing *Pay It Forward*, Catherine Ryan Hyde's goal was to write a good book. She never dreamed she could start a revolution in kindness.

> **The Pay It Forward Movement is the real-life reaction to the release of my novel in early 2000, followed by the creation of the Pay It Forward Foundation, followed by the Warner Brothers movie. I didn't write the novel expecting a social movement, but it's certainly been exciting to watch it grow.**
>
> **The purpose of the Pay It Forward Movement website is to bring together, in one place, as many real stories as we can. This serves several purposes. It helps the cynics see that Pay It Forward really is working, not just around the United States, but around the world. It brings much-deserved recognition to those doing the work, and puts the results of their efforts out in the open so others can be inspired. It's also a source of some good news for a change, a way to renew your faith in human nature.[8]**

The idea behind the entire movement of paying it forward is that when you do a kindness for a stranger and multiply that action through three more good deeds to others and then those people multiply it three more times, before long thousands and even millions of people are doing good with no hope of a payback.

The story continues to grow as Trevor's alcoholic mom, Arlene, played by Helen Hunt, challenges his good deed to bring Jerry, the homeless man, into their home and Trevor, in turn, challenges his mother's drinking. After a huge argument where Arlene slaps Trevor, he runs away and has a close call with a molester in the bus station, but is saved by Eugene.

When Trevor is interviewed on TV by a journalist who has tracked him down as the originator of the pay it forward movement, his mom realizes what a great thing her son has done. In his interview, Trevor explains his goal is to change the world with his pay it forward idea. However, he worries that other people may be too afraid to change their own lives in order to make the world a better place.

The story is very moving when Trevor is killed in a knife fight, defending another kid. Later that night Arlene and Eugene

NO SWEAT EXERCISE 34—PAY IT FORWARD

Directions: Now that you can see a real example of how you can make a difference in your life and impact the lives of many others by reaching your goals, it's time to put some of your own thoughts in writing. Grab your Goals Notebook and go to a quiet place where you can be alone with your thoughts. Open your notebook to the next blank page and write the title on the top line for the exercise. Next, mark out three lines. Allow yourself one line for each idea as you write out three ways you could change the world for the better and put your plan into action. If you find you're excited about this exercise, take time with your day planner to give your ideas a time and place to happen.

____

1. ______________________________________
2. ______________________________________
3. ______________________________________

witness thousands of people holding a candle vigil in their yard because they were inspired by Trevor and his pay it forward movement. Even though this film deals with many dicey subjects such as child abuse, the pain of an absent parent, and alcoholism, it is a believable story. The most interesting thing about this movie is that many people still feel today that it is the biography of a real kid.

Another young adult who has inspired others and made a difference is Craig Kielburger. He made it his goal to bring attention to the children who suffered due to the conditions found in child labor. One day when Craig was twelve years old, he picked up a newspaper and read the story of Iqbal Masih, a boy his age who had been murdered in Pakistan. Iqbal's death focused the world's attention on the terrible abuse of children who worked in the carpet-making industry. "I saw him as a hero for speaking out about child labor," says Kielburger. "I suddenly understood that a young person can make a difference."[9]

Mattie took action on September 11, 2001, in the only way he could—he wrote a poem. Bound to his wheelchair because he suffered from a rare genetic form of muscular dystrophy, but wanting to comfort everyone hurting in America, Mattie looked into his heart and wrote a poem that still moves us today. He met his goal that day to reach all Americans through the Internet when he sent it in to MyHero.com as his creative writing project. Today it can be found in his book, *Journey through Heartsongs*. Mattie considered the firefighters great heroes as they struggled to help all of the injured victims of September 11 at the World Trade Center, in the Pentagon, and at Shanksville, Pennsylvania, the site of the United Airlines (flight 93) plane crash.

"For Our World"[10]
by Mattie J. T. Stepanek
September 11, 2001

Before anybody
Says or does anything
That may hurt anyone else.
We need to be silent.
Just silent.
Silent for a moment
Before we forever lose
The blessing of songs
That grow in our hearts.
We need to notice.
Just notice.
Notice for a moment
Before the future slips away
Into ashes and dust of humility.
Stop, be silent, and notice.
In so many ways, we are the same.
Our differences are unique treasures.
We have, we are, a mosaic of gifts
To nurture, to offer, to accept.
We need to be.
Just be.
Be for a moment
Kind and gentle, innocent and trusting,
Like children and lambs,
Never judging or vengeful
Like the judging and vengeful.
And now, let us pray,
Differently, yet together,
Before there is no earth, no life,
No chance for peace.

Due to the surge of interest in Craig Kielburger's book, *Free the Children* has grown into a movement. Today it has grown into the world's largest network of children helping (other) children through education. Through the organization's unique youth-driven approach, more than 1 million young people have been involved in innovative programs in more than forty-five countries. Free the Children has an established track record of success, with three nominations for the Noble Peace Prize and partnerships with the United Nations and Oprah's Angel Network.[11]

In 1999, Craig, with his brother, Marc Keilburger, developed Leaders Today, which can open the door for you to step into another world. This organization offers "international training experiences to more than 350,000 youth every year. We bring our hands-on programs to schools and communities around the world, providing opportunities for both young people and adults alike to travel and learn through life-changing international volunteer trips." Leaders Today grew to become the worldwide leader in empowering youth by morphing into the Me to We Foundation. This all-embracing movement reveals the unique philosophy of Mark and Craig.

"Identifying the need for an alternative to the usual choices, [the Keilburger brothers] founded the Me and We family of social enterprises. Music, books, trips, clothing—a shamelessly idealistic new way of living, every day."[12]

Craig saw for himself the pain children endured as they worked day and night, and he felt compelled to tell their story. In his book *Free the Children*, Craig described the conditions he saw firsthand as he toured south Asia with Alam Rahman, a Canadian human rights worker.[13]

Michael Simmons is another young adult who has made a difference by reaching his goals. In 2003 when he was a student entrepreneur in college, Michael wrote a best seller, *The Student Success Manifesto: How to Create a Life of Passion, Purpose, and Prosperity*.[14]

Two years later, Michael formed a company with Sheena Lindahl called Extreme Entrepreneurship Educational Foundation. This has blossomed into a movement. Through the Internet the Extreme Entrepreneurship Corporation encourages other young adults to pursue their dreams and reach their goals using positive thinking and visualization. "Our goal here, our vision, is to reach a generation of people who can plan, prioritize and pursue their vision for life, who really care about what they believe in and they want to do."[15]

With these great examples of how successful teens can become when they meet their goals, it's time to envision your own success. How? When you write out your mission statement and your vision statement you'll incorporate the last two steps to reach your goals. Your mission statement is usually created first because you need it to formulate your vision.

Your mission statement is the declaration of what you are doing today to pursue your vision of the future.

Your vision statement describes the future—where you are going and what you want to do.

Let's look at the unique qualities of both the vision and mission statements to help you get your creative buzz flowing. The most important thing is not to stress out over writing your statements. Many people get hung up in this process of trying to determine what these two elements of mission and vision should be. Instead, let your feelings direct the flow of your thoughts. If you need a refresher, open your Goals Notebook and review No Sweat Exercises 32 and 33 where you allowed the flow of spirit to direct your actions.

GET INSPIRED

What do you want to do with your life? It is not an easy question to answer—and you shouldn't have to answer alone. Browse 43Things.com to find out what others want to do. You might find some goals you share. Click the "I want to do this" button to add a goal to your list. Got an idea for a new goal? Just type it in the text box on the homepage or at the bottom of any page on the site. Bam! Now, it's your thing.[16]

To complete this important activity you will do several exercises. As you allow one to build on another, before you know it, you'll have completed your mission and vision statements.

If you are in a group of students (or friends) and have been sharing this experience and book, now is the time to separate out and find a quiet niche where you can be alone with your thoughts.

In the event that some of you will tuck this book away in your library, remember to pull it out from time to time when you are in college or ready to enter into the job market. That's when you'll see how your goal-setting efforts have prepared you to fit into the working world and understand how this study relates to corporate strategic planning. Therefore we'll briefly review the corporate approach to defining a mission statement so you can access it in the future.

According to Susan M. Heathfield, a human resources specialist, "Both people and organizations need to establish a strategic framework for significant success . . . which consists of the following:

a vision for the future

a mission that defines what you are doing

values that shape your actions

strategies that zero in on your key success approaches

goals and action plans to guide your . . . actions.

Your . . . personal success depends on how well you define and live by each of these important concepts."[17]

MY MISSION STATEMENT FOR LIFE

Analyzing how a mission statement is used for strategic planning in the corporate world could get overwhelming. Many corporate

To combine a corporate approach for writing a mission statement with a teen viewpoint, you can go online to access the school agenda site Discover Zone.[18] This line of attack uses the Franklin Covey principles of values and leads you through a series of teen-friendly questions to help you form your mission statement.

Although effective, the process can be lengthy as it is divided into three segments. The first two are the Discover Challenge, where you describe your priorities, and the Great Discovery, where you find not only what matters to you most, but also your unique mission in life. The third segment consists of the actual paragraph where you write out your mission statement.

A more traditional approach adults might use for goal setting and writing a mission statement can be found through the philosophy of Earl Nightingale. A well-known radio broadcaster, Earl rose to fame in the 1960s when he joined forces with businessman Lloyd Conant to create the Nightingale-Conant Corporation, which was dedicated to helping people achieve success. The company's first recording was *The Strangest Secret*, by Earl Nightingale, which eventually went on to sell more than a million copies (and achieve a gold record status).

The corporation is still known as one of the world's largest producers of personal development and self-help programs, which offers dozens of programs by today's most influential speakers. The corporate philosophy holds that the "power to achieve the life of your dreams is in your hands—and the first step toward activating it is identifying the specific goals that will make your dreams real. After all, it's much easier to get what you want out of life when you know where you're going.

"A mission statement is only a paragraph long, but it has specific, measurable outcomes and a deadline for accomplishing that outcome. It's truly the best way to start your journey to success."[19]

seminars take an entire week to complete the process. However, because of journaling, and writing out your No Sweat Exercises, you have learned the basic principles of goal setting. That is all you need to write your mission and vision statements. Here is an example of my mission statement: *I am living my life's purpose as I bring hope to teens through my book,* Reaching Your Goals: The Ultimate Teen Guide, *and I further impart this spark during my author visits to schools and local bookstores.*

VISION STATEMENT: A FORCE TO SUSTAIN ME

According to Ms. Jones, a vision statement needs certain elements:

It is written down and visible where you can read it everyday.

It is written in the present as if it has already happened.

It covers a variety of activities and time frame.

It is filled with descriptive details that anchor it into reality.[20]

To see the difference between the two elements (mission and vision statements) let's first examine the vision statement described by Laurie Beth Jones in *The Path: Creating Your Mission Statement for Work and for Life*: "Your vision statement is the force that will sustain you when your mission statement seems too heavy to endure, enforce, or engage. All significant changes and intentions began with a vision first.

". . . Once you get clear about what you want, you will begin to attract help from multiple sources. . . . [Your vision] must be so clear and so powerful that its very magnetism and gravitational forces will literally pull it toward you."[21]

The vision and dream of your goal has always been with you. It's called "a force to sustain you" because it has been your inner hope that kept you moving during difficult times, tugging at your heart. Now you must pull away the outer skin and get to the real core of your desires. Here is an example of my vision statement: *I have reached so much success with my book,* Reaching Your Goals: The Ultimate Teen Guide, *that I am now preparing to appear on Oprah and teach "Creating Visual Goals with a Picture Map" to a national teen audience. I am also planning a national book tour where I will meet many of my teen supporters, as I sign their books and blow bubbles with them.*

What do you do next? You actually know the answer to that question, but here are some ideas to review.

- **Feed your interests; work the five steps to reach your goal and do the activities you've marked in your planner.**
- **Remember to always look for the signposts that will point you in the right direction.**

NO SWEAT EXERCISE 35—MY MISSION STATEMENT FOR LIFE

Directions: Now for a reality check in your life as a young adult — writing your mission statement. It is important to keep the process simple, otherwise you could feel weighed down. The bottom line is to keep in mind that you are only writing one paragraph, or even one line, that simply puts your goal into the present moment.

Treat this like any other No Sweat Exercise; open your Goals Notebook and write the title on the first line. Pick your most important goal and describe it as though you are completing it now. Voila! Your goal has become your mission statement.

If this process seems too confining for you, as in, "How can I possible write my goal using only one sentence?" turn it into a brainstorming project. Use the rest of the page to free write your mission statement. Then, boil down your ideas until you can rewrite them into one crystal-clear statement.

Ready? Set? Goal! Just start to write your paragraph and before you can sneeze twice, you'll have your mission statement in front of you.

____

____

____

____

____

- **Read over your Goals Notebook from time to time and see how your ideas have changed.**
- **Don't be afraid to expand a previous journal entry and keep up your daily journaling (even when you think you have nothing to write about).**
- **Listen and honor the secrets of your heart. If you don't, who will?**
- **Become responsible for your life and take pride that you are moving into maturity with a sense of purpose.**
- **Above all, love your life, be happy, and have fun being you!**

NO SWEAT EXERCISE 36—MY VISION STATEMENT: A FORCE TO SUSTAIN ME

Directions: Ready for the final push? Now, one more time turn to an empty page in your notebook. On the top line write the title of the exercise. Use approximately eight lines for your vision statement (which includes extra lines to rewrite it, if necessary).

To uncover your vision, trust in yourself and all of the work you have done in writing your mission statement. Allow every thought to tumble out because you are not looking for any particular order or sequence. Realize that the vision statement you are now writing is a bridge where your past and future come together.

To begin, simply freewrite as though you were journaling. Give yourself ten minutes. To put a final polish on this exercise, cut away some of the fluff and condense your vision statement to one short paragraph.

After you have finished that, print both your mission statement and vision statement on cards and in your day planner where you can read them often. You can paste them on your Treasure Map as well and turn them into an affirmation to say daily.

CONCLUSION: BE YOU!

No matter what your age, in looking back on the journey you have experienced through this book, you must admit that you aren't the same person you were when you started. You have changed. You can't be passive about your life because you've discovered what your dreams are, what your hidden goals have revealed, and what may lie ahead.

You now have the tools to mold your future in any way you wish. Never doubt yourself, even in your bleakest moment. Instead, remember how you felt while writing out your No Sweat Exercises—that you did have that spark of genius and that you felt it was real.

No one can make you successful but you. Discipline yourself to use your day planner daily, write down and read back your ideas, and find practical ways to make them happen. Believe your own ideas are unique.

Your goal is to be happy in life. Your challenge is to figure out how to be in the right place where you can do the right thing with the right people at the right time to accomplish your goal. As you put those pieces together and visualize what you want your life to become, you'll realize your life goal.

You are ready to go out and experience life and not be afraid to live in the moment. You are ready to reach within for inspiration and find the real you. Congratulations! The award goes to you!

Kayla is a real person, just like you. She left high school in her junior year to get a job, but she continued to attend evening

Kayla wins a scholarship.

classes for an entire year. Finally she went back to complete her senior year with her original class. She learned to overcome many obstacles but never lost sight of her goal. She realized her dream the day she graduated (with her class) and was awarded a scholarship to become a medical imaging technician. Today she attends college classes, and each day brings her closer to completing her training and reaching her goal.

I told Kayla what I am telling you. It is the message of this book. It's simply this—be passionate, be more, be yourself to the fullest! If you believe in your dream, you will meet your goal. Where you will be five years from now, ten years from now, and so on, is truly up to you. Trust in your destiny. Allow it to echo through the ups and downs of your life, calling you to become who you are meant to be.

NOTES

1. Wayne Dyer, *Inspiration: Your Ultimate Calling* (Carlsbad, CA: Hay House, 2006), 175.

2. There are many organizations where teens can volunteer. Here are sites that will give more information on a few of them:

   a. Pay It Forward Foundation, www.payitforwardfoundation.org/ (accessed March 6, 2007).
   b. "Make a Difference Day," USA Weekend, usaweekend.com/diffday/honorees/2006/060423intro_ca.html#top (accessed March 5, 2007).
   c. "Volunteer Opportunities for Teens," About.com: Teen Advice, teenadvice.about.com/cs/volunteering/ (accessed March 6, 2007).
   d. The Online Volunteer Guide: Especially for Teens, www.geocities.com/volguide/ (accessed March 6, 2007).
   e. Free the Children, www.freethechildren.com/index.php (accessed March 6, 2007).
   f. Peace Corps, www.peacecorps.gov/ (accessed March 6, 2007).

3. Kathlyn Gay, *Volunteering: The Ultimate Teen Guide* (Lanham, MD: Scarecrow Press, 2004), 107.

4. To read more about Mission Year and real stories of teens volunteering, go to Mission Year, www.missionyear.org/ (accessed March 3, 2007).

5. Dyer, *Inspiration*, 185.

6. Mattie J. T. Stepanek, *Journey through Heartsongs* (New York: Hyperion, 2002); *Hope through Hearsongs* (New York: Hyperion, 2002); *Celebrate through Heartsongs* (New York: Hyperion, 2002); *Loving through Heartsongs* (New York: Hyperion, 2002); and *Heartsongs* (New York: Hyperion, 2001).

7. "*Pay It Forward*," Moviefone, movies.aol.com/movie/pay-it-forward/8065/main (accessed March 3, 2007). The movie is based on the book

by Catherine Ryan Hyde, *Pay It Forward* (New York: Simon & Schuster, 2000). The book has been translated into twenty languages for publication in more than thirty countries and was chosen among the Best Books for Young Adults 2001 by the American Library Association.

8. Pay It Forward Foundation, www.payitforwardfoundation.org/ (accessed November 19, 2008); Nisandeh Neta, "Different New Year's Resolution," Inspirational Words of Wisdom, www.wow4u.com/passit/index.html (accessed March 3, 2007).

9. Jerrilyn Jacobs, "Peacemaker Hero: Craig Kielburger," My Hero, www.myhero.com/myhero/heroprint.asp?hero=c_Kielburger (accessed March 3, 2007).

10. Mattie J. T. Stepanek, "For Our World," My Hero, myhero.com/myhero/hero.asp?hero=m_stepanek2 (accessed December 15, 2006); Stepanek, *Journey*, 40.

11. Free the Children, www.freethechildren.com/index.php (accessed March 3, 2007).

12. Me to We Foundation, www.metowe.com/aboutus/history/ (accessed December 11, 2008).

13. Craig Kielburger and Kevin Major, *Free the Children: A Young Man Fights against Child Labor and Proves That Children Can Change the World* (New York: HarperCollins, 1998).

14. Michael Simmons, *The Student Success Manifesto: How to Create a Life of Passion, Purpose, and Prosperity* (New York: Extreme Entrepreneurship Education Corporation, 2003); www.successmanifesto.com/blogs/young-entrepreneur (accessed June 6, 2007).

15. Extreme Entrepreneurship Educational Foundation, www.successmanifesto.com/speaking/promo.html (accessed June 6, 2007). You can find more information on Michael Simmons in the following ways:

a. *The Student Success Manifesto: How to Create a Life of Passion, Purpose, and Prosperity* (New York: Extreme Entrepreneurship Education Corporation, 2003), www.successmanifesto.com (accessed December 11, 2008).
b. "Young Entrepreneur Journey," Success Manifesto, www.successmanifesto.com/blogs/young-entrepreneur/ (accessed June 6, 2007).

16. 43Things.com, www.43things.com (accessed June 12, 2007).

17. Susan M. Heathfield, "Build a Strategic Framework: Mission Statement, Vision, Values," About.com: Human Resources, humanresources.about.com/cs/strategicplanning1/a/strategicplan.htm (accessed December 15, 2006).

18. Discover Zone, discoverzone.com (accessed May 22, 2007)

19. "Our Free Mission Statement Builder . . . ," Nightingale-Conant, www.nightingale.com/mission_select.aspx (accessed June 13, 2007).

20. Jones, *The Path*, 73–74.

21. Laurie Beth Jones, *The Path: Creating Your Mission Statement for Work and for Life* (New York: Hyperion, 1996), 71, 76–77.

Resources

CHAPTER 1: WHAT ARE GOALS?

Brown, Les. *Live Your Dreams* (New York: William Morrow, 1992).
Graham, Stedman. *Nine Steps to Success: Teens Can Make It Happen* (New York: Simon & Schuster, 2000).
Jaffe, Azriela. *Create Your Own Luck: 8 Principles of Attracting Good Fortune in Life, Love and Work* (Holbrook, MA: Adams Media Corporation, 2000).
Jones, Laurie Beth. *The Path: Creating Your Mission Statement for Work and for Life* (New York: Hyperion, 1996).

CHAPTER 2: FIND YOUR PATH IN LIFE

Carson, Ben. *The Big Picture: Getting Perspective on What's Really Important in Life* (Grand Rapids, MI: Zondervan, 1999).
Covey, Sean. *The 7 Habits of Highly Effective Teens* (New York: Simon & Schuster, 1998).
Covey, Stephen. Institute for Principle-Centered Leadership. www.lecturenow.com/People/StephenCovey.htm (accessed November 19, 2008).
McGraw, Jay. *Life Strategies for Teens* (New York: Fireside, 2000).
Ponder, Catherine. *Open Your Mind to Prosperity* (Marina Del Rey, CA: De Vorss & Company, 1984).

CHAPTER 3: STAYING ON COURSE

Armstrong, Lance, with Sally Jenkins. *It's Not about the Bike: My Journey Back to Life* (New York: Penguin Group, 2000).
Choron, Sandra, and Harry Choron. *The Book of Lists for Teens* (New York: Houghton Mifflin, 2002).
Sukiennik, Diane, Bill Bendant, and Lisa Raufman. *The Career Fitness Program: Exercising Your Options* (Scottsdale, AZ: Gorsuch Scarisbrick, 1986).
Williams, GregAlan. *Boys to Men: Maps for the Journey* (New York: Main Street Books, 1997).

CHAPTER 4: TURN FAILURE INTO SUCCESS

Anderson, Dave. *The Story of the Olympics* (New York: HarperCollins, 1996).
Bloomfield, Harold. *Making Peace with Your Past: The Six Essential Steps to Enjoying a Great Future* (New York: HarperCollins, 2000).
Cameron, Julia. *The Artist's Way: A Spiritual Path to Higher Creativity* (New York: Putnam, 1992).
Carter-Scott, Cherie. *Negaholics: How to Overcome Negativity and Turn Your Life Around* (New York: Ballantine, 1990).
Ohno, Apolo Anton, and Nancy Ann Richardson. *A Journey: The Autobiography of Apolo Anton Ohno* (New York: Simon & Schuster Books for Young Readers, 2002).

CHAPTER 5: EMBRACE CHANGE TO MEET YOUR GOALS

De Angelis, Barbara. *How Did I Get Here? Finding Your Way to Renewed Hope and Happiness When Life and Love Take Unexpected Turns* (New York: St Martin's Press, 2006).
Havala, Suzanne. *Vegetarian Cooking for Dummies* (Hoboken, NJ: Wiley, 2001).
Heal, Dede. *The Starving Students' Vegetarian Cookbook* (New York: Warner Books, 2001).
Jenkins, Nancy Harmon. *Mediterranean Diet Cookbook: A Delicious Alternative to Lifelong Health* (New York: Bantam Books, 1994).
Johnson, Spencer. *Who Moved My Cheese?* (New York: Penguin Group, 1998).
——. *Who Moved My Cheese? for Kids: An A-Mazing Way to Change and Win* (New York: Penguin Group, 2003).
——. *Who Moved My Cheese? for Teens* (New York: Penguin Group, 2002).
McMartin, Grace J., ed. *A Recapitulation of Baba's Teachings: As Selected by Grace J. McMartin* (Hyderabad, India: Avon Printing Works, 1982).
Moosewood Collective. *Moosewood Restaurants Cook at Home: Fast and Easy Recipes for Any Day* (New York: Simon & Schuster/ Fireside, 1994).
Ray, Rachael. *365: No Repeats—a Year of Deliciously Different Dinners (A 30-Minute Meal Cookbook)* (New York: Crown, 2005).
Rensley, Carol Ann. *Nutrition for Dummies* (Hoboken, NJ: Wiley, 2005).
Stoll, Kristi, and Gidget Clayton. *Teen Vision: How to Find Your Passion and Realize Your Dreams* (Hillsboro, OR: Beyond Words, 2005).

CHAPTER 6: ACHIEVE YOUR GOALS WITH CREATIVE IMAGERY

Aiken, Clay, and Allison Glock. *Learning to Sing: Hearing the Music in Your Life* (New York: Random House, 2004).

Gawain, Shakti. *Creative Visualization: Use the Power of Your Imagination to Create What You Want in Your Life* (Novato, CA: Nataraj Publishing, 2002).

Goldstein, Hilary. "Required Reading: Adpolf." IGN Comics, May 2, 2005. comics.ign.com/articles/609/609520p1.html (accessed March 2, 2007).

Hallowell, Edward M., and John J. Ratey. *Answers to Distraction* (New York: Bantam Books, 1996).

——. *Delivered from Distraction: Getting the Most Out of Life with Attention Deficit Disorder* (New York: Random House, 2005).

Hill, Napoleon. *Think and Grow Rich Action Pack* (New York: Hawthorn/Dutton, 1968).

Irvine, Joan. "How to Make a Pop-Up." Makers Gallery. www.makersgallery.com/joanirvine/howto.html-7k (accessed January 7, 2006).

"Norman Vincent Peale." Wikipedia. en.wikipedia.org/wiki/Norman_Vincent_Peale (accessed June 6, 2007).

Peale, Dr. Norman Vincent. *Positive Imaging: The Powerful Way to Change Your Life* (New York: Ballantine Books, 1985).

Tezuka, Osamu. *Adolf*, volume 1: *A Tale of Twentieth Century* (San Francisco: VIZ Media, 1996).

——. *Adolf*, volume 2: *An Exile in Japan* (San Francisco: VIZ Media, 1996).

——. *Adolf*, volume 3: *The Half-Aryan Prince* (San Francisco: VIZ Media, 1996).

——. *Adolf*, volume 4: *Days of Infamy* (San Francisco: VIZ Media, 1996).

——. *Adolf*, volume 5: *1945 and All That Remains* (San Francisco: VIZ Media, 1997).

Tezuka Productions, Osamu Tezuka, and Jason D. Deangelis. Tezuka School of Animation: Learning the Basics (New York: Watson-Guptell Publications, 1999).

CHAPTER 7: CREATE VISUAL GOALS WITH A PICTURE MAP

Bachel, Beverly K. *What Do You Really Want? How to Set a Goal and Go for It: A Guide For Teens* (Minneapolis: Free Spirit Publishing, 2001).

"Bible." Wikipedia. en.wikipedia.org/wiki/Bible (accessed September 9, 2006).

Coelho, Paulo. *The Alchemist* (New York: HarperCollins, 1993).

——. *Warrior of the Light* (New York: HarperCollins, 2003).

Crystal, John C., and Richard N. Bolles. *Where Do I Go from Here with My Life?* (New York: Seabury Press, 1974).

Hay, Louise. *You Can Heal Your Life* (Carlsbad, CA: Hay House, 2005).

"Islam: The Koran." ThinkQuest. library.thinkquest.org/28505/islam/koran.htm (accessed September 9, 2006).

"Ministry University." Washington Post.com. education.washingtonpost.com/site/16192458001 (accessed June 12, 2007).

"Srimad Bhagavad Gita." Bhagavad-Gita. www.bhagavad-gita.org/ (accessed February 23, 2008).

Takatoka. "Symbols of Indigenous Peoples." Manataka American Indian Council. www.manataka.org/page29.html (accessed December 2, 2007).

Thompson, Gerry Maguire. *Meditation Made Easy: An Introduction to the Basics of the Ancient Art of Meditation* (New York: Sterling, 1999).

Thornton, Denise. *Teens with Disabilities: The Ultimate Teen Guide* (Lanham MD: Scarecrow Press, 2007).

University Ministry, studentaffairs.depaul.edu/ministry/jewish.html (accessed June 12, 2007).

Weissman, Darren R. *The Power of Infinite Love and Gratitude* (Carlsbad, CA: Hay House, 2007).

"The Written Law (The Torah)." Jewish Vertual Library. www.jewish virtuallibrary.org/jsource/Judaism/The_Written_Law.html (accessed December 11, 2008).

CHAPTER 8: MORE TOOLS FOR SELF-DISCOVERY

Cameron, Julia. *The Artist's Way Morning Pages Journal* (New York: Putnam, 2002).

Kranz, Linda. *Through My Eyes: A Journal for Teens* (Flagstaff, AZ: Rising Moon, 1998).

Mandino, Og. *The Greatest Salesman in the World* (New York: Bantam Paperbacks, 1983).

OgMadino.com, www.ogmandino.com/ (accessed June 9, 2007).

Ferrucci, Piero. *Inevitable Grace* (Los Angeles, CA: Jeremy P. Torcher, Inc., 1990), 62.

CHAPTER 9: CREATING GOALS WITH AFFIRMATIONS

Adrienne, Carol. *The Purpose of Your Life: Finding Your Place in the World Using Synchronicity, Intuition, and Uncommon Sense* (New York: HarperCollins, 1998).

"Barbara Morgan Talks with Students on Ham Radio." NASA (NASA's Teacher in Space program). www.nasa.gov/multimedia/podcasting/STS118_morgan_radio.html (accessed August 20, 2007).

Brown, Ona Mae. *Affirmacise! 101 Affirmations for Daily Living* (Chicago: Divine Order Communications, 1998).

The Christa McAuliffe Center, www.christa.org/main_page.htm (accessed December 10, 2006).

Franken, Al. *I'm Good Enough, I'm Smart Enough, and Doggone It, People Like Me! Daily Affirmations with Stuart Smalley* (New York: Dell, 1992).

———. *Lies and the Wrong Lying Liars Who Tell Them: A Fair and Balanced Look at the Right* (New York: Dutton Books, 2003).

———. *The Truth (with jokes)* (New York: Dutton Books, 2005).

Hay, Louise. *I Can Do It: How to Use Affirmations to Change Your Life* (Carlsbad, CA: Hay House, 2003).
———. *Meditations for Personal Healing* (Carlsbad, CA: Hay House, 2005), audio CD.
"Notes from the Universe." Tut's Adventure Club. www.tut.com/mmm.shtml (accessed December 10, 2006).
OnaBrown.com, www.onabrown.com (accessed October 10, 2007).
Shinn, Florence Scovel. *The Game of Life and How to Play It* (Carlsbad, CA: Hay House, 2005).
"Stuart Smalley." Wikipedia. en.wikipedia.org/wiki/Stuart_Smalley (accessed December 10, 2006).

CHAPTER 10: BEING IN SYNC WITH LIFE

Chopra, Deepak. *The Seven Spiritual Laws of Success, A Practical Guide to the Fulfillment of Your Dreams* (Novato, CA: Amber-Allen, 1994).
———. *The Way of the Wizard: Twenty Spiritual Lessons for Creating the Life Your Want* (New York: Harmony Books, 1995).
Dyer, Wayne W. *Change Your Thoughts–Change Your Life: Living the Wisdom of the Tao* (Carlsbad, CA: Hay House, 2007).
———. *The Power of Intention: Learning to Co-create Your World Your Way* (Carlsbad, CA: Hay House, 2004).
Hamilton, Bethany, www.bethanyhamilton.com (accessed April 15, 2007).
Maa, Sai. *Petals of Grace: Essential Teachings for Self-Mastery* (Crestone, CO: HIU Press, 2005).
The Purpose of Your Life, www.caroladrienne.com/ (accessed June 28, 2007).
"Quantum Physics: Paul Dirac." On Truth and Reality. www.spaceandmotion .com/physics-paul-dirac.htm (accessed September 6, 2006).

CHAPTER 11: THE LONG AND SHORT OF GOALS

Schwartz, Tina. *Organ Transplant, a Survival Guide for the Entire Family* (Lanham, MD: Scarecrow Press, 2005).

CHAPTER 12: READING THE SIGNPOSTS OF LIFE

Bolles, Richard N. *What Color Is Your Parachute? A Practical Manual for Job Hunters & Career Changers* (Berkeley, CA: Ten Speed Press, 1972).
———. *What Color Is Your Parachute? 2007: A Practical Manual for Job Hunters and Career-Changers* (London: Parachute Library, 2006).
———. *What Color Is Your Parachute? Workbook: How to Create a Picture of Your Ideal Job or Next Career* (London: Parachute Library, 2005).
Bolles, Richard Nelson, and Carol Christen. *What Color is Your Parachute? for Teens: Discovering Yourself, Defining Your Future* (London: Parachute Library, 2006).

Bragg, Richard. *I Am a Soldier, Too: The Jessica Lynch Story* (New York: Knopf, 2003).
Crystal, John C., and Richard N. Bolles. *Where Do I Go from Here with My Life?* (Berkeley, CA: Ten Speed Press, 1974).
Fedorko, Jamie, and Dwight Allot (illustrator). *The Intern Files: How to Get, Keep, and Make the Most of Your Internship* (New York: Simon Spotlight Entertainment, 2006).
Gay, Kathlyn. *Teens and Military Life: The Ultimate Teen Guide* (Lanham, MD: Scarecrow Press, 2008).
Military.com (information on benefits and tuition), edu.military.com/gibill/?ESRC=ggl_edu_miledu.kw&np=1 (accessed July 3, 2007).
Paquette, Penny Hutchins. *Apprenticeship: The Ultimate Teen Guide* (Lanham, MD: Scarecrow Press, 2005).
Peale, Dr. Norman Vincent. *Positive Imaging, The Powerful Way to Change Your Life* (New York: Ballantine Books, 1992).

CHAPTER 13: MOVING FORWARD WITH COURAGE

43Things.com, www.43things.com (accessed June 12, 2007).
About.com: Buddhism, buddhism.about.com/od/theravada/ss/BuddhismSS.htm (accessed April 24, 2007).
Dyer, Wayne W. *Inspiration: Your Ultimate Calling* (Carlsbad, CA, Hay House, 2006).
Covey, Franklin. *Sense of Purpose: Discovering your Personal Mission Statement* (Salt Lake City, UT: Franklin Covey, 1999).
Metcalf, Franz. *Buddha in Your Backpack: Everyday Buddhism for Teens* (Berkeley, CA: Seastone, 2002).
Ruiz, Don Miquel. *The Four Agreements* (San Rafael, CA: Amber-Allen, 1997).
Stein, David. *How to Make Monstrous, Huge, Unbelievably Big Bubbles* (Palo Alto, CA: Klutz, 2005).
Tezuka, Osamu. *Buddha*, volume 1: *Kapilavastu* (New York: Vertical, 2003).
———. *Buddha*, volume 2: *The Four Encounters* (New York: Vertical, 2003).
———. *Buddha*, volume 3: *Devadatta* (New York: Vertical, 2004).
———. *Buddha*, volume 4: *The Forest of Uruvela* (New York: Vertical, 2004).
———. *Buddha*, volume 5: *Deer Park* (New York: Vertical, 2004).
———. *Buddha*, volume 6: *Ananda* (New York: Vertical, 2004).
———. *Buddha*, volume 7: *Prince Ajatasattu* (New York: Vertical, 2005).
———. *Buddha*, volume 8: *Jetavana* (New York: Vertical, 2005).

CHAPTER 14: A NEW YOU WITH MISSION AND VISION

Gay, Kathlyn. *Volunteering: The Ultimate Teen Guide* (Lanham, MD: Scarecrow Press, 2004).
Hyde, Catherine Ryan. *Pay It Forward* (New York: Simon & Schuster, 2000).

Jones, Laurie Beth. *The Path: Creating Your Mission Statement for Work and for Life* (New York: Hyperion, 1996).

Kielburger, Craig, and Kevin Major. *Free the Children: A Young Man Fights against Child Labor and Proves That Children Can Change the World* (New York: HarperCollins, 1998).

Simmons Michael. *The Student Success Manifesto: How to Create a Life of Passion, Purpose, and Prosperity* (New York: Extreme Entrepreneurship Education Corporation, 2003). www.successmanifesto.com/speaking/promo.html (accessed June 6, 2007).

Stepanek, Mattie J. T. *Celebrate through Heartsongs* (New York: Hyperion, 2002).

———. "For Our World." My Hero. myhero.com/myhero/hero.asp?hero=m_stepanek2 (accessed December 15, 2006).

———. *Heartsongs* (New York: Hyperion, 2001).

———. *Journey through Heartsongs* (New York: Hyperion, 2002).

———. *Loving through Heartsongs* (New York: Hyperion, 2002).

FURTHER READING

Art and Creativity Books

Brookes, Mona. *Drawing for Older Children & Teens: The Internationally Acclaimed Method That Teaches You to Draw* (New York: Jeremy P. Tarcher, 1991).

Burns, Michael. *Digital Sci-Fi Art: A Step-by-Step Guide to Creating Stunning, Futuristic Images* (New York: HarperCollins, 2004).

Edwards, Betty. *The New Drawing on the Right Side of the Brain: A Course in Enhancing Creativity and Artistic Confidence* (New York: Jeremy P. Tarcher, 1989).

———. *The New Drawing on the Right Side of the Brain Workbook: Guided Practice in the Five Basic Skills of Drawing* (New York: Jeremy P. Tarcher, 2004).

Irvine, Joan. "How to Make a Pop-Up." Makers Gallery. www.makersgallery.com/joanirvine/howto.html-7k (accessed January 7, 2006).

Kobayashi, Junji. *Let's Draw Manga: Astro Boy* (New York: Digital Manga Publications, 2004).

Robert Sabuda.com, robertsabuda.com/ (accessed January 7, 2006).

Tezuka Productions, Osamu Tezuka, and Jason D. Deangelis. *Tezuka School of Animation 1: Learning the Basics* (New York: Watson-Guptell Publications, 1999).

Williams, Richard, and Imogen Sutton. *The Animator's Survival Kit: A Manual of Methods, Principles, and Formulas for Classical, Computer, Games, Stop Motion, and Internet Animators* (New York: Farrar, Straus and Giroux, 2001).

Windham, Ryder. *The Ultimate Visual Guide to Star Wars* (New York: D.K. Publishing, 2005).

Cookbooks

Havala, Suzanne. *Vegetarian Cooking for Dummies* (Hoboken, NJ: Wiley, 2001).

Heal, Dede. *The Starving Students' Vegetarian Cookbook* (New York: Warner Books, 2001).

Jenkins, Nancy Harmon. *Mediterranean Diet Cookbook: A Delicious Alternative to Lifelong Health* (New York: Bantam Books, 1994).

Moosewood Collective. *Moosewood Restaurants Cook at Home: Fast and Easy Recipes for Any Day* (New York: Simon & Schuster/Fireside, 1994).

Ray, Rachael. *365: No Repeats—A Year of Deliciously Different Dinners (A 30-Minute Meal Cookbook)* (New York: Crown, 2005).

Rensley, Carol Ann. *Nutrition for Dummies* (Hoboken, NJ: Wiley, 2005).

Journaling

Capacchione, Lucia, Ph.D. *The Creative Journal For Teens: Making Friends with Yourself* (Franklin Lakes, NJ: New Page/Career Press, 2001).

Capacchione, Lucia. *Visioning: Ten Steps to Designing the Life of Your Dreams* (New York: Putnam, 2000).

Rico, Gabriele. *Writing Your Way Through Personal Crisis: Pain and Possibility* (New York: Putnam, 1991).

Life Lists

Choron, Sandra, and Harry Choron. *The Book of Lists for Teens* (New York: Houghton Mifflin, 2002).

Espeland, Pamela. *Life Lists for Teens: Tips, Steps, Hints, and How-Tos for Growing Up, Getting Along, Learning, and Having Fun* (Minneapolis: Free Spirit, 2003).

Goddard, John. "The World's Greatest Goal Achiever." www.johngoddard.info/life_list.htm (accessed January 8, 2007).

Kaplan, Michael. "99 Things to Do before You Die: How to Make Your Own Life-List—and Start Achieving Your Goals." *Mens' Journal*, June 2005, 82–90.

Rogers, J. David. "JDR Life Lists." web.mst.edu/~rogersda/life_lists (accessed February 28, 2008.

"The *Smithsonian* Life List." Smithsonian.com. January 2008. www.smithsonianmag.com/travel/12596716.html (accessed February 28, 2008).

Magazines and Journals

Barnes, Biff. "Talk about Goals, Not Grades." *Parenting Today Magazine*, September 2003.

Browne, Joy. "How to Set Goals and Keep Them." *Parade Magazine*, March 18, 2007.
Boyer, David. "Computersmarts." *BottomLine/Personal*, February 1, 2006.
Charet, Francis X., and Hillary S. Webb. "Approaching Consciousness Studies." *New Perspectives*, no. 20 (Spring 2007).
———. "Decode Your Doodles." *Quizfest Magazine*, November/December 2005.
———. "Is It Time to Break Up with a Bud?" *QuizFest*, November/December 2005.
Ervolino, Bill. "Six Steps to Writing a To-Do List of a Lifetime." *Sunday Record* 1 (January 2006).
"Guideposts Editorial Guidelines." Guideposts. www.guidepostsmag.com/writers-guidelines/ (accessed December 11, 2008).
Joiner, Whitney. "Real Life: Heather's Story." *Seventeen* (June 2005): 99–100.
Kozlowski, Bettina. "Billy Corgan Comes Out of the Dark." *Conscious Choice* 18, no. 6 (June 2005).
Philip Morris USA. *Peer Pressure & Smoking* 2, no. 2. www.philipmorrisusa.com/en/prc/activities/downloadresources.asp (accessed January 6, 2007).
Stein, Joel. "Just Say Om." *Time Magazine* 162, no. 5 (August 4, 2003).
Wilson, MacKenzie. "Clay Aiken Had Conflicting Goals." AOL News www.aol.com/news/allmusicguide (accessed January 17, 2006).

ADDITIONAL INFORMATION

Camps and Summer Activities

Allen's Guide, www.allensguide.com/religious-camps/jewish-summer-camps/ (accessed October 10, 2007).
Awake, www.humanityinunity.org/SYMPLE/AudioVideoFiles/index.cfm (accessed December 18, 2007).
Higher Ground, www.carolinacamp.com/camp%20videos.htm (accessed October 10, 2007).
Omega Teen Camp, omegateencamp.org/dates-fees-register.htm (accessed January 2, 2008).

Careers without College

Assessment.com, www.assessment.com (seventy-one questions reveal ten areas of career interest that match your personality profile) (accessed November 28, 2007).
Guidance Associates, www.guidanceassociates.com/50bejopracawi.html (accessed November 8, 2005).
The Internet Public Library, www.ipl.org./div/teenpathways/ (Under "Search the IPL" type *Careers without college*. Watch for hidden fees!) (accessed November 8, 2005).
Keirsey.com, www.keirsey.com/cgi-bin/keirsey/newkts.cgi (accessed November 8, 2005).

Clubs and Organizations for Teens

Future Business Leaders of America (FBLA), www.fbla-pbl.org/index.asp (accessed March 2, 2008).
The Horatio Alger Foundation. *The State of Our Nation's Youth*: 2005–2006 Report. www.horatioalger.org/index.cfm (accessed November 19, 2008).
Sierra Student Coalition (SSC), www.ssc.org/ (accessed April 20, 2007).

Goal Setting

Brown, Les. *Les Brown—Life Story*. www.youtube.com/watch?v=oN01-B3oshg&feature=related (accessed January 12, 2008).
———. *Why People Fail*. www.youtube.com/watch?v=uekdv8SiTec (accessed February 28, 2008).
Extreme Entrepreneurship Educational Foundation, www.successmanifesto.com/speaking/promo.html (accessed June 6, 2007).
Hoagland-Smith, Leanne. "Tiger Woods, A Lesson—One Stroke At A Time!" ZeroMillion.com. www.zeromillion.com/personaldev/one-stroke-lesson.html (accessed April 19, 2007).
Simmons, Michael. "Young Entrepreneur Journey." www.successmanifesto.com/blogs/young-entrepreneur (accessed June 6, 2007).
Zigler, Zig. *Zig Ziglar—Setting Goals*. www.youtube.com/watch?v=Ae-VJ_lauCw (accessed December 21, 2007).

Goal Setting for School

Pacini, Victor. "Students Share their Goals and Dreams." www.victorpacini.com. (accessed May 24, 2007).
The Princeton Review. "Setting Goals for High School." www.princetonreview.com/college/research/articles/prepare/hsGoals.asp (accessed February 29, 2008).
Sanko, Manda. "Importance of Setting Goals in High School." www.associatedcontent.com/article/419876/the_importance_of_setting_goals_in.html (accessed February 26, 2008).

Historical Figures Who Met Their Goals

Jacobs, Jerrilyn. "Peacemaker Hero: Craig Kielburger." www.myhero.com/myhero/heroprint.asp?hero=c_Kielburger (accessed March 3, 2007).
"Martin Luther King, Jr., Civil-Rights Leader." www.lucidcafe.com/library/96jan/king.html (accessed November 5, 2006).
"Rosa Parks." www.girlpower.gov/girlarea/gpguests/RosaParks.htm,e-portals.org/Parks/ (accessed August 8, 2006).

Mission Statement

discoverzone.com (accessed May 22, 2007).
Heathfield, Susan M. "Build a Strategic Framework: Mission Statement, Vision, Values." humanresources.about.com/cs/strategicplanning1/a/strategicplan.htm (accessed December 15, 2006).
"Our Free Mission Statement Builder." www.nightingale.com/mission_select.aspx (accessed June 13, 2007).

Movies and Documentaries

A Cinderella Story. www2.warnerbros.com/acinderellastory/index.html (accessed May 12, 2007).
Eragon. www.eragonsite.com (accessed December 20, 2007).
Gandhi. www.imdb.com/title/tt0083987/ (accessed November 5, 2006).
Legally Blonde. www.legallyblonde.com/ (accessed March 3, 2007).
Napoleon Dynamite. www.napoleondynamitedvd.com (accessed January 5, 2007).
The Notebook. www.thenotebookmovie.com (accessed February 22, 2007).
Recycled Life. www.recycledlifedoc.com (accessed November 17, 2007).
Rocky. www.totalrocky.com/ (accessed June 7, 2007).
What the Bleep Do We Know? www.whatthebleep.com/whatthebleep (accessed March 2, 2007).
What the Bleep: Down the Rabbit Hole. www.whatthebleep.com/rabbithole/ (accessed March 2, 2007).

Out-of-the-Norm Learning Experiences

Greene, Rebecca. *The Teenagers' Guide to School Outside the Box* (Minneapolis, MN: Free Spirit, 2001).
Goddard College. www.goddard.edu/bachelorarts_individualizedstudies (accessed January 29, 2008).
"Famous High School Dropouts." www.increasebrainpower.com/high-school-dropouts.html (accessed June 28, 2007).
Premier High School ***discoveragenda***, 2002/03 edition (Bellingham, WA: Premier Agendas, Inc.). www.premieragenda.com (accessed January 8, 2007).

Quizzes

"Cool Quiz," www.coolquiz.com/myquiz/ (accessed February 28, 2008).
Quibblo.com, www.quibblo.com/tag/teens (accessed February 26, 2008).

Vision Statement

Create a Vision Statement. www.mindtools.com/pages/article/newLDR_90.htm (accessed November 17, 2007).

Volunteer Opportunities for Teens

The Bubel/Aiken Foundation. en.wikipedia.org/wiki/Clay_Aiken#American_Idol (accessed April 16, 2007).

Civitan International, www.civitan.org (accessed February 28, 2008).

Free the Children, www.freethechildren.com/index.php (accessed March 6, 2007).

Make a Difference Day. http://usaweekend.com/diffday/honorees/2006/060423intro_ca.html#top (accessed March 5, 2007).

Monarch Butterfly Migration. www.sierraclub.org/compass/2006/10/monarchy.asp (accessed November 17, 2007); www.nytimes.com/2006/10/03/science/03butter.html?_r=1&8dpc&oref=slogin (accessed November 27, 2007).

Mission Year, www.missionyear.org (accessed March 3, 2007).

The Online Volunteer Guide, www.geocities.com/volguide (accessed March 6, 2007).

Optimists International, www.optimist.org (accessed February 28, 2008).

Pay It Forward Foundation, www.payitforwardfoundation.org/ (accessed March 6, 2007).

Peace Corps, www.peacecorps.gov (accessed March 6, 2007).

"Volunterring Opportunities for Kids." http://teenadvice.about.com/cs/volunteering/ (accessed March 6, 2007).

PRODUCTS OF INTEREST

Affirmation Cards

Hay, Louise. *Power Thoughts For Teens: A 50-Card Deck* (Carlsbad, CA: Hay House, Inc., 2001); www.hayhouse.com/details.php?id=292 (accessed November 15, 2007).

Agendas and Accessories

www.dayrunner.com/webapp/wcs/stores/servlet/home (accessed December 19, 2007).

www.ecampus.com/bk_ detail.asp?isbn=0534534325&referrer=frgl (accessed November 7, 2006).

www.kingsford.org/powerschool/my_calendar_ical.pdf (accessed November 7, 2006)

palmtops.about.com/cs/pdafacts/a/Palm_Pocket_PC.htm (accessed December 19, 2007).
Power School, www.powerschool.com/ (accessed October 23, 2007).
www.premieragendas.com/ (accessed November 7, 2006).

Bubble Wands

"Bubble Wands." www.fleamarket1000.com/bubblewand.htm (accessed May 11, 2007).

Index

About the Author and Illustrator

This is **Anne Courtright's** first published work. She illustrated Tina Schwartz's *Organ Transplants: A Survival Guide for the Entire Family* (Scarecrow, 2005). Besides writing fiction for teens, Anne loves to draw and paint and work with teens who love to do the same. She lives on a small lake in the northern Chicago suburbs with her husband, two dogs, and a cat.

This is illustrator **Peg Raasch's** first book. As a child she painted sports posters for her dad, which fueled her dream to become an artist. After receiving an art degree, Peggy was an art manager for twenty years and kept a studio where she did both fine and graphic arts. The illustrations found in *Reaching Your Goals: The Ultimate Teen Guide* shows Peggy's love for incorporating humor into her art.